The Art of Connection

The Art of Connection

RISK, MOBILITY, AND THE CRAFTING OF
TRANSPARENCY IN COASTAL KENYA

Dillon Mahoney

UNIVERSITY OF CALIFORNIA PRESS

University of California Press, one of the most distinguished university presses in the United States, enriches lives around the world by advancing scholarship in the humanities, social sciences, and natural sciences. Its activities are supported by the UC Press Foundation and by philanthropic contributions from individuals and institutions. For more information, visit www.ucpress.edu.

University of California Press
Oakland, California

Library of Congress Cataloging-in-Publication Data

Names: Mahoney, Dillon, 1980– author.
Title: The art of connection : risk, mobility, and the crafting of transparency in coastal Kenya / Dillon Mahoney.
Description: Oakland, California : University of California Press, [2017] | Includes bibliographical references and index.
Identifiers: LCCN 2016030546 (print) | LCCN 2016035376 (ebook) | ISBN 9780520292871 (cloth : alk. paper) | ISBN 0520292871 (cloth : alk. paper) | ISBN 9780520292895 (pbk. : alk. paper) | ISBN 0520292898 (pbk. : alk. paper) | ISBN 9780520966239 (ebook)
Subjects: LCSH: Business communication—Kenya—Mombasa. | Artisans—Kenya—Mombasa. | Handicraft—Technological innovations—Kenya—Mombasa. | Digital communications—Kenya—Mombasa.
Classification: LCC HF5718.2.K4 M34 2017 (print) | LCC HF5718.2.K4 (ebook) | DDC 302.2096762/3—dc23
LC record available at https://lccn.loc.gov/2016030546

Manufactured in the United States of America

26 25 24 23 22 21 20 19 18 17
10 9 8 7 6 5 4 3 2 1

This book is dedicated to the Kenyan men and women who gave me their time and energy, their life stories, their views of their country and world, and their invaluable advice on how to structure this research and book.

CONTENTS

ILLUSTRATIONS

MAPS

FIGURES

ACKNOWLEDGMENTS

In addition to all of my research participants, to whom this book is dedicated, I would like to thank all of my teachers and advisors over the years. Since my first days in Kenya, I have received valuable support and mentorship from the School for International Training's staff based in Mombasa, and especially Athman Lali Omar, Hamisi, Ali, and Fatima. Fieldwork and language training were made possible by Princeton University's Program in Urbanization and Migration, Fulbright-Hays, and Rutgers University. This research could not have been conducted without my language skills, for which I thank Reuben and Lydia Jemase, Charles Bwenge, and John Mtembezi Innis. For the tireless dedication, mentoring, and editing of Angelique Haugerud, I offer a special thanks. I would also like to thank my other dissertation committee members, Dorothy Hodgson, David Hughes, Louisa Schein, and Christopher Steiner, for all of their insights and time spent discussing the material with me. And a final special thanks to all of the other advisors, teachers, and colleagues from Rutgers, especially Laura Ahearn, Barbara Cooper, Daniel Goldstein, James W. K. Harris, Fran Mascia-Lees, Alamin Mazrui, Bonnie McKay, and Richard Schroeder.

This book would not have been possible without the permission of the Kenyan Government, to which I am grateful. I would like to thank the staff at the Institute for Development Studies and Isaac Nyamongo and the staff of the Institute for African Studies at the University of Nairobi for a strong and helpful academic affiliation. I am also very grateful to the staff from the Kenya National Archives in Nairobi and the National Museums of Kenya for help, support, and feedback. I am particularly indebted to Mudathir Ahmed Abdulkarim, Purity Kiura, Haleem Hassan (for twice saving my laptop from a virus), Mzalendo Kibunjia, Wycliffe Marende, Emmanuel Ndiema, and Ahmed Mohamed Omar.

I would also like to thank the University of California Press and its editorial staff for helping me make this book a reality, especially Barbara Armentrout, Stacy Eisenstark, Zuha Khan, and Reed Malcolm. I am grateful to the *African Studies Review* and the *Political and Legal Anthropology Review* for allowing me to reproduce material here. A special thanks is also due to Janet McIntosh and others who reviewed my work and gave me excellent feedback and comments. And a thanks to Bill Nelson for the great maps.

Finally, my academic colleagues at Rutgers and USF, students and TAs, close friends, and family were supportive throughout this entire process, providing me at times with important intellectual, financial, and moral support. I am particularly indebted to my parents and sister: James, Marilyn, and Nora Mahoney. And to Hauwa Adeniji, Donna Auston, Albert Badokufa, Sharon Baskind-Wing, Reeanne Bates, Margit Njoki Bertalan (the best photographer I know), Elizabeth Bird, Rosie Bongiovanni, Chelsea Booth, Sasha Bostick, David Brunner, Stella Capoccia, Ginny Caputo, Heide Castañeda, Fatimah Williams Castro, Jennifer Haunani Chong, Nicolas Clauvelin, Sheryl Cousart, Lisa Danish, Siad Darwish, Cassandra Decker, Deniz Daser, Joseph Debiec, Neema Deche, Tara Deubel, Lori Dibble, Gary Dida, Bria Dunham, Andrew and Betty Eisenberg, Megan Ference, Gabrielle Fondiller, E. J. Ford, Andrew Gerkey (thanks for keeping me sane all those years), Kennedy Gitu, Ted Gold, John Goodson, Assaf Harel, David Himmelgreen, Kevin and Davis Jemase (for keeping me up on Kenyan pop culture and Sheng and always reminding me of how uncool I am), Tayo Jolaosho, Chaunetta Jones, Tristan Turtle Danger Jones, Christopher Kelliher, Dana Ketcher, Chals "Junior" Kitonyi, Stan Kivai, Jacqueline Kowa, Laura Leisinger, Alex DeLaricheliere Lancey, James Pkemoi Lololita, Ken MacLeish, Meredith Main, Sarasij Majumder, Marlaina Martin, Scott Matter, Emily McDonald, Rahim Abdul Mohammed, Nancy Moinde (can't thank you and your boys enough!), Noelle Molé, Gabriel Mootian, Boaz Moseti, Harrison Munga, Grace and Esther Shirū Mwangi, John Napora, Benjamin and Celine Neimark, Stephen Nyaga, Kioko Nzioka, Atieno Obure, Moses Oganda, Katie Orlemanski, Prasanthi Pavuluri, Lisa Poggiali, Jeremy Prestholdt, Nell Quest, Ryan Quinlan, Kaniqua Robinson, Benjamin Schneider, Sheela Sekhar, Debarati Sen, Lawrence Shaw, Montserrat Soler, Angela Steusse, Satsuki Takahashi, Leslie Walker, Ramin Weaver, Linda Whiteford, Bradley Wilson, John Wing, David Wright, Kristina Dziedzic-Wright, Kevin Yelvington, Becky Zarger, and all those I have forgotten to name—my most sincere thanks.

ONE

The Art of Connection

AN INTRODUCTION

> Now it is so much easier and better because of the Internet and
> cell phones. It is really incredible. In the old days, there were
> always problems with communication and nothing seemed to
> work right. Before these things, you had to arrange everything
> ahead of time: When to call. When to be at the pay phone. What
> time it would be. It was very problematic because communicat-
> ing was so difficult.
>
> CRAFTS EXPORTER, NAIROBI
> *(Author's Interview, January 9, 2006)*

SINCE 2000, FEW VISITORS TO URBAN EAST AFRICA could help but
experience the popularity and usefulness of cell phones and Internet cafés.
These new technologies were at the center of a cultural negotiation and performance of modernity, decorated with the advertisements and billboards of
service providers selling access to new means of communication and social
and economic connection. Corporate marketing of new digital technologies
to Kenyans in the twenty-first century was dangling the chance of economic
success and social mobility before those who had long been denied full and
equal participation in world affairs and economic development. The possibilities were as numerous as the unanswered questions: How were the obvious benefits of new digital technologies being distributed? Were the marketing slogans empty promises, or could these new technologies help boost the
economy by jumping more Kenyans into the global economy? To what extent
do education, age, gender, ethnic background, and personal connections continue to shape peoples' lived experiences of risk, success, and failure?

To answer these questions, I spent nearly fifteen years interviewing and
following Kenyan crafts traders and exporters to see how they adapted new
digital technologies to their business strategies at a time already characterized
by economic insecurity, informality, and immobility. The importance of new

digital technologies to my research participants must be understood within this context. This book is, therefore, more than just a study of digital technologies in Kenya. It is also an exploration of Kenya's tourism and crafts industries, the history of cooperative development in Kenya, and the lived experiences of risk and insecurity that characterized the lives of my research participants as they struggled to maintain business connections during a time of economic upheaval. Because of this, my research shifted frequently from Mombasa's roadsides to the city's Internet cafés, cooperatives, and tourist venues.

Throughout this time, I have remained interested not just in the digital component of the research but in the broader context of Kenya's handicrafts, or "curio," industry of ethnic and tourist arts.[1] Kenya's tourism and crafts industries are not only economically substantial, but they also play a central role in representing and producing knowledge about Kenya and Africa for the rest of the world. This book focuses on the Kenyan exporters, intermediaries, and production organizations that are the foundation of Kenya's crafts industry, including the popular product lines of Kisii soapstone and Kamba (or Akamba) wood carving.[2]

Unlike new digital technologies, which represent globalization and modernity, Kenyan crafts and carvings have typically represented Kenya as "local," "natural," "indigenous," "tribal," "ethnic," or "traditional." Kenyan arts and crafts are rarely signed by individual artists and are more typically marketed through ethnic product lines like Kamba wood carving and Kisii soapstone. By labeling this handmade art as ethnic crafts, it aligns with classic colonial understandings of Africa as "primitive," closer to nature, or still "developing." It is no surprise that most Kamba woodcarvings feature either a tribal-looking figure or a wild animal, saying more about the legacy of colonialism than Kenyan culture.

But beneath the façade, Kenya's art traders and exporters are modern businesspeople who have spent well over a decade adapting cell phones and other digital technologies and apps to their business models. They are anything but local or small-scale. Kenyan businesspeople today are carrying on centuries-old traditions of East Africans working as intermediaries in the global economy (see Prestholdt 2008). By no means are digital technologies suddenly connecting Kenyans to the rest of the world for the first time. The shock value of the typical media trope of an African holding a cell phone is rooted in popular assumptions about culture and change. Considering East Africa has been a center of international trade for centuries, it should not surprise us to see Kenyan traders using the latest technologies. This book is an invitation to think critically about the deeper politics of such images and take a deeper look into the lives of the East African men and women who are very much connected to new digital technologies and have long been active players in the global economy.

As I discuss in the next chapter, Mombasa is not only East Africa's biggest port, but also an ancient city that has for centuries been a center of contact and connection. Cross-cultural connections have a long history on the East African coast, although the power dynamics of those who are meeting and interacting are constantly changing (McIntosh 2009; Meiu 2011). The lived experiences of connections and interactions that make up what we often abstractly call the "global economy" have always come with a fair amount of what anthropologist Anna Tsing calls "friction": "the grip of worldly encounter" (2005:1) or "the awkward, unequal, unstable, and creative qualities of interconnection across difference" (4). The challenge to ethnographers is to recover the noncorporate components of globalization and the stories of those who lack power but have "presence" in the world today (Sassen 1998:xxi).[3] Kenya's art traders and exporters are just such noncorporate and often immobile yet transnational actors who, despite being politically and economically disempowered, play an important role in representing Kenyan culture to the rest of the world while also shaping the culture of Kenya's small-business economy.

The research in this book also speaks to two separate but related topics of debate in African studies today: Afropolitanism and the Africa Rising narrative. The image of a cell phone in the hand of an African has been a dominant trope of the Western media since the turn of the twenty-first century. This image has also been used prominently to support the Africa Rising narrative.[4] In 2011 and 2012, both the *Economist* and *Time* magazines ran cover stories titled "Africa Rising."[5] Ironically, in 2000, the *Economist* had titled a cover story about Africa "The Hopeless Continent."[6] *Time* is no newcomer to the Africa Rising narrative, having published an Africa Rising cover story in 1988, just four years after a 1984 cover story titled "Africa's Woes."[7] In all of these cases, the complexity of Africa's history and diversity is erased through the creation of singular entity: Africa. Through this denial of the right to history and complexity, Africa and Africans are relegated to a position where they can be understood only within the binary of Afro-optimism and Afro-pessimism. Despite sounding positive and optimistic, the Africa Rising narrative frames Africa as either rising or falling, moving forwards or backwards.

The image of the Maasai herdsman walking through the savanna while speaking on a cell phone and the accompanying stories of poor Africans revolutionizing their lives with phones and mobile money have amused Western readers and supported the Africa Rising narrative. I do not deny the significance of herdsmen having access to new mobile communication technologies. But we must think carefully about who is producing the Africa Rising narrative and the images that accompany it. I look forward to more herder selfies on social media. But as several analysts have pointed out, much of the Africa Rising hype (and the accompanying statistics) come from North American and European investment banks, whose directors view Africa as an exciting and risky new frontier for investment (Lemma 2013).[8] As the continent that maintained a respectable, growing gross domestic product (GDP) through the most recent global financial crisis, Africa has become for the international banking community, in Lemma's (2013) words, "a brand, a product to be packaged and sold on the merits of its financial worth." Despite the excitement about a growing African middle class and growing GDP in many African countries, a majority of Africans are still regularly affected by poverty (see also Ellis 2011a).

In this book, while I am eager to represent Africa and Africans as modern, global, and connected—and my research participants most certainly were—their lives are not romantic. Connecting to the global economy has proved an insufficient pathway out of poverty. Rather, connecting to the global economy and relying on new technologies for doing international business has come with all types of new risks. I am, therefore, challenged to carefully balance optimism with reality in the way I represent people's lives and experiences here.

Analysts and critics of Afropolitanism are similarly faced with the challenge of balancing optimism with reality. In brief, the idea of Afropolitanism is rooted in a departure from racialized and static thinking about identity to construct alternative, proud, modern, and mobile African identities unified through an aesthetic of cultural and symbolic blending and hybridity (Dabiri 2014; Mbembe 2007).[9] Afropolitanism is rooted in creative innovation and mixing, the "traditional" images and tropes about Africa having always been constructions (Mbembe 2007). In many ways, Afropolitanism is a form of resistance to disparaging Western tropes about Africa, like those famously described in the biting satire of Kenyan writer Binyavanga Wainaina in his now-famous "How to Write about Africa" (2006). Wainaina sarcastically instructs the reader: "Never have a picture of a well-adjusted African on the cover of your book. . . . An AK-47, prominent ribs, naked breasts: use these."

He continues, "If you must include an African, make sure you get one in Masai or Zulu or Dogon dress." An important aspect of Afropolitanism is the production of counterrepresentations to tropes of Africa as impoverished, violent, and tribal. The Afropolitan is modern, global, and connected.

But as with the discourse of Africa Rising, Afropolitanism has also been critiqued for elitism and the central role consumerism plays in its cultural assemblages. Emma Dabiri (2014) has argued that this exclusive consumerism sidelines Afropolitanism's more important insights into race, modernity, and identity. While Afropolitanism has succeeded in giving a voice to Africans, she writes, the narratives of the underprivileged are still largely missing. Referring to Afropolitanism as the "handmaiden of the Africa Rising narrative," she points out that when one searches for *Afropolitan* on Google, many links take you to luxury lifestyle magazines and shops selling jewelry, art, and new types of Afropolitan designs.

Originally catering to white tourists, even Kenya's decades-old crafts industry, which has always also had some customers among the African middle class and bourgeoisie, has adapted to the demand of Afropolitans. Kenyan artisans and craftspeople—especially those who are Afropolitans themselves—are now proudly producing Afropolitan aesthetics through jewelry, fabrics, and handbags that are being sold to both the African middle class and the rest of the world. While these new markets and economic opportunities have the potential to be liberating and empowering, we must remember that they also come with new risks and contradictions. I see this book as an opportunity to further evaluate Afropolitanism and the Africa Rising narrative by providing the stories of the marginalized and underprivileged African traders whose businesses are economically central to producing crafts for Afropolitans and are making at least some analysts say that Africa is, indeed, "rising."

Davis was one such trader.[10] Born in Western Kenya in the early 1970s, he moved to Mombasa at the age of sixteen and soon found employment selling curio art. After ten years working outside Fort Jesus, Mombasa's most frequented tourist attraction, selling handicrafts and carvings to tourists, Davis lost his roadside kiosk in a wave of municipal demolitions in January 2002. But with the help of a cell phone and a personal e-mail account, he found that he could maintain long-term connections with overseas buyers even after being abruptly displaced from his prime location outside of Fort Jesus. Using his cell phone and e-mail to access customers meant Davis was no longer doing business at the whim of the Mombasa's tourism industry. Instead, he was able to shift his business almost entirely into exporting, although only because of connections he had made along the roadside during face-to-face interactions in a predigital age.

Examining a variety of such individuals' experiences allows a more robust understanding of how Africans have adapted new digital technologies to their lives. During my time in Kenya, I was concerned with traders' economic histories in relation to state policy and to local and global events and trends. For example, in another reversal of fortunes, by 2007 Davis could no longer afford his website and had stopped receiving orders from his American and British customers. His major foreign client in the United States, who had even supplied him with his own ATM and business cards, told him quite directly (although through e-mail) that his services would no longer be needed and that his employment was being put on hold indefinitely. The U.S. economy was declining, the dollar was weak, and with fewer Americans traveling and spending money on small souvenirs, the company was cutting back on orders from their overseas suppliers. With no orders and no income, he was suddenly stranded—ejected from the international networks in which he had been a major actor. He had even lost his beloved mobile phone to a moneylender who took it as collateral until the money he had lent to Davis was returned.

In 2014, Davis was struggling to raise chickens to sell eggs to a local tourist hotel.[11] He had been one of the first Kenyans to bridge the "digital divide" but struggled to find an economically productive use for the smartphone I had bought him. He regretted that I could no longer stay with him when I visited Kenya because the small room he shared with two other men was neither secure nor spacious. The economic success he had once experienced was a thing of the past. Amid all of the hopes of Africa Rising and his previous optimism—for jumping scales into international markets, meeting new buyers, and realizing the potential of new digital technologies—Davis found himself between mud walls and under a rusty roof. His story and those of the nearly one hundred other carvers, artisans, traders, and shop vendors I interviewed for this book illuminate the contradictions, hopes, and anguish of so many aspiring Kenyans competing within an economic environment that despite seeming more free and internationally connected is by no means stable or secure.

The insecurity and challenges experienced by Mombasa's small-business class are not new and are rooted in a history of migration and shifting development models. Beginning in the 1950s and continuing through the 1970s, Kenyans from Nairobi, Machakos, and Kisii Districts (now counties) found the trade in handicrafts and carvings very lucrative in the coastal port and tourism hub of Mombasa. With substantial state assistance and insistence, organizations like Mombasa's Kamba woodcarving and Kisii soapstone cooperatives became the foundation of Kenya's handicrafts, or curio, trade during the 1970s and 1980s (see chapter 3). Thousands of mostly Kamba-speaking men from rural Eastern Province, many of whom remain active in carving today, spent decades developing connections with international buyers through the Kamba woodcarving cooperative's showroom and wholesale shops. Many older cooperative members I interviewed had stories of the "glory days" in the 1970s and 1980s, when the woodcarving cooperative's profits allowed poorly educated carvers to make a living and educate their siblings and children. While unique, Kenya's crafts cooperatives have a story similar to that of many thousands of other cooperatives in the country: they had early success, they are remembered nostalgically, and they have now become flooded with an unmanageable number of young people looking for employment.

Kenya's nine thousand registered cooperative societies supported over 2.5 million people in 1999 (Kenya 2002:37). But by then, the cooperatives' relationship with the central government was rapidly changing. Kenyan government support of cooperatives through direct assistance and subsidized services ended with the passage of the Co-operative Societies Act and the Sessional Paper No.6 of 1997 on "Cooperatives in a Liberalized Economic Environment." This act officially marked end of the government's obligation to assist and subsidize cooperatives by making them "free enterprises" forced to compete directly with other privately owned businesses (Kenya 2002:37; Muthuma 2012). While additional legislation was later passed in 2003, 2004, and as recently as 2008 to try to reverse some of the damage and create better government oversight and regulation of cooperatives, the "liberalization" of Kenya's cooperatives just prior to my research greatly increased economic insecurity and instability for everyone in Mombasa's crafts industry.

In addition to cutbacks in support for cooperatives, the municipal government's inconsistent approach to the city's informal and roadside economy was another major source of insecurity in the city. While traders were allowed to remain in a semiformal state along the roadsides through the 1990s, the politicized demolition of at least ten thousand roadside kiosks in Mombasa in late 2001 and early 2002 illuminates the problem of inconsistent and contradictory government policy in regulating the economy, particularly the microenterprise, or "informal," economy. Further, the political tensions surrounding the demolitions and other political activities often played on ethnic tensions in the migrant city. As I will discuss, the demolition of Mombasa's roadside kiosks in Mombasa continued a trend practiced since colonial times of removing marginalized and disadvantaged traders from Mombasa's downtown roadsides. The demolitions further isolated migrant traders and craftspeople like Davis from the potentially lucrative curio and tourism industries while simultaneously politicizing ethnic identities. The ethnic aspect of these political tensions and how they shaped my research participants' sensibilities and strategies is central to the story told in this book.

During the same years that Mombasa experienced its roadside kiosk demolitions (2001–02), access to cell phones and Internet expanded rapidly,[12] providing many disenfranchised traders like Davis with a potential means to negotiate and overcome the many political and economic barriers to enterprise and industry development. By 2005 and 2006, all of the thirty crafts exporters participating in my study were regularly using their cell phones and e-mail for business. But as Davis's story demonstrates, new digital technologies alone are not sufficient for the expansion of Kenya's handicraft industry or growth in profits for producers and small-scale traders. Rather, the stories of the individuals I have followed since 2001 point to the continuing importance of patron-client relations, education, and ethnic politics in shaping successful strategies. Personal connections and networks are as important as ever in an age of social networking, with mobile apps like Facebook, WhatsApp, and M-PESA often reproducing inequalities and the advantages of the wealthy and the well-connected.

Yet the Africa Rising hype around the importance of new digital technologies for economic development and mobility remains in the minds of marginalized and immobile individuals like Davis, who blames himself for his businesses' failure. The dual emergence of digital hype and mobility hype (or the digital-mobile) has been a fundamental aspect of neoliberal globalization in Kenya, with all of its contradictions. Marketers have actively associated digital technologies with freedom and mobility in advertisements and on billboards. For example, a 2006 advertisement for a Kenyan cellular provider featured an image of a young girl hanging from a tire swing and read simply, "Experience Freedom." Associating digital technologies and the new economy with abstract ideas such as freedom is an effective branding and marketing strategy that masks the increasing informality of the economy. Further, this new informality as an organizing logic for small businesses in cities around the world (Roy 2005), while an offshoot of neoliberal thinking, both subverts *and* preserves state power (Hansen 2014; Goldstein 2016). The state has minimal responsibility over regulating the economy, but it has the justification to intervene and tax at will. Just as Mombasa's roadside kiosks had enjoyed a semilegal formality before being violently removed when it became politically expedient (see chapter 3), so too a new generation of Kenyans occupies a semiformal economic space based not on access to urban roadsides but to international networks and mobile technologies. With this shift, the risk from direct government interaction has been mitigated. The new danger lies in becoming dependent upon a fickle global economy and precarious long-distance connections for doing business. Meanwhile, the roadsides that were once lined with kiosks and small shops are now decorated with billboards and advertising for various telecom companies.

Risk is inherent in an informal economy, where the state has withdrawn and the responsibility to manage risk has been left to individuals. Risk has long been theorized as a driving force in a globalized world or during a period of late modernity (Beck 1992, 2000; Giddens 1991). But as the economy changes, so do the risks. With a few important exceptions, there is still little anthropological literature on the precarious nature of new digital technologies and how they relate to risks—both their mediation and their encounter. Scholars have written extensively about how the modern global financial system has globalized risk (LiPuma and Lee 2004) and about the value Western businesspeople and bankers place on investing in "risky" marginalized environments (Orta 2013). Yet risk is not an objective measure but a social construction and in a state of constant flux. Indeed, it seems that what Mary Douglas and Aaron Wildavsky asserted in the early 1980s still holds true today: that due to the uniqueness of individuals' situations, "substantial disagreement remains over what is risky, how risky it is, and what to do about it" (1982:1). Kenyan businesspeople struggling in this new age of the digital-mobile and microinformality have much to teach us about risk and how risk relates to experiences of connection and mobility (and immobility).

The recent increase in mobilities research, often termed the "mobility turn" or the "new mobility paradigm," has been helpful for its focus on the performance of mobility and the power relations that shape individual experiences of mobility and immobility.[13] I am particularly drawn by Nina Glick Schiller and Noel Salazar's call to "move beyond the ready equation of mobility with freedom by examining not only movement as connection but also as an aspect of new confinements and modes of exploitation" (2013:190). The stories in this book are meant to demonstrate how new types of mobilities and opportunities available to struggling Kenyan traders come with not just new types of risks but also new forms of informality and exploitation, a new identity politics, and a new ethics and moral understandings of economic development.

AFRICAN ART AS GLOBAL COMMODITY

During my first months in Kenya as an undergraduate, it was not African art but the art traders, with their precarious livelihoods and their innovative strategies, who really fascinated me. Of course, being able to turn their precarity into my novelty was evidence of my own privilege. But I have continually been drawn to Kenya's art traders because their stories have allowed me to, as James Ferguson has suggested, "conceive, theoretically and politically, of a 'grass-roots' that would be not local, communal, and authentic, but worldly, well-connected, and opportunistic" (2004:394). Kenya's curio traders and other small-scale tourism operators were modern businesspeople with dreams of moving out of Kenya and operating transnationally as empowered social and economic actors. But the individual stories of semilegal entrepreneurs who are central to the global economy are often purposefully silenced. As Christopher Steiner writes, "the African art trader has been relegated by silence to an invisible cog in the wheels of a complex transnational market—a market which functions because of, *not* in spite of, the African middleman" (1994:10).

Writing about the commercial or economic side of the African art trade seemed surprising and counterintuitive to many Americans with whom I discussed my research. African art in North America and Europe is generally understood to represent a romanticized, precolonial ritual setting that was ostensibly free of the political and economic pressures that structure the world today. But it is important to remember that Kenya's handicrafts industry is rooted in colonialism and economically substantial. The woodcarving component alone was estimated during the mid-1990s to earn as much as US$20 million annually (Choge, Cunningham, and Ellery 2005, citing Obunga 1995 and Choge 2002). While it is nearly impossible to calculate the number of carvers, sanders, decorators, and vendors working in the woodcarving industry, Raymond Obunga (1995) estimated during his mid-1990s survey that there were 60,000–80,000 active carvers in Kenya with over 400,000 dependents (see Choge, Cunningham, and Ellery 2005:33).

One way to construct an ethnography that pushes beyond earlier anthropological preoccupations with bounded social systems or the "tribal unit" has been to follow the change of a commodity's meanings through its "social life" from production to consumption (Appadurai 1986; Steiner 1994). As Sidney Mintz (1985) did with sugar and Eric Wolf (1982) did with numerous commodities, the contributors to Arjun Appadurai's (1986) collection on the "social life of things" sought to examine the movement of commodities around the world and thus the *process* of change of objects' meanings as they circulated. African woodcarving industries, as Steiner (1994) has demonstrated, are a fertile ground for such studies (see also Jules-Rosette 1984). Kenya's handicrafts industry is just one example of many such industries that are struggling to adjust to the challenges of the global economy.

Kenya's crafts industry is especially interesting because it has long been at the center of global conversations about the meanings of Africa—as both an idea and a place—and its relationship with the rest of the world. Objects are, for example, assigned meaning when placed in the home or the "curio cabinet," as the artifact is removed from the public space of the museum to a private, domestic space. This practice has a long history. The continued terming of Kenya's commodified carvings and crafts as *curios* is traceable to the initial categorization of African art by Europeans as "curiosities," or objects that were considered "worthy neither of scientific investigation nor aesthetic appreciation" (Steiner 1994:108). Often termed *ethnic and tribal arts,* these arts and crafts have long figured into generalized cultural comparisons that hinged on underlying ethnocentric assumptions of cultural evolutionism. Using art to place diverse human cultures into an evolutionary hierarchy was useful to Europeans and Americans during the nineteenth and twentieth centuries "because [art] constituted ... the ultimate measure of human achievement" (Phillips and Steiner 1999b, 7). As Ruth Phillips and Christopher Steiner described, "The presence or absence of 'true art,' defined as free creation unfettered by functional requirements, could be used as a kind of litmus test of the level of civilization a group of people had supposedly achieved" (1999b, 7). Art informed nineteenth-century debates about whether Africa was rising or falling in the same way that digital technology does today. I would suggest that the image of an African holding a cell phone has become the litmus paper of twenty-first-century African achievement.

While the initial twentieth-century demand for African art, especially in France, was limited to the Cubists, a curiosity about Africa following the First World War helped slowly stimulate demand for African art among European consumers in other sectors of society (Steiner 1994:4–5).

Particularly with the onset of mass international tourism following the Second World War, ethnic and tourist arts became what Phillips and Steiner call "a special category of exotica, . . . constructed not just to represent the idea of the handmade, but also to display iconographic motifs and forms that signified 'old' ways of life imagined as simpler and more satisfying" (1999b:13). As Europe modernized through the twentieth century, exporting ideas and dreams of technological breakthrough and global economic integration, the art of the non-West provided the "Others" and their handmade, unsigned crafts against which white Euro-American intellectual-tourists could compare themselves for reassurance of their own modernity and civility.[14]

Kenya's handicrafts industry is inseparable from its tourism industry and the tourist imagination (Salazar 2011). Kenya's tourism industry is one of the oldest in Africa, first gaining fame in the early twentieth century for its big-game hunting.[15] Because tourism in Kenya has generally been accepted as an economic boon and a valuable asset to the national economy, tourism development was initially subsidized by the government, especially in the form of transportation infrastructure to connect the parks and beaches to Mombasa and Nairobi (Ondicho 1999:49–51). Kenya, long the center of international capitalism and investment in East Africa (Miller and Yeager 1994:3; Cooper 2002; Leys 1975; Throup 1987), came to dominate East African tourism after the 1947 establishment of the East African Tourist Travel Association (EATTA) (Alila and McCormick 1999; Ndege 1992; Sindiga 1999; Ondicho 1999). This regional association was based in Nairobi and was considered to privilege the development of Kenyan tourism over Uganda and Tanzania within British East Africa (Alila and McCormick 1999:7).[16]

After independence in 1963, President Jomo Kenyatta's government followed the colonial lead and developed Kenya as one of Africa's most popular tourist destinations. During the 1960s, international tourism was largely seen globally as enabling economic development and therefore a public good. The United Nations, for example, declared 1967 International Tourism Year (Crick 1989:315). That same year, the U.S. government gave $3 million to Kenya for tourism development, most of which went to strengthening infrastructure in Nairobi and Mombasa (Akama 1999:15). By 1969 tourism took the place of coffee as the country's single largest source of foreign exchange.[17] Large government-supported bodies such as the Kenya Tourism Development Corporation (KTDC), the Industrial and Commercial Development Corporation (ICDC), and the Development Finance Company of Kenya (DFCK) became important actors during the early independence period, when development policy was focused on enabling the government to carefully control investments (Leys 1975:131–32).[18]

These investments in infrastructure created the slate upon which the messages of Kenyan tourism could be written and consumed by the world's leisure class. The constellation of symbols and language central to Kenyan tourism "is as much a structure of power as it is a structure of meaning," writes Edward Bruner (1991:240). In Kenya, much of that meaning and representation is produced, conveyed, and consumed through arts and crafts sold to tourists. The vendors of those crafts, therefore, have a certain degree of power and influence over the messages of Kenyan tourism.

Kenya's tourism and curio industries initially derived their symbolism from images of "tribal" Maasai pastoralists and wildlife motifs, largely because these were the stereotypical images of Africa desired by white Westerners and tourists. These relatively tame primordial images successfully marketed Kenya through the 1970s and 1980s, when the young nation was perceived internationally as "an 'island' of stability in a 'sea' of political turmoil in the African continent" (Akama 2002:8). These early depictions were firmly rooted in the British colonial imagination and had been nurtured by the colonial settlers, administrators, and travelers who were Kenya's initial tourists and the original consumers of Kenya's carvings and crafts. To meet this demand, Kenyan artisans and businesspeople had first begun developing new products to sell specifically to the British following the First World War. By Kenyan independence in 1963, major networks for the production and distribution of arts and crafts connected Kenyan artisans and cooperatives to the rest of East Africa and the world.

The desire and allure underlying Western curiosity about Africa and its art had not dissipated by the end of the century. In a discussion of late twentieth-century museum presentations of African art, Steiner (1996) discussed how African art still relies upon a process of mystification and discovery to be palatable and desirable for Western consumption. He describes how African art, while often unchanging in form, has continued to be represented for the American public (specifically in New York City museums and exhibitions) as a newly discovered form of primitive art that is proof that Others are capable of exotic masterpieces. Steiner compared New York City's late-twentieth-century attraction to African art to that of the 1930s, arguing that the production and reproduction of images of Africa in the West relied on a continual erasing and rediscovery of Africa's past. It is, indeed, the erasure of Africa's past that has allowed the singular concept of "Africa" (or Africa

Rising) to emerge as a sociocultural reality in the early twenty-first century. This erasure also speaks to the illusion and mystification inherent in the presentation of all African art, although my research participants were slowly shifting away from presenting Africa as a place of wild animals, tribal peoples, and colonial discovery toward representing it as a connected but marginalized place in need of help.

I often asked myself whether revealing rather than erasing the recent history and economic realities of Kenya's crafts industry potentially damages the value of the art itself. Not necessarily, I have concluded; value is always a slippery construct. Products labeled as Fair Trade, for example, generate value by explicitly informing altruistic consumers about production conditions (see chapters 6 and 7). In later chapters I will discuss the phenomenon of marketing marginality, or revealing producers' marginality or poverty to attract altruistic customers.[19] Amid this tension between revelation and obfuscation, ideas like transparency, trust, and ethics would also become central to traders' strategies for brokering the meanings and the value of the arts and crafts they sold.

TRANSPARENCY AND THE ART OF CONNECTION

In this book, I use "art of connection" in two primary ways. In one sense, it is a means by which businesspeople create and maintain economic ties, in the case of my research participants, after being physically displaced. In other words, it is an economic strategy or series of strategies involving both material transactions and symbolic performances. Digital technologies are central to these evolving strategies for maintaining business connections and for producing representations of connection and transparency. Digital technologies also expand the types of connections that can be repeatedly made at multiple scales: between intermediaries and their local, regional, and global networks; between producers and consumers over great distances; between producers and consumers in face-to-face encounters; and between citizens and states. As much as the art of connection is about enabling mundane business transactions and face-to-face interactions, it is also about fantasy, idealization, illusion, and obfuscation. The art of making and maintaining connections looks very different for producers than it does for Kenyan exporters, intermediaries, or overseas buyers.

In a second sense, the art of connection is an artistic motif that has become very popular since the 1990s. The art-of-connection motif, to which I return in chapter 7, displays interhuman connection, often through abstract anthropogenic forms that lack gender or race. These carvings and sculptures generally depict balanced connection, or even equality. As I argue in chapter 7, they are popular among Kenyan vendors as well as tourists and buyers because they depict an ideal of egalitarian global connectivity that is free from the constraints of racial or gender inequality. One might even call these sculptures and their ideals Afropolitan. While these sculptures are fundamentally ideological—we indeed live in a world structured by racial, gender, and other forms of inequality—they artistically display the importance of and value placed upon equality and transparent and trusting connection in the world today.

While transparency is experienced in fleeting moments, it is crucial for forming the connections (especially long-distance, digital connections) essential to economic survival, risk management, and the balancing of multiple identities and affiliations in the modern world. In an age of neoliberalism, transparency has globally become a powerful form of intervention into a world of understandable and controllable relations (Ballestero 2012, 160; Bessire 2005; Gaonkar and McCarthy 1994; Hetherington 2011). Nongovernmental organizations (NGOs), for example, work under the guise of transparency to rationalize their interventions. As Martin Webb has argued, "the work of transparency activists is directed at producing an 'ethical scene' in which their poor clients are encouraged to understand themselves as potentially empowered citizens of a nation wounded by corruption and bad governance" (2012:206). Transparency, an idea based upon a deceptively simple visual metaphor, is rooted in illusion and has a deep politics that ethnography can help us to better understand (Ballestero 2012; Hetherington 2011; Poggiali 2016).

I am interested in the connections between digital technologies and transparency, and particularly the idea that digital technologies will make relationships among long-distance traders or between citizen and state more transparent. I have found that rather than having any automatic impact, new digital technologies like cell phones challenged long-distance traders and exporters to appear transparent in ways they may previously have not had to. Long-distance impersonal business has brought a new challenge of trust. New linguistic and symbolic practices—from web-page designs to business cards—have become essential for negotiating inequality over distances and making and maintaining new connections—or the art of connection.

The best example of the production of a sense of transparency as central to the art of connection comes in the form of the Fair Trade sticker, ethical branding, or what I refer to as "NGO aesthetics" and the marketing of marginality.[20] Fair Trade's ethical philosophy involves connecting craftspeople and producers directly to Western importers, thus bypassing intermediaries (Reichman 2008:108). But in addition to the implicit assertion that buyers are being connected directly and fairly to nonexploited producers, Fair Trade companies also regularly claim that their crafts are made by "single mothers," "disabled girls," or "homeless children" as a way to attract altruistic buyers who want to participate in African "development." It is generally assumed that these marginalized artisans are treated fairly, although *fair* is rarely clearly defined, and even when it is (such as by Fair Trade labeling organizations), there is insufficient oversight. What makes this economically profitable from the perspective of the Kenyan crafts traders and exporters is that now they can attract customers by presenting their often exploitative business practices as transparent. They can openly market that the products they are selling are being made by marginalized and exploited groups.

In other global industries, such as textiles, this search for the cheapest labor to maintain the highest profit margins is known as the "race to the bottom" (Klein 2002; Rudra 2008; Tonelson 2002). Naomi Klein has documented how corporate lifestyle-branding works to obfuscate the realities of the sweatshop labor that actually drives the global textile industry. But the Fair Trade brand is different. It succeeds by not only erasing the exploitative realities of the global economy but revealing the realities of marginality and need. The only remaining challenge for intermediaries is to erase their potentially exploitative existence, or render themselves invisible. This is crucial to avoid fears of exploitation among customers.

Not only do most Kenyan carvers and craftspeople make very little money, but even the exporters and intermediaries—the actual people who apply the Fair Trade stickers—live lives that are surrounded by insecurity and shaped by the uncertainties of Kenyan politics and the global economy. If a trader is ever slow to adapt and innovate, competitors can quickly use their advantages to cut him or her out of the business (as with Davis). Individual entrepreneurs with personal connections were generally the fastest to adapt cell phones and e-mail to their businesses, setting the stage for intense competition with the more established workshops and cooperatives (see chapter 6). Throughout this competition, the Fair Trade sticker has continued to represent a transparent, ethical, and trusting relationship that makes the intermediary and the exploitative realities of production invisible. By balancing revelation and obfuscation—what is revealed and what is not—Kenyan art traders can produce a sense of trust and transparency that is central to the art of connection.

In summary, I use and have observed transparency being used in two ways. First, from a more emic perspective, being transparent implies being ethical or trustworthy. The word *transparency* itself has had great significance in Kenya since at least the 1990s, and it is often used within a political context as the opposite of corruption. When applied to the economy, *transparency* suggests trust, honesty, and fairness. A business might be seen as ethical because it is transparent with its customers and employees. But traders, governments, and corporations alike can produce a sense of transparency today in order to simplify very complex and potentially exploitative economic networks and their political realities. Transparency as the deployment of an ethical scene emphasizes intelligibility and simplicity over complexity, which brings us to the more complicated usage of transparency.

In a second, more etic sense, transparency is also about erasure or strategic invisibility. Transparency, Andrea Ballestero (2012) has argued, is about much more than making the opaque visible. For example, with the application of a Fair Trade sticker, Kenyan exporters are not only revealing but also simplifying complex economic realities by branding them as "ethical." By doing so, they render their own roles as potentially exploitative intermediaries invisible, leaving the eventual consumer with the opportunity to purchase not just a material commodity but a direct connection to a needy artisan. Therefore, while transparency can make the opaque *visible*—by revealing the marginality of artisans to attract altruistic buyers—performing or producing a sense of transparency can also serve to erase complex economic realities and render potentially exploitative intermediaries *invisible*. Transparency, therefore, is not just about revelation but also erasure. The art of connection relies upon maintaining trust by balancing revelation and obfuscation.

Transparency thus becomes central to the art of connection, both through the idealistic connections depicted in the artistic motif and in the form of the new branding and symbolic strategies used by traders to maintain the fleeting notions of trusted long-distance connection in the minds of their business partners and the eventual consumers. Clever labeling and branding tactics—which also involve removing all the original labeling placed on products by the actual producers—are essential for exporters and intermediaries to maintain their jobs and positions within the commodity chain. The art of connection I discuss in this book is, therefore, a story of how disadvantaged Kenyan exporters and intermediaries balance the intimacy and distance afforded by new digital technologies to perform trusting and ethical connections and practices while erasing unappealing political and economic realities (such as ethnopolitical violence) and the complexity of the commodity chain itself.

This book speaks to ethnicity in Kenya—its tenacious reifications and conflicts, its lived realities, and the efforts to challenge ethnic divisiveness (see Bravman 1998; Lynch 2011; McIntosh 2009; Osborne 2014). Beyond being dutiful presentations of political and economic history, the first several chapters of this book focus specifically on situating ethnicity in Kenya. But the stories I tell are not just of conflict and reification of difference but also of how businesspeople have struggled to overcome ethnic divisiveness to find economic success and to manage risk. The businesspeople who participated in my research were operating within an extremely insecure and risky political and economic environment. As ethnic identities were politicized by Kenya's political elites in feuds over election votes (especially in 1997 and 2007–08), traders I knew who depended upon tourism and economic stability became perturbed by ethnic or "tribal" rivalries and performances.

Meanwhile, Kenyan art that showed the nation to be modern, changing, and new, represented Kenya as welcoming to tourists without playing on labels, brands, and symbols that were often politically sensitive. It appealed to tourists on its own terms, as modern or worldly with a cosmopolitan identity and neither "tribal" nor "traditional" in either a cultural or economic sense. Although John Comaroff and Jean Comaroff have demonstrated in their book *Ethnicity, Inc.* (2009) that ethnic symbolism has a powerful value when marketed in a neoliberal era, I found that ethnic tension in Kenya was one of many reasons for crafts producers and traders to de-ethnicize their products and downplay ethnic or "tribal" symbolism. Ethnicity can generate value in the world today, but only in relation to the lived realities of ethnic conflict as experienced in real-world locales and contexts. As I will discuss, it is at times advantageous to replace the ethnic brand with the Fair Trade label.

PROJECT DESIGN, LANGUAGE, AND METHODS

This book is the product of a longitudinal study and my long-standing relationships with people who could be termed informants or research subjects.

I prefer to use the term *research participant* because terms like *informant* deceptively suggest that such individuals were passive subjects in the overall project and simply gave me information or were observed. The research was in many ways a collaboration between me and the Kenyans who steered and directed my lines of inquiry. This ethnography is also the result of my ability (or inability at times) to stay in contact with traders for more than a decade as I worked to continue my studies and research and they tried to sustain and expand their businesses. Digital technologies played a central role in my ability to keep in touch with participants, breaking down the oft-described boundary between "the field" and "the home."

At the core of this research and my own exercise in international social connectivity was my ability to communicate and use language to my benefit rather than allow it to be a hindrance. Fluency in colloquial Kenyan Swahili and overall linguistic flexibility gave me the social mobility needed to live and function within the array of communities found in urban and semiurban coastal Kenya. Urban and well-educated Kenyans tend to be multilingual, usually knowing at least conversational English and Swahili as well as other indigenous or foreign languages. I found that many urban Kenyans, especially those from multiethnic areas of Nairobi and Mombasa or those who had gone to school with Kenyans from around the country, knew at least some of the language of their parents' ethnic group (or groups), as well as bits and greetings of Kikuyu, Luo, and the languages of other large Kenyan ethnic communities. Kenyans with whom I interacted daily, ranging from roadside vendors to academics, found it peculiar that a foreigner like me would take interest in the local languages of Kenya. But Kenyans tended to view my language skills positively if for no more reason than the novelty, and language became an important way to demonstrate that I was not just another tourist. I could explain my interest in language by pointing out that it was, indeed, my job to know the bits and pieces of Giriama, Kikuyu, and Luo that were slipped into everyday speech in Mombasa just as it was theirs to learn enough German, French, and Italian to greet the variety of foreign tourists that frequent Mombasa and conduct a simple business transaction with them. I also felt it was important to conduct interviews in people's first languages so that they could feel comfortable expressing themselves. As a result, many of the quotes in this book are translations from Swahili or, more commonly, a mixture of Swahili and English.

My research began in early 2001, when I lived in the Hermes Hotel in downtown Mombasa and walked ten minutes to Fort Jesus daily to sit and chat with the roadside vendors and tour guides.[21] At the time I was studying Swahili intensively as a twenty-year-old study-abroad student. Those first months of research were spent on the roadside or in the park outside of the fort, playing chess and checkers, getting rained on, and primarily just talking and telling stories. I learned about Swahili slang and Kenyan popular culture while explaining how Americans *really* felt about George W. Bush and who *really* killed Biggie and Tupac (both questions I was regularly asked in the early days of research). Beyond developing rapport and cultural competency, my goal was to understand the basic components of the traders' businesses, how they had come to occupy their dilapidated roadside structures, and how they related to the residents of the immediate Old Town community. I also considerably expanded my knowledge of Swahili and developed strong friendships with many of the vendors, who were in some cases as interested in being friends with a young American as I was in learning about their livelihoods.

As I got to know the Fort Jesus curio traders better, I realized that they offered an interesting window onto larger social and economic processes in Mombasa, largely challenging the simple arguments about coastal ethnopolitical allegiance and conflict. For example, Davis was a vendor whose father was Luo and whose mother was Kisii but who spoke Kikuyu (in addition to Kisii, Swahili, and English) fluently after growing up in Nairobi. As a result, while he lacked a formal education or wealth, Davis had several situational ethnic identities to draw upon. His ethnic identity carried a great deal of ambiguity, challenging the notion that ethnic categories in Kenya were rigid and inflexible.

Wanjiru, a woman of eighteen when I first met her in 2001, was socially categorized as Kikuyu despite the fact that she was born and raised in Mombasa and did not speak Kikuyu fluently. In 2005 she self-identified as one of the *Mombasani,* a term used by many young Kenyans in Mombasa from noncoastal ethnic groups who stressed that they had no home other than Mombasa. While she and other Kenyans were often seen as migrants or outsiders on the Kenyan coast, claims to tenure and belonging along Mombasa's roadsides were complicated (see chapter 2).

Other curio vendors like Simon, born in 1978, had migrated to Mombasa in the mid-1990s from near the town of Samburu in Kwale District of Coast Province. He had lived in Mombasa for less time than either Davis or Wanjiru, but he was generally categorized by the government, scholars, and local communities as a "coastal person" (*mpwani*) and a Mijikenda, whereas the others were seen as migrants or "upcountry people" (*watu wa bara*).

The contradictions of ethnoregional identity were numerous, and the iro-
nies were pervasive around the tourism industry and curio trade, which sold
its own form of "tribalism" to a Western audience through Kamba woodcarving, Maasai beadwork, and Kisii soapstone. This was despite the constructed
nature of these categories and the fact that Kenyan handicrafts were often
made by individuals from backgrounds other than those of the labels used to
market the art. The traders lining the roadside outside of Fort Jesus in 2001
represented to me all of the complexities and contradictions not just of identity but also of economic necessity for Mombasa's struggling businesspeople.

When the kiosks that provided the basic infrastructure for the population
of my original study were demolished with the rest of Mombasa's roadside
structures in December 2001 and January 2002 (see chapter 3), the new regime
of economic change and urban "cleaning" began to steer my project. The ethnic
politics and tensions that surrounded elections and events like the kiosk demolitions were also central to the stories I collected. I had initially been interested
in the realities of conducting a business along the roadside in urban Mombasa.
Now my research participants, many of whom could barely keep in touch with
me by phone or e-mail, were struggling to find any opportunity available.

The importance of cell phones and e-mail access to my participants at this
particular time of crisis was something that I felt needed emphasis, especially
as Kenya would soon be dubbed Africa's "Silicon Savanna" (Perry 2011). A
longitudinal research design allowed me to follow the larger patterns of how
digital technologies and economic changes influenced traders and their business strategies. Rather than sidelining new tools like cell phones and the
Internet, I decided to bring them to the forefront of my research agenda,
making the impact of new communication technologies a central component
of my Fulbright-funded, year-long dissertation research project (2005–06; see
Mahoney 2009).

Beginning in 2005, I began to focus (in person or remotely through contacts) on three research zones: (1) Mombasa's Old Town outside of Fort Jesus;
(2) Changamwe, home to the Kamba and Kisii cooperatives, Magongo Curio
Market, and many of my research participants; and (3) the beaches of the
North Coast, including the tourist venues and informal economic networks
built up around the public beach locally known as "Pirates" after a local club
and performance venue. In 2005 and 2006, I rented an apartment in the middle of Mombasa Island overlooking the city's football stadium and roughly
geographically in the center of my three research zones, allowing me daily
access to each. In 2007 and 2008 I lived just north of Mombasa in the area

between Kikambala and Mtwapa, and in 2014 I stayed in the city very close to the train station. On many mornings, I would ride with other commuters into downtown Mombasa, alight at the General Post Office, buy a newspaper and walk down Makadara and Nkrumah Roads toward the Town Hall, municipal offices, and Fort Jesus. After a few hours of chatting with the vendors as they set up their businesses and began their days, I would head back toward the Post Office to catch a *matatu* to Changamwe. Coming back into Mombasa in the late afternoon usually afforded enough time to eat before heading to the North Coast for the evening (see map 1, in the next chapter).

I have also frequently made excursions across East Africa to track down economic networks that I had found converging in the port city. I have spent considerable time conducting informal surveys in Lamu, Malindi, and Nairobi, and my research has at times taken me to areas of Machakos, Wamunyu, Kitui, Tabaka, Kisii, Kisumu, Lunga Lunga, and Arusha, as well as to small shops throughout the United States. These trips were important for contextualizing the production groups and intermediaries I found in Mombasa.

In total, well over 150 individuals participated in the research on which this book is based. Of those participants, a majority were involved in the curio industry as carvers or traders, although many had no direct connection to the handicrafts business. Roughly one-quarter of eventual research participants were part of the research beginning in 2001, while the rest were slowly added with time and through snowball sampling. While most of those who participated were male, more than twenty women participated. As I will discuss in future chapters, although men were historically at the center of the carving industries, and the populations of Kenyan cities have been disproportionately male since the colonial era, women have found their own niche in the crafts industries making certain products like baskets and beadwork or as vendors along roadsides or on beaches. I am indebted to the Republic of Kenya for allowing me to conduct this research and to everyone who participated in this research, and I feel a great burden in trying to represent their experiences as best I can.

A NOTE ON NAMING

To further complicate the task of writing about ethnicity in Africa, many categories, politically constructed or not, exist as linguistic or geographic entities. For example, "Swahili" people are called the *Waswahili* in the Swahili language, and their language, *Kiswahili*. Kenya's coast is also often simply called the Swahili Coast, despite the minority status of Swahili in the region. This is a separate issue from the old question "Who is a Swahili?" (see Eastman 1971), the answer to which is largely historically and geographically dependent. While it is necessary to refer to ethnic communities in this book, I only do so with hesitation. My goal is not to problematically essentialize ethnic communities that are themselves colonial constructions and under continual contestation and negotiation. Rather, I wish to capture and represent the linguistic and political realities I found. To give another example, Kamba speakers are called *Wakamba* in Swahili and *Akamba* in their own language, Kikamba. It is therefore common to hear the Kamba cooperative called the Akamba cooperative. For convenience, I have used the common English root terms *Swahili, Kamba,* and *Kikuyu* to refer to ethnic communities and languages. But this is an admittedly imperfect attempt. I have tried to problematize ethnic categories when possible, and I have noted in backnotes cases that are less clear.

Because of the sensitivity of some of this book's topics, I have omitted or changed all the names of traders and research participants to maintain their anonymity. The names of most cooperatives and organizations, however, are real. In most of these cases there was little I could do to hide the identities of the workshops or cooperative groups. If I felt my representation would be of no harm, I decided to use the real names of websites, groups, and workshops. In some cases, however, they have been changed.

Another problem arose in naming the types of wood carved. Anthony Cunningham has raised this issue regarding the wood carved and sold across East Africa, asking: "When you are told that a wood is mahogany, ironwood or ebony, for example, which one of the 30 tree species commonly called 'mahogany,' 100 species called 'ironwood' or 40 species called 'ebony' do you think this refers to?"[22] To further complicate the linguistic reality, most trees and woods sold in Kenya have names in Swahili and other African languages as well as in English. The very dark-colored African blackwood, for example, is called *mpingo* in Swahili. *Mpingo* in turn is translated into English as "ebony," even though African blackwood *(Dalbergia melanoxylon)* is not a "true ebony" of the *Diospyros* genus. In a similar case, the wood most preferred by the carvers, called *muhugu (Brachylaena huillensis)* and usually translated as "mahogany," is actually a hard guava wood and not a "true mahogany" (Jules-Rosette 1984:119). However, because these woods are commonly sold and marketed as "ebony" and "mahogany," I often use the same terms as the traders and note any inconsistencies in the backnotes.

How have preexisting inequalities along lines of education, age, gender, ethnic background, and personal connections been reproduced historically? What role does a history of British indirect rule and cooperative development play in shaping how Kenyans from diverse backgrounds understand and navigate the risks and opportunities created by new digital communication technologies? The next two chapters of the book blend history and ethnography to give the reader a fuller understanding of the historical struggles over belonging in Mombasa.

In chapter 2, I explore the history of social inequality and the conflicting discourses of marginality predominant in the city. One view shared by many struggling migrants holds that they have been denied their rights as Kenyan citizens. Another represents various coastal communities that have been actively disenfranchised and manipulated by both the colonial and postcolonial governments of Kenya. Both groups make claims to land and political representation in Mombasa—one from a national perspective and one from a regional perspective. This comparison frames a decade of individual stories of ethnic insecurity and the struggle to access cooperatives and municipal markets, local and international economic networks, tourist hotels and beaches, and ethnic neighborhoods and communities. This chapter is also important for providing background on ethnic politics and tensions that were so central to the precarious economic environment in which my participants were competing.

Chapter 3 then traces the development of Kenya's tourism and handicraft industries from their roots in twentieth-century British colonialism. I draw on archival as well as ethnographic data collected just before the 2002 demolition of Mombasa's roadside kiosks, which form the starting point for the larger longitudinal study. I focus on the array of experiences of Mombasa's roadside traders of diverse backgrounds as they struggle with the privatization and segregation of urban residential and commercial space both before and after the demolitions.

Chapter 4 engages with the theme of economic informality and economic regulation in Kenya. In 2002, Mwai Kibaki was elected on an anticorruption platform that stressed job creation, telecom liberalization, "city cleaning," and increased revenue collection. I am interested specifically in how the relationship between the informal economy and the Kenyan state changed during Kibaki's presidency (2002–2013), particularly in Mombasa and among my research participants. I am concerned with how residents of Mombasa, including those who work around the tourism industry, understood their rights and economic opportunities following waves of urban kiosk demolitions between 2001 and 2004. I also use detailed ethnographic examples and economic histories to demonstrate the effects of government attempts to license and tax coastal handicrafts traders and tourism operators.

Chapters 5 and 6 explore the impact of new digital technologies on artisans, exporters, and cooperative organizations. Chapter 5 provides a comparison of Simon and Davis, two traders who developed very different strategies after the demolition of the roadside kiosks. Building on my argument about the importance of risk for assessing new mobilities developed in chapter 5, chapter 6 explores the ideas of transparency, Fair Trade, and "ethical" development. I argue that the art of connection in an economically informal age when digital technology has become essential is rooted in the production and maintenance of a sense of trust and transparency, however illusory.

In chapter 7, I turn to changes in the aesthetics and forms of the art itself to demonstrate how connected and savvy Kenyan traders have adapted to an ever-changing and diverse tourist demographic, including Afropolitans. Can the community of Kenyan culture brokers alter the notion of what constitutes an "authentic" experience of Kenya through their economic strategies and the shifting aesthetics of the art they sell? In questioning a singular and static notion of an authentic Kenya or Africa as produced through tourism and tourist art, I explore how Kenyan tourist art and handicrafts have been marketed in new and creative ways: as Fair Trade, as a particular tree species, or as representing modern global interconnectedness. I focus on the art-of-connection motif and its artistic representation of an ideal of egalitarian and transparent human interconnection acceptable to both tourists and Kenyan vendors.

I conclude with a discussion of what the experiences of Kenyan traders and culture brokers can tell us about globalization, development, and digital-power divides today. Talking strictly of a *digital* divide in Kenya distracts attention from the historical formation of social inequality and masks the actions of certain powerful political, corporate, and development elites. This masking is an important aspect in the illusion of transparency so artistically mobilized today by innovative East African entrepreneurs.

TWO

Mombasa Marginalized

CLAIMS TO LAND AND LEGITIMACY
IN A TOURIST CITY

Nearly everyone arrives on the coast at Mombasa, a much more
enjoyable place to spend time than Nairobi. Kenya's second city
is a tropical centre par excellence: steamy, lazy, at times unbeliev-
ably dilapidated, but genial.

RICHARD TRILLO
The Rough Guide to Kenya *(2002:441)*

I WAS INITIALLY DRAWN TO Mombasa and its Old Town for reasons
similar to those that have enticed hundreds of thousands of American and
European travelers to visit the Kenyan coast every year since the late 1960s.
Our predictable imaginations, desires, and spending habits were the economic foundation of Mombasa's tour guides, hawkers, and the occupants of
the roughly twenty wood-and-sheet-metal kiosks that were built on the roadside outside of Old Town's Fort Jesus. These structures and their occupants
were the focus of my initial study in 2001, during which time I befriended
many of their resident art vendors who were selling Kisii soapstone and
Kamba wood carvings, as well as handmade baskets, paintings, and jewelry.

I found it easy to emerge from even a brief foray through Mombasa with
two quite different stories of the social landscape. On the one hand, the city
has since the 1960s been a major international tourism hub, a destination for
European beach prowlers, American safari seekers in transit, and a multitude
of international cruise lines navigating the western Indian Ocean. Even
among Kenyans, Mombasa occupies an imaginative space of vacation,
warmth, and welcome, as summed up by the oft-heard phrase "Mombasa
raha" (Mombasa fun). Tourist art adorns even local bars and Internet cafés
in the city, and until recently a sign in French, Italian, German, English, and
Swahili welcomed visitors entering Mombasa from the airport, Nairobi, and
the continental mainland. During my stay in Mombasa, tens of thousands of

FIGURE 1. Mombasa's public beach on a Sunday. Kenyans often enjoy being tourists in their own country and visit the beach to swim, ride a camel, or simply enjoy the breeze. Photo by author, 2003.

tourists from Nairobi and "up-country" would descend upon Mombasa during the Easter and Christmas holidays, filling hotels, nightclubs, and beaches alike (figure 1; domestic tourism will be discussed further in chapter 7.).

But despite the promise inspired by depictions of Mombasa's warm climate, leisurely way of life, and slow pace, for centuries the port city was called Mvita, a name often translated as "place of war."[1] Indeed, as much as Mombasa's history is one of cosmopolitan sociocultural mixture and sharing, the interactions that have defined the city's social politics have taken place within the context of larger structures of violence and inequality such as slavery and colonization. Mombasa has most recently been in the Western press not as a hot spot for tourists but as a site of human and drug trafficking as well as terrorism (Kithi 2006; Mayoyo and Wabala 2006).

Since 2001, there has been constant fluctuation between representations of Mombasa as an ideal, pristine tourist destination and as an insecure city of travel advisories and warnings. Neither chaotic nor irrational, these events and experiences of the city were part of a larger pattern with deep historical roots. The underlying ethnopolitical tensions in Mombasa provide the backdrop for my larger study of curio vendors' use of digital technologies, particularly as they struggled to find secure ways to do business.

As recently as 2014 and 2015, there were constant warnings about security in Kenya and particularly Mombasa. It reminded me of June 2003, when I traveled to Mombasa just months after the United States had invaded Iraq and less than a year after a hotel just north of Mombasa had been bombed.

Both times, travel advisories and warnings of possible terrorist attacks and political violence hurt the tourism industry and created a palpable tension.

But by 2014 and 2015, the spatial organization of the crafts and tourism industries had dramatically changed. Businesspeople were no longer lining the urban roadsides but were instead much more mobile, operating with cell phones, websites, and carefully constructed business cards. The art of connection that had existed in the predigital era along Mombasa's roadsides was quite different from that which emerged in later years. This chapter addresses the earlier importance of connecting to the roadside, to Mombasa's local tourism industry, and to tourists with whom businesspeople could interact face-to-face.

Whereas tourism had been Kenya's leading source of foreign exchange in the late 1980s, the industry's promise was shaken in the early 1990s. The return of multiparty politics in 1991–92 meant turmoil and violence for many Kenyans, especially in strategic cities like Mombasa, where social stratification had long been politicized and new opposition parties became outlets for decades of frustration. Although the 1990s were an important period for the development of Kenyan democracy, the economic downturn and political violence shattered many hopes of economic development and modernization.

Beginning in the early 1990s, the ruling party, the Kenya African National Union (KANU), increasingly turned to violence to silence the political opposition. In the early 1990s, KANU targeted the Islamic Party of Kenya (IPK) in Mombasa in order to divide and destabilize Muslim unity, which it saw as a direct challenge to its political dominance (HRW 2002; Oded 2000; Wolf 2000:141–42). Amid the turmoil, tourists and investors stayed away, and the tourist city of Mombasa slipped into a state of persistent insecurity. For example, in 1993 the IPK organized a strike that paralyzed Mombasa, making it arguably one of the most successful in Kenya's postcolonial history (Mazrui and Shariff 1994:152). In Old Town, battles raged as narrow streets were blocked, and petrol bombs were hurled at easily ambushed police vehicles. Kenya's coastal tourism hub remained a ghost town as heavily armed riot police patrolled the rainy streets with dogs. Such events cast fear of economic collapse into tour operators, investors, and Christian migrants, who often spoke to me about the political violence surrounding the government's muzzling of the IPK as the beginning of the political-economic precariousness that would haunt them for the next several decades.

President Moi and KANU had an extra challenge on the coast preceding the 1997 general election, as it was Moi's final legal term as president and

Mombasa had become a bastion of political opposition. The call for constitutional reform was getting louder, and stipulations had been added that would make it more difficult for Moi and KANU to emerge victorious in both national and local elections.[2] Meanwhile, the corruption in Mombasa's local affairs had become more obvious to the voting population, and there was a noticeable decline in living standards in the city and across the country.[3] Tourism had been declining since the beginning of the 1990s, and investors had begun to move out of Mombasa town to the walled protection of coastal resorts. By 1997, migrants from up-country Kenya were seen "ipso facto, [as] opposition supporters" in Mombasa, which had the potential to politically unite up-country migrants and coastal Muslims, such as IPK supporters, against Moi and KANU (Wolf 2000:148).

On the night of August 13, 1997, a Kamba curio vendor and research participant named Andrew returned to Likoni on Mombasa's South Coast after work. He had been playing cards in a small bar next to the police station before heading home earlier than usual. But upon arriving home, a complex of rooms where he lived with other Kamba, Kisii, and Digo men (some Muslims from the coast and others Christians from up-country), he heard shots from the area of the police station he had just left. As he recalled, he and his neighbors had no idea what was happening, and they spent the night in fear with their doors locked and the lights off.

During that first night of violence, raiders attacked the Likoni police station, killed six officers, stole over forty guns, and then went on a violent rampage through the neighborhoods on Mombasa's South Coast (HRW 2002:39). Andrew told me that some of the men with whom he had been socializing earlier in the night had been hurt or killed during the violence. He had avoided it by only minutes.

The raiders targeted primarily Christian Kamba, Kikuyu, Luhya, and Luo migrants living in Likoni, just south of Mombasa Island (see map 1). The tense issue of land tenure and ownership on the coast, as well as issues of access to public jobs, had led many to blame unemployment and underdevelopment on an "'invasion' of 'up-country' businesspeople" (Wolf 2000:142). In addition to the six police killed the first day, six civilians were killed and hundreds of others were beaten and maimed severely with multiple machete wounds (HRW 2002:61). Following the attacks on the police station, raiders went house to house threatening up-country migrants. Some who testified to Human Rights Watch admitted using language, greetings, and accents to identify people's ethnic backgrounds. As Andrew explained to me several years later: "We did not know what it was about since there was very little problem between coastal and up-country people. We were all poor. There were all types of rumors about who it was, but Kenyans are peace-loving people. Whatever this was, it was a matter of politics."

A Kisii curio vendor whom I interviewed in 2005 had lived in Likoni since the 1970s and remembered the first night when the raiders came to his house. As was typical in the area, several families of diverse Kenyan ethnic backgrounds resided in his housing compound, each in a separate room. The raiders banged on the doors and forced everyone outside at gunpoint. They lined up the inhabitants and asked them to declare their "tribe" or ethnic background (*kabila* in Swahili). The man with whom I spoke explained that those coming from southwest Kenya, like him, were told to kneel down while those of coastal background remained standing. But the Luo men, he told me, were beaten severely rather than told to kneel. They were all finally told, "Ukitoka bara, ondoka kesho" (If you are from up-country, leave tomorrow).

He immediately contacted his brother, who was a policeman in Mombasa and who came to help him evacuate his property and family using a police vehicle. When the raiders returned the next morning, they began shooting at the police, who were still helping my research participant remove furniture from his home. He abandoned most of his property, he told me, and headed straight to Changamwe, on the mainland to the west of Mombasa Island (see map 1), and had never returned to Likoni in the nearly ten years since then. It helped to have a police vehicle, he said in 2005 from his family's one-room home in Chaani, a neighbourhood in Changamwe. "This is where I came," he said. "I moved straight in here. I salvaged only what you see. And I was very lucky."

These types of stories were fresh in the minds of the traders and tour operators I interviewed in the early years of my research, although it was in their economic best interest to keep these stories far from the ears of tourists. Election years were regularly feared because of the potential for violence and the loss of business. Even if the violence did not immediately or directly affect individuals' daily lives, Kenyans were very much aware that travel advisories issued by such countries as the United States or Great Britain could cripple business. These advisories have repeatedly hurt Kenya's tourism and crafts industries. Indeed, one of the major reasons for individuals to "jump scales" into the international crafts business was to break their dependence on tourist arrivals.

The art of connection I describe in this book is shaped by this context of pervasive insecurity. Not only were traders moving away from downtowns and a dependence upon tourist arrivals, the art they sold also began to change in form and symbolism. A vast majority of traders and entrepreneurs I interviewed downplayed their ethnic backgrounds and the ethnic or "tribal" symbolism in their art. For these aspiring Kenyan businesspeople, ethnicity was a matter of politics and not something they sought to promote. But at the same time that respondents downplayed ethnic conflict, their stories, which begin in this chapter, also demonstrate how susceptible they were to the ramifications of ethnic politics in Kenya. This is essential for understanding the messiness of the lived experience of ethnicity in Kenya that symbols and presentations of transparency are so important for simplifying.

This chapter provides an opportunity to explore the risks and economic ups and downs that have shaped the lives of Mombasa's residents and the struggles to create a form of Kenyan nationalism on the coast. While risk is omnipresent in contemporary societies (Beck 1992, 2000), risk itself is a social construct and is in constant flux (Douglas and Wildavsky 1982). To contextualize the risks confronting my research participants, I provide a historical background on identity and belonging in Mombasa before turning to the complexity of ethnoreligious identity among my initial research participants. My goal is to reveal the complexity of ethnoreligious identity I encountered. While I explain the main ethnoregional divides in Mombasa, I also discuss how crafts traders sought security through multiethnic unity and an ethical, national sense of citizenship in opposition to the chaos and violence that so often dominated headlines. In the predigital age, there was an art to connection, although it looked quite different from what I would find in later years. This chapter allows the opportunity to discuss the situation when I first began my research, when the crucial connection for vendors was to Mombasa's Old Town tourism industry and tourists with whom they could interact face-to-face.

COASTAL IDENTITY POLITICS

Deriving from the Arabic word *sahil* or *sawahil* (coast),[4] *Swahili* is a historic Indian Ocean term for the inhabitants of various city-states along the East African coast from Somalia in the north to present-day Mozambique and Madagascar in the south. Since the colonial era, the Muslim community of Mombasa's Old Town has been well-known not necessarily as representative of Mombasa and the Kenyan coast but as the last surviving remnant of

Mombasa's original, or indigenous, inhabitants and rulers. Further, the present minority status of Muslim Swahili on the coast has nurtured a tendency to characterize the Swahili as an inherently marginalized people. For example, after reviewing the history of Swahili society on the East African coast, Mark Horton and John Middleton wrote that the Swahili "have been used, exploited, and largely discarded by both colonial powers and the independent governments of Kenya and Tanzania, so that the term *Swahili* has come to refer to a marginalized and internally divided category of people without any obvious sense of single political identity, an 'Other' conceived as a means of self-definition of those who so define them" (2000:14).

Since colonial times, when applied by outsiders to people of the coast more generally, the term *Swahili* has indexed a type of backward laziness and an underdeveloped marginality that often places responsibility on the Swahili people themselves (see Mazrui and Shariff 1994; Waaijenberg 1993; Willis 1993). By marketing the coast region as a destination of leisure populated with unchanging and often highly sexualized Others, the Kenyan tourism industry has continued to appropriate and commodify an exotic version of Swahili culture and aesthetics (Kasfir 2004). Coastal Kenya's dynamic history of cultural exchange and cosmopolitanism is typically either romanticized or washed away to create a blank slate for tourist consumption. As Sidney Kasfir noted, tour operators rarely rely on foreigners' interest in stone towns and Swahili culture but rather on "the Indian Ocean's warm water, coral reefs, and white sand beaches" (2004, 322), a setting she compares to the Caribbean, where tourists spend little time away from their beach resorts. As a result, when tourists do encounter local Kenyans, it is generally during what Kasfir describes as "optional forays to restaurants and souvenir stalls" (322).

Having been politicized long before the onset of mass tourism in Kenya, Swahili is a flexible social category.[5] I have experienced *Swahili* being used with a variety of meanings depending upon the context. One self-proclaimed Swahili tour guide working outside of Fort Jesus once told me that you were Swahili if you were a coastal Muslim who liked to swim and who was a fan of football (soccer). The qualifications for being a Swahili of Mombasa are ever-changing and as complex and contested as anywhere else in East Africa.

Since at least the eighteenth century, the inhabitants of Mombasa Island were organized through their own kin and patron networks as a political entity known as the Theneshara Taifa, or Twelve Tribes (Berg 1968; Swartz 1991), although the Swahili word *taifa* is best translated as "nation." Most subgroups of the Theneshara Taifa are identified by the Swahili names for

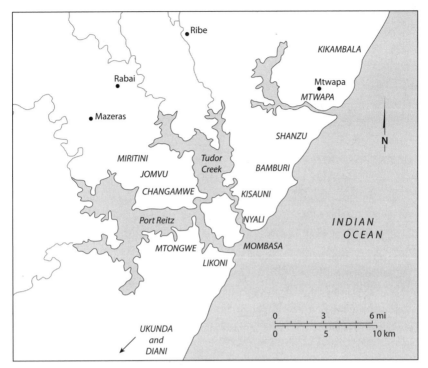

MAP I. Mombasa Island and the immediate vicinity. Rabai and Ribe were the sites of the respective Mijikenda *kaya*. Kisauni, Changamwe, and Likoni were, along with the island's Mvita, the four constituencies of Mombasa District during most of my early research. (Mombasa is now a county, and there are now additional constituencies.) The outlying settlements, such as Mtwapa and Mazeras, were officially outside of Mombasa city but were still important residential areas for people working in Mombasa. Many of these names refer to both places and groups of people, subgroups of both the historic Mombasa Swahili and the Mijikenda.

people of various other coastal settlements outside of Mombasa Island, such as Mtwapa, Kilifi, Kilindini, or Changamwe (see maps 1 and 2; Berg 1968, 45; Swartz 1991).[6]

Like Mombasa's Theneshara Taifa, the predominantly non-Muslim Mijikenda of the immediate coastal hinterland are also a confederation of closely related ethnolinguistic groups.[7] *Mijikenda* itself means "nine" (*kenda* or *chenda*) "towns" (*miji* or *midzi*),[8] although the term has been used to refer to the non-Swahili coastal groups of Mombasa's hinterland only since the 1930s and 1940s as a result of the formation of the Mombasa-based Mijikenda Union (Willis 1993:28). Before that time, the people of the coastal interior were called either the *wanyika* ("people of the bush," a derogatory term) or

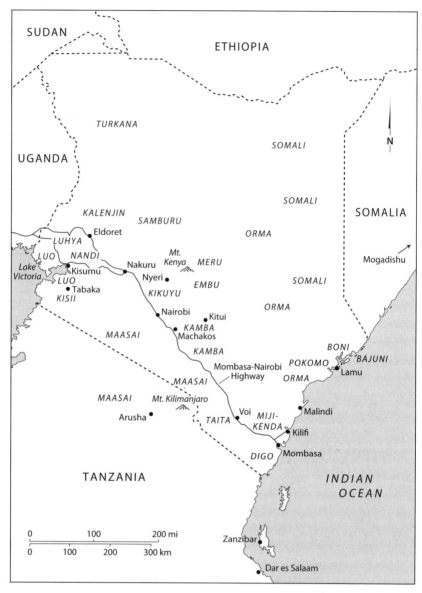

MAP 2. Kenya within East Africa. The ethnic groups shown are in rough estimations of the locations where the British found them living in the late nineteenth century. These groups have since moved throughout Kenya and East Africa, although these particular areas are still considered by some to be their "home" areas. The map also shows the location of Mombasa with respect to Nairobi to the northwest, Dar es Salaam and Zanzibar to the south, and Malindi and Lamu further north on the coast. Kamba carvers tended to come from the area just southeast of Nairobi, and Kisii carvers were from near the town of Tabaka in western Kenya.

the residents of one of the many *kaya,* or fortified settlements of the Mombasa hinterland (Spear 1978; Willis 1993).[9] Whether discussing the Theneshara Taifa Swahili of Mombasa or the various communities of the coastal interior, the important point is that before the early twentieth century, identity and belonging were flexible and subject to complex gender, labor, and trade relations among all of these communities (Waaijenberg 1993; Willis 1993).[10]

While never a dominant Swahili city-state until the Portuguese conquest and the building of Fort Jesus in the 1590s, Mombasa's unique geography has made it a highly contested port of entry into the coastal hinterland, historically attracting diverse populations from throughout the region (often as refugees). Small and easily defensible, Mombasa Island is only five square miles, roughly two miles across at its widest and three miles long (see map 3). The island and its immediate surroundings are not exceptionally fertile since coral lies just below the topsoil and the ground holds little water. Rich in fish until very recently, the sea was traditionally the primary source of protein for Mombasa's communities, making settlements sustainable even if politically or geographically isolated from the hinterland communities.

A few miles inland from the coast, the land climbs into a steep ridge, which provides a fertile and well-watered area, rich for growing crops and historically cultivated with sorghum, rice, and later maize by the residents of the Mijikenda kaya (Willis 1993:21–2).[11] This fertile agricultural region of forested hills extends only a few miles before becoming dry and slowly turning into the Taru Desert (Willis 1993:21; Brantley 1981). This vast area of dusty red soil receives very little rainfall and was a crucial deterrent to passage until the British crossed it by rail in 1897, reaching Voi on the western edge in December of that year (see map 2; Miller 1971:315).

Before the onset of late nineteenth-century British colonialism, intensive trade had already powerfully shaped East Africa's political and economic organization (Miller 1971). Slaves, ivory, and gold were the most valuable exports from East Africa, and the most common imports to the region were cloth, beads, and brass wire—commodities often brokered by South Asian and European merchants through Zanzibar (Miller 1971; Prestholdt 2004:763, 2008). The interior trade in what is now Kenya was long in the hands of traders from Kaya Giriama (Mijikenda) in the Mombasa hinterland in partnership with Kamba speakers working primarily through Kitui, who by the mid-nineteenth century were conducting business directly with Mombasa's merchants (Brantley 1981; Krapf 1860, 144; Steinhart 2000). Beginning in the 1840s, large Kamba caravans began regularly arriving in

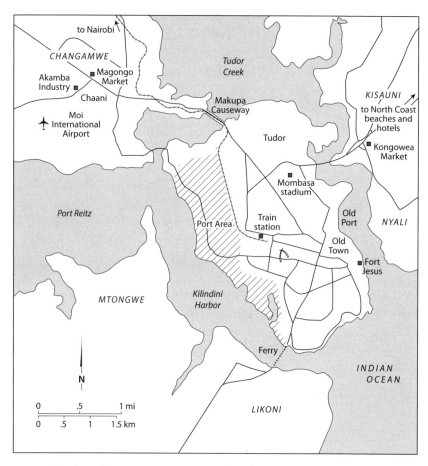

MAP 3. Mombasa City. Most mass tourism is found on the north and south coasts, particularly between Bamburi and Mtwapa to the north, past the wealthy enclave of Nyali. Changamwe is the primary connection to Nairobi and is home to Moi International Airport, Akamba Industry Co-Operative Society, and many export-processing zones.

Mombasa carrying hundreds of ivory tusks (Kimambo 1970, 81).[12] Not long before the onset of British rule,[13] Arab and Swahili traders began to penetrate deep into the Kenyan interior, making it the unique northern path to the Rift Valley and lakes region for traders looking for alternatives to the southern routes (Miller 1971).

Despite the economic success of traders from Kitui and elsewhere in the far interior, as recently as the turn of the twentieth century the colonial administrators viewed the Muslim population, which provided an immediately accessible labor pool, as the most fit for many of the jobs they needed done in Mombasa, whether as porters, managers, or even policemen (Willis 1993:110). But beginning in 1906, as British investment in Mombasa's port increased, the city's Muslim "Swahili" changed in the eyes of the British "from civilized allies into the anti-social dregs of Mombasa" (Willis 1993:110–11). By 1910 the British were actively constructing the Swahili as lazy, listless, and a lost cause (Willis 1993:111). As Willis (1993) has described in detail, discourses and rumors that constructed the Swahili as a "contagion" allowed the British to keep Mombasa's urban Muslims from trading and owning land in the hinterland. Idleness and immorality would become discursively associated with the Swahili as the British and other Africans from the hinterland viewed them as a contaminating influence (Willis 1993).

The result of this British reconstruction of what it meant to be Swahili was that Mombasa's long-term Muslim inhabitants increasingly organized themselves as Arab and therefore *non-African* and non-Swahili (see Nabende and Musalia 1999; Salim 1973). Official census figures for the coastal population covering the fifty years before independence in 1963 showed a consistent increase in the number of "Arabs" and a corresponding decline in the number of "Swahili," a fact James de Ver Allen suggested "could only be accounted for by huge numbers of the latter reclassifying themselves as the former" (1993, 8).

The Special Ordinance of 1910 made clear that while Muslims of Asian or Arab ancestry could make private land claims, all other land belonged to the Crown, and the inhabitants of such land were officially labeled "squatters" (Cooper 1980; Kanyinga 2000; Waaijenberg 1993; Willis 1993).[14] Under the premise of protecting the Africans of the Mombasa hinterland from being cheated, it forbade private landowners on the coast from selling land and gave legal right to most of this land to coastal Muslims—ostensibly Arabs and, therefore, non-Africans. But while the subgroups of the Mijikenda had communal land set aside for them, urban Muslims who could not attain the coveted Arab status were denied a communal reserve. For example, the colonial attorney general ruled that the Theneshara Taifa Swahili of Mombasa were neither "a tribal entity" nor agriculturalists, but private actors to be treated as such (Willis 1993:125).[15] After initial efforts at gradualism and the use of Arabs and Swahili in establishing the protectorate, colonial officials eventually taxed much of them into poverty (Cooper 1980:234). By failing to build an adequate transportation infrastructure on the coast, the British quickly marginalized the region surrounding Mombasa, especially in comparison to Nairobi and Kenya's central highlands (Cooper 1980:234).

The pivotal turn in the twentieth-century "Arabization" of Mombasa's Swahili came with their official recognition as Arabs by the colonial government in 1952 (Oded 2000:63). This meant that they were taxed and voted as Arabs, particularly during the important preindependence elections of 1957 and 1961 (Oded 2000:63).[16] Independence in 1963, however, brought a new challenge to coastal Muslims, who had worked tirelessly during the colonial period for the coveted nonnative status. After independence, reversing this political distinction was essential for urban Muslims on the coast to maintain claims to land and indigenous labor in independent Kenya (Waaijenberg 1993:18–19).[17] In the Kenya of the 1960s, residents with Arab status or ancestry had to reaffirm their Kenyan and African citizenship to support their occupation of land and the economic privileges gained or retained during the colonial era. When Swahili became Kenya's national language in 1969, it was only after fierce debate and opposition (Mazrui and Shariff 1994).[18] For example, Kenya's first attorney general Charles Njonjo declared, "Swahili is just as foreign to Kenya as the English language" (Mazrui and Shariff 1994:79). Despite concessions that were made to coastal elites during Jomo Kenyatta's presidency (1963–78), leading politicians made frequent statements reminding the Swahili that they were actually Arabs and that their land claims had a precarious legality (Mazrui and Shariff 1994:143). This helps to explain why it was mentioned in the Mombasa District Monthly Report of August 1965: "Persons originally registered as Arabs are still frequenting this office trying to have changes effected on their Identity Cards so that they read Bajun instead. It is regretted that this procedure was suspended some time ago."[19] Again in 1968 it was recorded that "with legislation enacted amending the Trade Act, Immigration Act, and Transport Licensing to give more opportunities to citizens, there was a notable rush by people of Arab origin to change their identities to African. This did not prove to be easy as it appears on the surface."[20]

The independence-era politics of the 1960s largely positioned Mijikenda tenants and squatters against "Arab" and "Swahili" landowners, no longer simply differentiated by religion since many Mijikenda (particularly Digo and Giriama) converted to Islam while retaining their ethnic identities (Kanyinga 2000; Parkin 1989; Salim 1970; Waaijenberg 1993; Wolf 2000). While many Mijikenda preferred *majimbo*-ist, or federalist, governance, because of the numerical majority of the Mijikenda within Coast Province, many Swahili and Arabs living in the coast's urban centers were in favor of *mwambao*-ism, a political platform that proposed the separation and independence of the ten-mile coastal strip that had been originally leased to the British government by the Sultan of Zanzibar in the 1890s (Salim 1970; Wolf 2000). Mixtures of the federalist and secessionist platforms would repeatedly reemerge in the decades following independence, most recently in the form of the Mombasa Republican Council (MRC) in the years leading up to the 2013 general election (see Goldsmith 2014). But as in 1963, after persistent division among coastal peoples of different ethnic and religious backgrounds, neither the federalist nor the secessionist positions would succeed, as power was repeatedly centralized in Nairobi and the neighboring Central Highlands.

Following independence, as political power and economic development consolidated in Nairobi and away from the coast, conflicts continually developed as landless coastal people blamed up-country migrants, particularly those from the areas around Nairobi, for the perceived shortage of coastal land (Kanyinga 2000:117).[21] Feeding off of these tensions, ethnic as well as regional identities were heavily politicized during the 1970s and 1980s, as migrants from densely populated areas in the interior continued the nearly century-old tradition of moving to Mombasa and the Kenyan coast in search of work (Kanyinga 2000; Mazrui and Shariff 1994; McIntosh 2005; Oucho 2002; Wolf 2000). During the elections of the 1990s, political tactics were used to divide and disenfranchise Muslims (in 1992) as well as poor squatters and migrants (in 1997).[22] During the violent 2008 elections, Kenyans from both coastal and up-country regions targeted Kikuyus from Kenya's Central Province (assumed to be supporters of incumbent President Mwai Kibaki; see Mueller 2008), while in the period before and after Kenya's 2013 elections, the MRC united many coastal Kenyans in a call for coastal secession (Goldsmith 2014).

These conflicts have come in patterns that mirror Kenya's larger national political divisions. Mombasa's case reminds us that Kenya's ethnic groups are of different sizes and have highly variable access to resources, historically and today. In Kenya, a national consciousness has developed unevenly among the various social groups and regions of the country (Haugerud 1995:40). Different ethnic communities have had very different experiences of the Kenyan state and perceptions of the Kenyan nation. These unstable politics played an important role in shaping the experiences of my research participants as they struggled in business and life in a diverse Indian Ocean city.

The tensions surrounding ethnic politics pushed many modern Kenyan businesspeople to downplay ethnic differences within Mombasa. Despite the obvious tensions, my research participants would often insist that Kenyans were a peace-loving people. This was at first confusing to me since ethnic networks and politics were clearly so central to Kenya's economic and political climate. But I also knew how important it was for traders working around the tourism industry to represent Kenya as a peaceful and welcoming destination. The images of Kenya and Africa they produce and sell to tourists must simplify complex realities and appear transparent and honest. This challenge is not unlike that facing Afropolitans or the Africa Rising narrative today, struggling to stress the positives of the African experience while coping with many of the realities. The art of connection discussed in this book has emerged out of this context of Mombasa as a city of violence, a city of peace, and most importantly, a city of connection.

MOMBASA, A CITY OF CONNECTION

I first arrived in Mombasa in January 2001 as a student participant in a study-abroad program during my junior year in college. I remember landing in Mombasa's Moi International Airport and feeling the East African coast's signature humidity as if I had stepped into a cloud. I felt a distinct shock driving through what I would later learn were the neighborhoods of Changamwe, across Makupa Causeway, and onto Mombasa Island itself—an island surrounded on three sides by mainland. I remember slowly riding along Jomo Kenyatta Avenue and into the central business district before descending down Nkrumah Road, through the square outside of Fort Jesus, and into the Old Town (see map 3). Fort Jesus (figure 2), built by the Portuguese and later used and modified by various Omani, Swahili, and British governors of Mombasa, became a museum and tourist attraction only after Kenyan independence in 1963. With the rise in Kenyan tourism in the late twentieth century, Fort Jesus had been significantly renovated and rehabilitated to become the coastal headquarters of the National Museums of Kenya (NMK). Since the 1970s, Fort Jesus has consistently ranked as one of the most frequented tourist sites in Kenya, among international tourists and Kenyans alike (see Kenya 2003, 2005a). The area immediately outside of Fort Jesus was the southern edge of the most concentrated historic Swahili settlement in Mombasa and the area where I stayed during my first weeks in Kenya.

Mombasa's streets were informal social and economic marketplaces in which young white Americans were assumed to have large amounts of both symbolic and economic capital, although initially we did not necessarily

FIGURE 2. Fort Jesus, looking east toward the Indian Ocean. Photo by author, 2006.

understand why or how. Every day the other students and I were required to navigate passage through the square outside of Fort Jesus, an obstacle course of salespeople, agents, and tour guides, who aggressively offered a variety of services and commodities. Taxi drivers would call to us repeatedly with hands raised in the air, pleading to give us a ride. The tour guides grabbed at our clothes and called us *rafiki,* Swahili for "friend."

Amid the apparent chaos, the least intimidating place seemed to be the kiosk-lined roadside (figure 3) furthest from the fort, which loomed seemingly undisturbed over everything. The far side of Nkrumah Road opposite the fort bordered the Mazrui Cemetery, the final resting place of several governors of Omani descent who had struggled to order Mombasa's highly politicized and internationally connected economy during the eighteenth and nineteenth centuries. The space between the Mazrui Cemetery and the fort's towering yellow walls remains a landmark site of interaction between the privileged and the underprivileged, commanding the attention of most visitors to the city. From the roadside outside of the cemetery, around fifteen Kenyan men and women sold an assortment of small crafts, baskets, jewelry, and wood and soapstone carvings, almost all of which could be found in other major cities and tourist sites around the country. Tourists and travelers bought these small material representations of Kenya or Africa to take home and use to demonstrate their cosmopolitan sensibilities and worldly experiences. I also entered into such consumption patterns and was interested in Kenyan arts and crafts, having read about the impact of African masks and

FIGURE 3. Fort Jesus curio vendors lining Nkrumah Road outside of the Mazrui Cemetery, which is hidden beneath the trees behind the kiosks. Fort Jesus is out of sight directly to the left of the photographer. Photo by author, 2001.

motifs on celebrated European artists such as Picasso, Matisse, and Braque (Steiner 1994:4–5; Kasfir 1999a). I found that giving money to an art vendor working along the roadside felt good in the sense that I was helping someone who was working hard or admirably pursuing a familiar American ideology of pulling oneself up by the bootstraps.

I was fascinated by both the diversity of vendors selling the art and the variety of products being sold (see figures 4–8). Certain wooden kiosks were full of colorfully painted soapstone sculptures, carved into the shapes of animals, bowls, chess sets, or abstract interconnected figures. Other vendors specialized in what I would come to know as Kamba woodcarving, which consisted of a variety of wooden masks and carved animals, bowls, and figurines. Still other kiosks sold printed T-shirts, colorful fabrics known locally as *kangas* or *kikois*,[23] woven sisal bags, small carved pieces such as boxes, stools, and bookends, as well as a variety of beadwork adorning sandals, earrings, necklaces, and bracelets.

These commodities had semiethnic roots. Because the main soapstone quarries were in Tabaka in Kisii District, most of those carving or selling soapstone tended to come from the Kisii (or Gusii) ethnolinguistic group,

FIGURE 4. A Fort Jesus curio vendor holding a carved giraffe mask. Photo by author, 2001.

FIGURE 5. A curio vendor watching over his shop outside of Fort Jesus, where he sells mostly painted soapstone carvings. Photo by author, 2001.

FIGURE 6. A Fort Jesus curio vendor displaying a variety of woven baskets, carvings, and textiles. Photo by author, 2001.

FIGURE 7. A tabletop curio vendor in Mombasa. Especially at the beaches and along roadsides, it is still common to find vendors selling from small tables they set up daily rather than from kiosks. Photo by author, 2001.

FIGURE 8. Curio vendor reading *Vibe* magazine to pass the time at his kiosk filled with many types of soapstone carvings. Photo by author, 2001.

although most members of this community had nothing to do with soapstone. The first to start carving and selling wood carvings of animals and caricatures of Maasai warriors in the early twentieth century were Kamba-speaking men from Wamunyu, in the heart of Ukambani ("Kamba country"). But even within the Kamba community, a family or personal connection was needed to access these economic networks and to get started in the business. Baskets and beadwork depended less on geographically specific raw materials and were produced by craftspeople, typically women, from a variety of ethnic communities; carvers tended to be men.

Taken together, Kenya's crafts industry offered an alternative perspective on the country's ethnic diversity. While both the tourism and crafts industries had long used ethnic imagery as a marketing tool, the peaceful multiculturalism displayed through the artwork and various product lines seemed remarkably separate from the ethnopolitical tensions that were apparent in newspaper headlines and the anxious comments of people with whom I spoke. There were also many diverse perspectives on the very real economic implications of ethnic networks within the industry. Certain groups had clear advantages while others were left marginalized.

I found that the same individuals who would actively downplay ethnic tensions would make long arguments about their own marginality and their own ethnic rivalries. Individuals from every group or background would regularly make their own claims to economic space and legitimacy in Mombasa. Not only was this a necessity, but I was often seen as an authoritative witness to their claims. These claims, which were rooted in socially constructed categories and local, regional, national, and even continental scales, were an essential part of maintaining a connection to Mombasa as well as to me the foreigner. Such claims also pointed to the frictions and tensions that accompany connection in an interconnected world. While the term *globalization* came to prominence in the 1990s for its hopeful forecast of a multicultural world free of borders where everyone would be mobile, mobility does not necessarily equate to greater freedom and can lead to new forms of exploitation and risk (Glick Schiller and Salazar 2013).

CLAIMS OF UP-COUNTRY MARGINALITY

Once they knew they had my ear, up-country migrants often relayed their stories of marginalization at the hands of the coastal elite, especially those of the Indian- and Arab-dominated business community. Through such stories, migrants made their claims to rights over coastal land, despite being from noncoastal ethnic groups. For example, Mama Wanjiru (Wanjiru's mother), an ethnic Kikuyu born in Nairobi, came to Mombasa to live with her father's older brother in 1978 after both her parents passed away (author's interview, Oct. 27, 2005, Mombasa).[24] Her uncle had lived on a plot of land in Mombasa's middle- and working-class Tudor residential estate (see map 3), which she told me he had purchased with money saved from a lifetime of dock work begun in the 1940s. Her uncle died not long after her arrival in Mombasa, and soon three men she referred to as "Arabs" (*waarabu* in Swahili) produced a title deed, claiming the plot she had inherited was theirs. Mama Wanjiru interpreted the challenge from the Arab landowners to be a part of a larger pattern of Kikuyu dispossession following the death of Kenya's first president, Jomo Kenyatta (in 1978), and the replacement of his client base by that of Daniel arap Moi.

It is true that during the first years of Moi's presidency there was a dramatic restructuring of patron-client networks within Kenya (Barkan 1993; Miller and Yeager 1994; Throup 1987). From the time he became president through the 1980s, Moi pushed many Kikuyu out of prominent civil service positions throughout the country (Barkan 1993:88). Ever the populist in theme, he replaced them with members of so-called disadvantaged or marginalized groups, particularly his fellow Kalenjin but also numerical minorities such as the Swahili and immigrants from South Asia and the Middle East living on the Kenyan coast. This replacement of Kenyatta's patronage networks with Moi's own clients played out in Mombasa as the replacement of Kikuyu with Moi's signature South Asian clientele.

As Mama Wanjiru interpreted it, the "Arabs and Swahilis" saw an opportunity to take whatever Kikuyu migrants to the coast had attained. She took those making the claims to court, where their deed was declared a forgery. But they returned, threatening to burn her house if she stayed. Out of fear, she abandoned the property to the developers. She relayed her anxiety to me twenty years later, saying there had been a wave of such attacks at the time, when many Kikuyu and migrants from up-country were "burned out."

This type of ethnic rivalry and competition was typical among the stories I heard, especially from those who had been competing in the curio business for several decades. At independence in 1963, at least forty "mostly Asian [i.e., Indian]-owned variety and souvenir" shops lined the streets of Mombasa's central business district, all but two of which targeted a mainly pedestrian tourist market (De Blij 1968:129–30). Although by the 1970s, Kamba, Kisii, Kikuyu, and other Kenyan traders had begun selling along Mombasa's roadsides, South Asian traders continued to run most of the large art boutiques and formal shops.

But unlike the highly contested roadsides of the central business district (like those of Moi Avenue [formerly Kilindini Road]), Mombasa's Old Town was long closed to the vending of curios. The 1962 Master Plan for the city of Mombasa reported: "Although possibly the greatest tourist attraction in Mombasa, it is rather significant that no curio or other purely tourist shops exist within the Old Town" (NMK 1990). The arrival of vendors outside of Fort Jesus was somewhat more recent and tells its own story.

Many curio vendors with whom I spoke referred to the area outside of Fort Jesus as *msitu* (a forest) before their arrival. This was at least partially due to what many viewed as the urban and ostensibly non-"African" "Arab" culture of Old Town's Swahili inhabitants. Through such stories and constructions, these traders metaphorically cut back the orientalized jungle that Old Town represented to them, opening it up and making it accessible for tourism and tourist consumption.[25] Their move into Old Town was seen by non-Muslim curio traders as the taming of a wild part of the Kenyan coast. This is ironic since Mombasa's Old Town is one of the oldest urban areas in Africa, dating back centuries. But by claiming that they and their ancestors (as opposed to the Swahili) had long been traders and laborers on the coast, vendors from noncoastal ethnic backgrounds argued through daily conversations and the products they sold that *they* were the ones (as opposed to the local Swahili) who had done the important work of not only building but now also "civilizing" Old Town and Fort Jesus, thereby making these sites accessible to tourists and the Kenyan nation.[26] Building on colonial stereotypes of the coast and the Swahili as undeveloped and lazy, many such migrant traders felt they were at the forefront of steering national development by bringing a strong work ethic to what some saw as a foreign and culturally backwards corner of their country.

As the story went, through the 1970s a solitary Kikuyu woman was the only individual to sell goods—baskets and shells—to tourists outside of Fort Jesus. By all accounts she was well-known and locally accepted.[27] While men tended to dominate the production and sale of carvings of both soapstone and wood, baskets and beadwork were often made and sold by women. Born and raised in Nairobi, this woman first sold sisal bags in 1972 from a wooden structure built on a small plot about fifty yards in front of Fort Jesus's main entrance on the roadside between the fort and the colonial-era Mombasa Club. The land itself was owned by the National Museum at Fort Jesus, but apparently nobody minded an older Kikuyu woman selling items to passing tourists. At the time, the only other vendor in the area was a Digo man who fried and sold cassava brought from Likoni to Mombasa's south.[28]

In 1979, the woman employed her fifteen-year-old grandson, Njoroge, to supply her regularly with sisal *kiondo* bags from Nairobi.[29] When she passed away in 1988, Njoroge moved permanently to Mombasa and took over his grandmother's modest business, mixing wood carvings, paintings, and other items with the shells and baskets she had sold for sixteen years. Njoroge would become a close research participant as he operated from his shop outside of Fort Jesus. He was a Kikuyu trader from the first family to tap the area's tourist market, and in his mind, a proud Kenyan as deserving of access to Mombasa's tourist market as anyone. He was also openly recognized by migrant vendors and Old Town locals as the vendor who had been there the longest. He is also one of the few who still remains with his shop at the time of printing.

Mama Wanjiru was the first person to sell curios from the roadside outside of the Mazrui Cemetery across Nkrumah Road from Fort Jesus, which was on municipal, not museum, land (author's interview, October 27, 2005,

Mombasa). When she arrived in 1984, she settled in next to the cassava vendor; Njoroge's grandmother was the only other curio vendor outside the fort but was operating on museum land on the other side of the square. There was a tradition of female Kikuyu traders working in urban Kenya during the decades following independence. This was particularly true among landless Kikuyu who had migrated away from Central Province and Nairobi beginning in the 1960s. Although many Kamba and Kisii vendors had wives and daughters who tended their farms in rural Kenya while they plied the curio trade in Mombasa, many Kikuyu families and women like Mama Wanjiru did not have any stake or support network in rural Kenya.

After abandoning her uncle's plot in Tudor, where she had run a small kiosk selling beer, Mama Wanjiru and her husband—who had a stable but low-paying job in a tourist hotel—had moved into a small middle class apartment not far from Fort Jesus. She had first tried selling curios along Moi Avenue, but the competition was too high, and the male vendors made it difficult for her to sell. She said she was surrounded by men, a Kisii man on one side and a Luhya man on the other, who resented the competition she brought and were generally "rude," using sexist comments to bully her out. She said police would also harass her, disapproving of a Kikuyu woman working along Moi Avenue in public and threatening to arrest her for prostitution. Such demonizing of urban businesswomen in Africa, which continues to be used to police economic and gender boundaries, has a long history stretching back to the colonial era (Hodgson and McCurdy 2001).

When her first daughter, Wanjiru, was born in 1982, Mama Wanjiru would take her for walks to the fresh air around Fort Jesus. During one such trip she met Njoroge's grandmother, another Kikuyu woman struggling to make a living along Mombasa's roadsides. Unlike along Moi Avenue, where curio traders had operated as hawkers or from roadside kiosks for decades, Njoroge's grandmother told her that outside of Fort Jesus she "could not sell enough."

But Mama Wanjiru told me that once there were two Kikuyu women working outside of the fort, one with a young daughter, young men from the immediate Old Town neighborhood came and told her that she had to leave. With little love for the people of Old Town, she told me, "Those Swahilis, they are bad people with hate in their hearts. They don't want to let people have a chance." Out of fear, she would leave her kiosk empty at night, selling only what she could carry to work during the day. In desperation, she went to the Mombasa Municipal Council, who sold her a license for her kiosk.

When she returned to sell from the roadside across from the fort, local Old Town residents confronted her again and insisted that she move or they would destroy her shop. But she countered them by revealing that she had a municipal license. As I would find in many cases, consistent licensing and regulation was often the key to economic security. "They never came back and never burned me out," Mama Wanjiru told me proudly in October 2005, more than twenty years later.

MAKING COASTAL CONNECTIONS

Several other Kikuyu women, one of whom was married to a local Swahili man and had converted to Islam, followed Mama Wanjiru's example and built small kiosks along the roadside outside of the Mazrui Cemetery. By the late 1980s, even local Swahili men and women from Old Town began building kiosks along the roadside to operate or to rent to coastal Mijikenda or migrant up-country vendors. In 1988, a Kisii entrepreneur named Nyambuto built numerous kiosks and storage sheds in the remaining spaces, leaving the entire roadside facing the fort lined with sheet-metal-and-wooden structures of varying sizes and shapes (figure 9 shows the rebuilding of a kiosk). Almost all of these sold carvings, paintings, and crafts to tourists visiting Old Town and Fort Jesus.

The Kenyans I first encountered working outside of Fort Jesus in 2001 helped me appreciate the complexity of ethnic and religious diversity within Mombasa's roadside economy. They also showed me that claims to land, legitimacy, and marginality were rooted in the ethnoreligious politics of the city. Gender, age, and family networks were clearly also important factors inseparable from these ethnoregional claims. By the time of my initial research in 2001, two women from up-country Kenya—one Kikuyu and one Luo—had converted to Islam through marriage. This type of flexibility and diversity that characterized the socioeconomic relations outside the fort was generally seen as a good thing by those I interviewed. Davis, who was not religious himself and was of mixed ethnic background, tried to explain this to me in one of the first interviews I conducted. Our conversation went as follows:

DAVIS: Actually, I don't see the differences we have here. We have Mijikendas here. We have people from up-country. Now, we begin to have some Swahilis also here. I am happy. I would like it to be like total

FIGURE 9. Men rebuilding a kiosk outside of Fort Jesus. Despite their lack of uniformity, a great deal of money was invested in the maintenance of the kiosks. Photo by author, April 2001.

mix of Swahili, Mijikenda, there are people from up-country. Indians, that would sound better. Yeah, I would like that.

AUTHOR: You mean in this group here?

DAVIS: Yeah, I would like that very much, because if I see we just end up being just one specific tribe just dominating an area . . . that would be dangerous. If we have just a mixture of everyone here, I personally become happy because I know there is security. You would like to harm that place and you think, no, I have a brother that owns a store there. (Author's interview, April 18, 2001, Mombasa)

At the time of the interview, Davis had almost finished buying his kiosk from its original builder, who was a local Muslim woman from Old Town and from whom he had rented the shop for nearly ten years. Hassan, his neighbor to one side, was the only young Swahili man selling in the row of kiosks outside the Mazrui Cemetery. Davis called him a "good guy," and they regularly watched each other's shops when one went to lunch or to meet someone elsewhere during the day. As Davis put it, "He is not like the other young Swahilis who do drugs and steal things" (author's interview, April 18, 2001, Mombasa).

Hassan, who was twenty, was not from Mombasa, although his mother was born in the city. His father lived in Kilifi to the north and worked as a wood-carver in the recently revived Swahili wood-carving tradition. Hassan had moved to Mombasa from Malindi to live with his mother's brother and sell some of the Swahili-style wood carvings to the tourists outside of the fort. He did admit that Swahili men generally did not like selling crafts to tourists, but he argued vehemently that it was not because of laziness but because they had other business interests (author's interview, April 22, 2001, Mombasa). It was often difficult for Muslims from Mombasa's Swahili community to access the curio business for religious reasons. As several people explained to me, because Islam is a religion historically rooted in the criticism of idolatry, its teachings understandably cause many Muslims to take offense to curio art that represents animal and human forms.

While several kiosks were owned by local Muslims of Mombasa, very few of these owners worked in their shops. As a result, one conclusion that could be drawn from a quick survey of tour operators and curio vendors was that few coastal people or Swahili were invested in tourism or the curio business, as Carol Eastman (1995) found. My research suggests that the situation is much more complex. The Swahili business class was heavily invested in the kiosk economy outside of Fort Jesus. However, only a few young Swahili men actually worked there in person. Most Muslim men outside of Fort Jesus worked as tour guides, who were associated with drugs and theft and did not have a good reputation among the roadside traders. When Hassan built his kiosk, he knew that he would have to handle complex social politics and heavy competition from people who had been in the business in that location for much longer than he had. But he had a family connection to a local Swahili wood-carving workshop, and Fort Jesus was an exciting place to work. He got to interact with rich people every day.

The traders even had their own organization, which represented continuing attempts to gain formal representation as legitimate and legal businesspeople occupying the roadside outside of Fort Jesus. Everyone was aware of how precarious their economic situation was, especially considering how divisive ethnic politics could quickly become. Their solution was to cooperate and work together as a multiethnic organization that actively downplayed the tensions in Kenya. They all depended on the idea of a cohesive Kenyan nation where *hakuna matata* (there are no problems or worries). This downplaying of trouble, which remains important today, was central to the art of connection along the roadside long before the digital era. When I began this research, the most important connection for the traders was to the roadside, to Old Town, and to the face-to-face interactions with tourists on which they depended.

TRANSPARENT COOPERATION AS ART OF
CONNECTION

When I first started doing research outside of Fort Jesus in 2001, the vendors had recently formed an organization called the Fort Jesus Curio Group. Most of those who worked selling crafts outside the fort were group members, although few of the absentee owners joined. There was no obligation to join, and some of the vendors chose to wait and see if the group was successful before joining. According to the chairman, a thirty-five-year-old Giriama man from north of Mombasa, the group was organized around the ideals of security through diversity and transparent cooperation. This was the best strategy for mitigating risk, he told me (author's interview, April 26, 2001, Mombasa).

Of the twenty-one kiosks outside of Fort Jesus during the first half of 2001, sixteen lined the roadside outside of the Mazrui Cemetery along Nkrumah Road facing the north wall of Fort Jesus. The others, such as Njoroge's, were located on museum land across the square. In all of those shops, I counted thirty-one individuals in my original 2001 census who had some sort of economic investment in the kiosk-based curio economy. Twenty-four participated in my research. I never met the remaining seven people, all of whom were absentee kiosk owners. Unable to meet with them in person, I obtained information about them from their employees and other members of the Fort Jesus Curio Group.

Of the seven absentee owners, one Kamba and two Kisii owners had formal employment outside the curio industry and hired other men to work in their shops. I was, however, very familiar with their employees. The remaining four owners were identified for me as simply "Swahili," although as I have already discussed, this is a slippery term that generally just refers to a Muslim person from the coast. Two of these owners were women who lived in nearby Old Town. The third was a man living in Old Town but originally from Lamu. The fourth was Hassan's uncle, who was originally from Malindi and who also ran a Swahili wood-carving workshop in Mombasa's Old Town.

Of the twenty-four people who were active research participants in 2001, the most prominent kiosk owner was Nyambuto. He was a Kisii man from the site of the soapstone quarries in Tabaka, and he was the absentee owner of four kiosks (although he did check on the kiosks fairly regularly when he was in Mombasa). He used his personal connections to the quarries to regularly supply soapstone carvings to his employees located outside of Fort Jesus and on Moi Avenue near Mombasa's famous giant elephant tusks that stretch across the major roadway connecting the port to the downtown.

The other six kiosks located outside of the Mazrui Cemetery were owned by five Kikuyu women and one Kikuyu man. The women included Mama Wanjiru and her daughter Wanjiru, Mama Wachira, and Elizabeth (all of whom will be discussed in later chapters). All of these Kikuyu owners came in person daily to sell from their shops, making them a unique demographic. Three of the Kikuyu women had moved to the coast from Nairobi; the other two women and the man were born and raised in Mombasa.

In addition to Njoroge's shop, the other two shops that were built on museum land were owned by Muslim Swahili men. The older was originally from Lamu on Kenya's far northern coast and the younger, Jamal, was from the local Old Town community. Through personal connections, they had been able to secure small plots on museum land next to Njoroge's grandmother's original location. Along with Njoroge's shop, they are the only shops still located directly outside of Fort Jesus. The roadside economy painted a fascinating picture of the social complexity of the small-scale African business class in Mombasa, with the owners being made up of Kikuyu businesswomen, local Swahili residents, and entrepreneurs already heavily invested in the crafts industry.

Some of the vendors rented the kiosks from which they sold their own items. Davis was in the process of buying his kiosk from the owner, but since he was still paying off the owner in April 2001, I initially included him in my census as a renter. It took him over two years to slowly pay off the 75,000 Kenya shillings (US$1,000) to purchase the small wooden structure, which he finally did just a few months before the kiosks were demolished (see chapter 3). Davis was Kisii according to his identity card, although he had never lived in Kisii District. Another renter, Ronald, was a Luo man who had grown up in Nakuru and had lived in Mombasa since graduating from Mombasa Polytechnic with a degree in accounting. He had taken over his kiosk from his sister, who had run the shop before him, renting it from Mama Wanjiru. The third renter was a Giriama man in his thirties who came from Kilifi District to the north of Mombasa and rented his kiosk from a local Swahili woman from Old Town. While it existed in other markets, I did not find a single case of double renting, whereby one individual rents a kiosk from the owner only to rent it again to another trader.

On the bottom of the economic ladder were those who were just employed to sell things from the kiosks. These individuals had the least capital and were the most economically desperate. They were usually paid a low monthly salary and given the option of making additional money by selling items above a certain "preferred price." All of these employees were men: Andrew was a Kamba man from the town of Kitui, which more than a century earlier had been a major hub for the ivory trade. Two others, Dennis and Boniface, were brothers from Kisii who grew up near the soapstone quarries in Tabaka and worked for their uncle, Nyambuto, the prominent kiosk owner. They claimed regularly that they had been carving soapstone since the time they could walk, although almost all soapstone carving actually took place in Tabaka at the quarries. Hassan, the twenty-year-old Swahili man who would later build his own kiosk, had recently moved to Mombasa from Malindi to work in his uncle's kiosk. A disabled young Digo man from Likoni to the south of Mombasa did his best to sell from his crutches and chair, which were set up in his shop. Two Giriama men from Kilifi District were also employed in various kiosks, as were three Duruma men, who were brothers from the small town of Samburu in Kwale District not far west of Mombasa along the road to Nairobi. Several of the brothers will return in the next several chapters.

I decided to include Omar, a fourth Duruma brother, in my survey although he did not have his own kiosk but instead sold from a small roadside table that he would set up every morning. It was actually Omar who had initially told me, during a discussion spent sitting in the shade by his roadside table when we were both in our early twenties, that the Fort Jesus curio vendors would be an interesting topic of study for a young American student. "Study us," he had told me. At the time of writing, Omar is one of the few who still regularly sets up his table outside the fort.

In sum, of those individuals who either owned or worked or were invested in the curio economy outside Mombasa's Fort Jesus in April 2001, eight were coastal Mijikenda (three Giriama, four Duruma, one Digo), seven were Muslims of the Kenyan coast who either self-identified or were identified by others as Swahili, seven were Kikuyu, six Kisii, two Kamba, and one Luo (although these were slippery categories), for a total of thirty-one individuals, all Kenyan, working in this one small section of Mombasa's kiosk economy and curio industry.

Owners were usually not present and generally had access to either formal employment or their own capital for operating small businesses. Such businesspeople tended to own their kiosks as a side investment, and many did not belong to the Fort Jesus Curio Group. The significant exception was the Kikuyu owners; they worked in their kiosks on a regular basis and tended to sell a more diversified variety of wood carvings, baskets, soapstone, and jewelry. It is also significant that of the eight Mijikenda—all of them men—who were selling curios outside of Fort Jesus in 2001, seven were employed on commission or low salary. There were clear correlations between ethnicity and class, with Kikuyu and Swahili men and women at the top as owners, young men from up-country renting, and migrants and young coastal Mijikenda men at the bottom. The traders provided a glimpse of the ethnic power dynamics as well as the interethnic cooperation that existed within a small piece of Mombasa's roadside economy.

Although many of the Kikuyu women in the group had an economic advantage as kiosk owners with superior access to capital, the chairman pointed out that many of these women—or "*mamas*" as he called them—had taught the younger men how to make beadwork and how to run a business. At times they even acted as surrogate kin to younger migrants to Mombasa from up-country or elsewhere on the coast (author's interview, April 26, 2001). I found social relations to be generally characterized by openness, flexibility, and pragmatism. When questioned directly, most traders working outside of Fort Jesus told me that there was very little tension brought by ethnic or religious differences. From its inception, there had been a stated ideal to make the Fort Jesus Curio Group egalitarian through diversity. Some of this came from the necessities of the situation. But there were countless stories of interethnic cooperation.

After moving to Mombasa from Kilifi in 1991 at the age of 18, Kazungu, who was a coastal Giriama, had found employment working with a Luhya trader originally from western Kenya. He sold a variety of curio products from a kiosk located near Uhuru Gardens and Moi Avenue's elephant tusks. Despite their differences in ethnoregional background and economic power, Kazungu could not say enough good things about his original employer, who he claimed had taught him all the tricks of the trade, including where to buy the cheapest soapstone and wood carvings. In 1995 when the curio business in Mombasa began to decline with the continued influx of migrants from up-country, rising unemployment, political insecurity, and a steady decline in tourists, Kazungu's employer left the business. But before doing so he helped Kazungu find a job working in a kiosk for a Kisii trader selling soapstone outside of Fort Jesus.

The kiosk was jointly owned by one Kisii and one Kamba man. Neither worked selling curios themselves, but they found it profitable to maintain the shop to supplement their formal incomes made in Mombasa. The kiosk was divided evenly down the middle with one half displaying Kamba wood carvings brokered by Andrew—a self-identified Kamba trader from Kitui—and the other covered in Kisii soapstone carvings, sculptures, and chess boards sold by Kazungu. Despite the ethnic difference, Kazungu and Andrew were close friends who had much in common. Both of them were born on farms in 1973 and both came to Mombasa in 1991 after nearly completing primary school. Since even their salaries were identical, the main difference between the two was that Andrew chose to live among other up-country migrants in Likoni to the south while Kazungu lived in the largely Mijikenda town of Mtwapa to the north.

The Fort Jesus Curio Group's chairman, a Giriama man of thirty-five, told me that he did not feel there was any hierarchy based on income, age, or gender within the group. Advantages were acquired through "work ethic," as he put it (author's interview, April 26, 2001). I almost always witnessed mutual respect among the vendors during the weeks I spent with them in the first stage of research in 2001. This is not to say that there was not still competition and animosity between certain individuals. But from my experience, minimizing conflict and cooperating when necessary was a way of developing new networks by investing in one's own security through the group. Further, cooperating and never allowing rivalries to develop into public arguments was important for performing to tourists the important image of a Kenya populated by friendly people, where "hakuna matata" rang true.

Most importantly, many traders remarked to me in 2001 and in later years that "the curio group worked." In this case, *worked* implies that it had allowed them to occupy for many years an inherently risky economic space and connect to the local tourism industry. But that had been possible only through interethnic cooperation. While ethnicity in Kenya is clearly an economically and politically salient issue, Kenyans will appeal to ideals of diversity to downplay ethnic conflict and generate economic security.

Still, the traders were also fiercely competitive with one another, and each individual member of the Fort Jesus Curio Group was under daily pressure to reassert a claim to legitimacy along the roadside. It was when questions of belonging and legality arose that discussions of ethnic difference became suddenly heated. The discourses of identity and belonging produced through such discussions and everyday banter were framed by the deeper fears and worries of economic insecurity and competition that had shadowed and shaped the culture of the roadside vendors.

Ethnic or "tribal" identity in Kenya is extremely complex and rooted in history and politics.[30] My method for determining ethnic identity was usually direct questioning, and in almost every case I was given a direct response. Such questions also often highlighted problems with typical categorization and shed light on broader ideologies and stereotypes of ethnic difference. Ethnic identities in urban Kenya are slippery and only meaningful within particular social contexts. Identity and community belonging are especially difficult for migrants without a connection to a rural "home" community. In Kenyan cities, having a "home" community is central to peoples' identities. Davis, who had lived on the coast since 1994, stressed in 2005 that despite his up-country ethnic identity, he felt like a coastal person, particularly when it came to politics. He told me, "I am Kisii, but I have lived in Mombasa for a long time and I know this place. I can't just go to Kisii. I don't have those connections. If my business is burned out, I could maybe go to Nairobi since I know people there. But for now, this is home" (author's interview, October 7, 2005, Mombasa).

In addition to arguments based upon belonging and indigeneity, people of different communities were often stereotyped within the context of ideals of capitalism and competition. Work ethic was frequently mentioned in discussions of ethnic difference, especially among migrants who were not from the coast. My interviewees often took time to describe themselves or members of their ethnic communities as hard-working. These were discourses of personhood, as individuals made claims not just to identities but ways of being (Karp 2002). Others were, not surprisingly, disparaged for being lazy. Comparing his hard work to others' laziness was especially important for someone like Davis, who struggled to find a home in Kenya while also believing strongly that there was security in diversity. In his late twenties and with his array of situational ethnic identities, Davis told me:

> This is individual competition. . . . You have to work very hard to survive. . . .
> If you are just sleeping, or you just do this sometimes, there is nobody
> who will wait for you to wake up. That is the competition I am talking
> about. That's why I'm saying like, Swahili, in the coastal region, they are
> kind of lazy. And they should accept that their major problem is that "we
> are being lazy" and "we have to adjust that and join others' struggle for
> life." And then I think it would be fine. (Author's interview, April 18, 2001,
> Mombasa)

Ronald, a twenty-five-year-old Luo curio vendor and kiosk renter, echoed Davis's views on the problems of Mombasa's economy:

The Swahili, they are lazy because they can't manage to do a job like this. They cannot come and sit here from morning until evening. He can do it from, let's say nine in the morning to twelve. Then he goes home, sleeps a little bit, he comes back from two o'clock to four. If he gets a little money, he buys *miraa*[31] and goes and sits there (gesturing to the park outside the fort). He calls it a holiday. But us, we must struggle. I think because we come from very far. But them, their home is here. Everything is here. Their family is here so they can't go hungry. They don't pay for lunch, they go home to *mama*. But somebody like me, I have only my sister here, or sometimes some people, they don't have anybody. It's you for yourself. Your other family members are very far, so you must struggle. (Author's interview, April 27, 2001, Mombasa)

It is important to note that the Fort Jesus curio vendors confronted Swahili men who were mainly either operating as tour guides or "beach boys" outside of the fort or were taking some time to relax and sit in the neighboring park. The discourse on Swahili laziness came not just from their daily experiences but as the continuation of early colonial discourses and stereotypes about urban Muslims of the coast. Digging deeper, the stories I heard from migrants were also a direct response to the prominent political discourse heard at the coast that Swahili marginality was a product of up-country migrants having taken coastal jobs. Curio vendors' claims of Swahili laziness were, therefore, not necessarily meant to argue that the whole Swahili community was lazy. It was, instead, an attempt to reshape the discourse around marginality on the coast. While many academics and politicians equate the Swahili with marginality (Horton and Middleton 2000:14; Mazrui and Shariff 1994; Wolf 2000), both up-country migrants and coastal Mijikenda had their own counternarratives that they deployed in opposition to the dominant discourse. The result was a complex and often contradictory set of ideas and understandings of belonging in Mombasa that simultaneously assigned marginality a certain symbolic capital while fueling fears of possible political instability.

Many scholars have examined the late-twentieth-century development of Swahili ethnonationalism on the Kenyan coast in opposition to a negligent central government (Goldsmith 2014; Mazrui and Shariff 1994; Ntarangwi 2003). On the roadsides in Old Town I was witnessing the production of a multiethnic Kenyan nationalism and a sense of ethical national citizenship in opposition to ethnoterritorial claims made by coastal people. Asking traders about their migrant status often started debates about whether any Kenyan could indeed be considered a migrant within his or her own country. Such questions were particularly problematic for long-distance and regional traders who regularly traveled and did business throughout Kenya but depended upon the port.

Davis, who had moved to Mombasa from Nairobi at the age of sixteen, argued in 2003: "There are no migrants in Kenya. It's ridiculous. In Kenya you should not have migrants" (author's interview, June 10, 2003, Mombasa). Davis's use of the word *should* makes his statement particularly interesting by showing that he clearly accepts that migrants are still a socially significant demographic within the country. He supported his opinions with examples of discrimination he had experienced when looking for employment and housing in Mombasa. But he was also staking a claim to his right to do business on the coast by arguing that he was first and foremost a Kenyan and not a migrant while also arguing that his migrant status had marginalized him and therefore made him more deserving of opportunity. Such contradictions seemed central to many claims to land and legitimacy in the tourist city.

The verbal battles and endless chatter between curio traders and tour guides outside of Fort Jesus also cast light on the identity politics and power dynamics along the roadside. Both curio vendors and tour guides were competing for tourist dollars, and I regularly witnessed tour guides demanding commission or a "tax" (*ushuru*) from vendors. Guides would also frequently interrupt a transaction between a tourist and a vendor, demanding commission from traders for attracting customers. Skimming off the vendors' profits became an informal job for local men outside the fort, and it generated its share of animosity. Yet many of the guides from the local Old Town community told me on separate occasions that they felt it their "right" (*haki*) to demand ushuru from the curio traders. The vendors typically responded that the problem with the local guides was simply that they were "lazy beach boys without a beach," as one vendor put it.

In truth, a visitor's typical first experience of the square outside of Fort Jesus involved a self-described "guide" who attached himself, often unwanted, to a group or individual visiting the fort. The discourse produced by these guides was often (though not always) uniquely Swahili and coast-centric. The guides were aware of competition from other sites on the coast as well as from the game parks and Nairobi, and they used their roots in Old Town as their claim to legitimacy and coastal authenticity. Unlike other tourist destinations on the East African coast, such as Zanzibar or Lamu, Mombasa was more open to contestation from migrants from the mainland. It was, therefore, more important for local Swahili tourism operators to reaffirm both the coastal nature of Mombasa and their authentic belonging in such an environment.

I often heard short phrases during tour guides' interactions with tourists, as the Swahili language was commonly used to entice tourists into an authentic experience of the coast or Kenya as a whole. There were phrases such as "Mombasa *raha*" (Mombasa fun), "Lamu *tamu*" (sweet Lamu), or simply, "Mombasa is surrounded by coral reefs while Nairobi is only surrounded by Maasai." The choice was offered to the tourist in simple terms by the guides, who presented themselves as people connected to the heart of Mombasa and authentic coastal culture. They were not dealing with the same risks as the migrant vendors, and they showed little interest in finding security through the promotion of multiethnic nationalism. To the contrary, theirs was a discourse of ethnoterritorialism, or "baptismal essentialisms," that often irked the curio vendors (McIntosh 2005). As one guide told me in September of 2005, Old Town was a neighborhood with "real culture," producing ideas of authenticity while using them to market his own neighborhood to foreign tourists and himself as the ideal guide.

In general, the local tour guides who hung around the square outside the fort, often intoxicated, were also simply much louder than the vendors, taxi drivers, and other passersby. They regularly controlled the space by yelling and waving back and forth to one another as if something was always happening. One of the common phrases used by the tour guides operating outside of Fort Jesus was "Kibokoni kiboko yao!" It referenced a neighborhood near the fort named Kibokoni and was essentially a statement that Kibokoni is excellent or exceptional. It was used primarily by self-proclaimed Swahili men from the local community to perform their belonging—not just to Mombasa but to the location where they daily competed and operated next to the curio vendors, many of whom had not been born and raised on the coast.

For migrant curio vendors of diverse ethnic backgrounds, the challenge was to produce and perform their own ideas of what it meant to be Kenyan for both tourists and those around them. The wearing of jewelry and clothing in the colors of the Kenyan flag or the reciting of well-known slogans used to market Kenyan tourism, such as hakuna matata, functioned to ease curio vendors into economic spaces that were not necessarily as calm and problem-free as marketed. Hanging a Kenyan flag inside of one's kiosk next to a picture of the president—as required by law in formal shops—allowed traders to market Kenya as an attractive tourist destination for the consumption of leisure and to demonstrate their economic legitimacy on the roadsides of Old Town and urban Mombasa. This was, again, key to connecting to the roadsides, Old Town's tourism industry, and international tourists themselves.

But despite these attempts and the Fort Jesus Curio Group's appeal for security through diversity, the underlying tensions remained. One just had to question who the *real* coastal people were or who were indeed the most marginalized in Mombasa to spark a very interesting set of arguments in which everyone was invested.

"*REAL* COASTAL PEOPLE"

Sidelined by claims made by coastal Swahili and up-country migrants, coastal Mijikenda—possibly the most politically and economically marginalized— were also most frequently left voiceless in the debates over marginality and belonging. In her study of essentialist language ideology in Malindi, Janet McIntosh has stressed that connections between language, ethnicity, and religion are not timeless or primordial but a "distinctly local formulation that has emerged from a series of historical shifts on the coast" (2005:152). Characterizing the sociopolitical situation on the Kenyan coast as a "crucible of inequality," McIntosh has described how many Giriama (a subgroup of the Mijikenda), caught between the coastal–up-country binary, simultaneously hope that "up-country people living on the coast might be heavily taxed or barred from working there" while "Arabs and Swahilis alike might be 'sent back to Arabia'" (2005, 155). The young Mijikenda men in my study were well aware of the advantages held by some up-country traders, although I rarely heard words of direct animosity. As one Giriama vendor named Kahindi told me: "It's a huge advantage to come from up-country. But it's a problem of us Africans, Kenyans, that people put so much emphasis on *kabila* [tribe]. They help each other out and favor each other. Kisiis, they do it with soapstone. And it helps to be Kisii because you need to go up-country to get the raw materials. It's easy. And if you want to speak to the other people selling at the beaches, the Kambas have taken over everything" (author's interview, July 26, 2003, Mombasa).

While Kahindi accepted that the members of many ethnic communities had developed their own market niches that they controlled through language and favoritism, he was not against Kenyans migrating to Mombasa. He pointed out that soapstone could be obtained only in a very isolated area of southwestern Kenya, around which Kisii-speaking communities had lived and worked their farms for generations. Many of the Kamba vendors on the beach had been working there since the 1960s and often sold products on commission for family members who were carvers in one of the several primarily Kamba wood-carving cooperatives located in Kenya. However, continually using the terms *up-country* and *coast* to frame the discussion allowed Kahindi to claim that he was a *real* coastal person. Arguments by individuals of Mijikenda heritage that they were indeed the *true* people of the coast (as opposed to migrants or even the Swahili) were common and shed light on the continuing importance of ethnoterritorialism and autochthony (or local rootedness) at the coast and in a world of global connections (McIntosh 2009; Geschiere 2009).

Despite regularly pointing to politics as the *real* problem, members of the broader coastal Mijikenda community like Kahindi also revealed a certain animosity toward the coastal Muslim or Swahili elite. Opinions often depended upon the location on the coast from which the individual migrated. Many Giriama traders from the Kilifi and Takaungu area who had migrated to Mombasa from further north spoke disdainfully about the Mombasa Swahili and at times even identified more firmly with migrant traders from noncoastal regions of Kenya. For example, Kahindi, who said he was simply from "the reserve" in the Kilifi-Takaungu area, told me despondently: "But if you go there, the Mazruis own everything." While he insisted to me that the Swahili were, indeed, an ethnic group (*kabila*) that included the prominent Mazrui family, he added that they were "very small in number. But they like to think they are *wengi sana* [very many]." "The people of the coast are the Mijikenda," he stressed (author's interview, July 26, 2003, Mombasa).

Out of such arguments, binary formulations of laziness and hard work informed the discourse around ethnicity, inequality, and marginality in Mombasa. The Swahili have long been defined as a marginalized group, although their complexity is rooted in their history as Mombasa's most established occupants and businesspeople. Migrants regularly claim to be harderworking and yet regularly discriminated against by "lazy" coastal Swahili. With potentially the most to lose, up-country people in Mombasa often try to downplay ethnic tensions and grievances on the coast because they have the most to lose from ethnoterritorial politics. Meanwhile, the coastal Mijikenda, who are arguably the most marginalized and have a strong claim to indigeneity and autochthony, have the least voice and potential for political manipulation. As I will discuss throughout the rest of this book, these identity politics would influence economic strategies and the arts and crafts vendors sold.

As coastal marginalization continues in Kenya, the idea of marginalization has itself become politicized and central to identity and to claims to land, legitimacy, and political representation in Mombasa. Traders and migrants learned about the importance of making claims to marginality, and some of this sensibility remains in their self-presentation on the global market (see chapters 6–7). During the early days of my research, these fundamentally political discourses were produced and reproduced along the roadsides outside of Fort Jesus, although usually in Swahili and away from tourists' ears.

Despite these contested claims, Mombasa's roadside-kiosk economy also allowed for the development of important cross-ethnic, inclusive socioeconomic communication and cooperation. It was within the context of pervasive ethnopolitical insecurity that these average Kenyans of diverse backgrounds formed an organization that could not be targeted for representing only a single ethnoregional or religious community.

This chapter has described the predigital art of connection I found among roadside crafts traders and tour operators. At this time, one had to rely on face-to-face interactions along the contested roadsides. The connection to the roadside and to Mombasa's Old Town were essential. Traders from up-country tried to downplay ethnic differences and stress that Mombasa was a safe and welcoming place free of worries. Yet clearly these were somewhat illusory statements rooted more in hope than reality. The art of connection involved pushing for economic formalization from the Kenyan government and the production of a peaceful Kenyan multiculturalism and a hakuna-matata sensibility, even if that was not a reflection of the actual economic culture of the competitive urban roadside. But the attempts to organize that I describe were taking place within an informal and semilegal economic setting that had been allowed to exist only while politically expedient. As I will discuss in the next chapter, the economic restructuring and political changes of the 1990s would culminate in the "city cleaning" and urban demolitions of the late-Moi and early-Kibaki years, as patron-client relations and networks would shift once again, and the attempts and goals of the Fort Jesus Curio Group would become only nostalgic memories.

THREE

———

Crafts Traders versus the State

IN DECEMBER 2001 AND January 2002, during the lead-up to the 2002 general election, politicians closely affiliated with ruling-party KANU led the demolitions of between ten thousand and fifteen thousand roadside kiosks in Mombasa. Some claimed it to be "city cleaning" and "beautification" so that Mombasa might be granted full "city status." Others, such as Mvita MP Shariff Nassir, told the occupants of the roadside kiosks that he wanted them to "go home." While the demolitions were officially framed as a matter of public policy, there were clear undertones of ethnic politics.

If the previous chapter captured the predigital need for connection to Old Town's roadsides and tourists, this chapter highlights additional violence and insecurity—often with an ethnic undertone—that accompanied the dramatic changes that would be experienced in Mombasa's urban environment and felt throughout Mombasa's crafts industry. It is impossible to appreciate the impact of new digital technologies and the emergent strategies for maintaining socioeconomic connections without appreciating the radical shifts in the urban economy that began in December 2001, less than a year after I began my research. From an aesthetic point of view, Mombasa's roadsides have become much cleaner and safer since the removal of the roadside kiosks. The city, in many ways, looks much better, and Kenya's economy has rebounded dramatically since the desperation of the 1990s. But these changes came at a cost, both politically and economically.

The demolitions came at an important time of transition from Moi's political patronage networks to those of Mwai Kibaki. While the political change was largely welcome across the country, the violence and restructuring accompanying the transition were part of a larger pattern of political and structural violence that would come to haunt the crafts and tourism industries, as well as many other industries that relied upon small urban businesses and entrepreneurs. In many cases, Moi's close allies resorted to a desperation politics as they tried to retain whatever power they could. As in other parts of Kenya, in Mombasa this transition was resisted, as local and national parties sought a new equilibrium.

Since the 1970s, Mombasa's roadside kiosk economy had blossomed under KANU rule. It is clear from government documents in the national archives that Mombasa's Municipal Council and KANU politicians were personally involved in creating and maintaining Mombasa's semiformal and semilegal roadside economy for personal and pragmatic reasons. The thousands of kiosks that lined Mombasa's roadsides had remained largely untouched for decades, allowing small businesspeople to operate in a state of semiformality that allowed municipal authorities to create jobs and generate revenue. But Kenyan businesspeople invested in the kiosk economy were constantly at risk of losing this relationship or of being betrayed by the same politicians who had enabled their initial success.

The demolitions that began in December 2001 were led by Shariff Nassir, a close ally of President Moi, at least partially because the ruling party assumed that the migrants who worked in and owned the kiosks would "go home," to use Nassir's words, and vote elsewhere, thus tipping the scales in KANU's favor. With the 2002 election approaching, the light-skinned Nassir tried hard to project himself as the leader of the Mombasa coastal "Swahili" community. Yet when he told migrants to leave Mombasa and "go home," many shook their heads and asked where exactly they should go. Many migrants had no home to which they could return. Further, the strict political and ethnic lines found in divisive political discourse were not always realities on the ground. Ethnicity and identity were much more complex in Kenya than politicians like Nassir would have had people believe. Maybe not surprisingly, Nassir, who had been previously heralded as the "King of the Coast," would lose the 2002 election by a landslide, as voters demonstrated their support for the opposition throughout Mombasa's four constituencies.

But despite the outcome, the demolitions that preceded the election meant the loss of thousands of small shops, the end of organizations like the Fort Jesus Curio Group, and a radical change in the way the coastal tourism and crafts industries would be organized. The demolitions impacted not just these industries but everything from the sale of electronics to secondhand clothing. The economy was radically altered as the roadsides were "cleaned" and a new wave of economic formalization characterized the relationship between small-scale businesspeople and the state. For many entrepreneurs invested in the global crafts trade, this was the final straw that pushed them toward new technologies, jumping scales into global markets, and investing in export and wholesale businesses that were not spatially dependent upon a connection to the city center. The demolitions were central in altering traders' relationship to space and place and in shaping the new and emergent twenty-first-century art of connection I describe in this book.

One goal of this chapter is to provide some of the broader history of Kenya's tourism and craft industries, their emergence in Mombasa, and their relationships with local governments. Since the 1960s and the early days of Kenyan mass tourism, when cruise ships arrived at the port and tourists strolled past roadside kiosks to the central business district, the spatial configuration of Mombasa's tourism industry has changed considerably.[1] Mombasa's case as a port city helps to demonstrate the larger international and regional patterns of land privatization, land grabbing, and land accumulation by dispossession brought by neoliberal reforms and policy (Harvey 2005:178–79). For Harvey (1989:295–96), the breakdown of spatial barriers has made capital more sensitive to variations among places, as specialized destinations have differentiated themselves so as to attract capital. "The result," Harvey (1989) writes, "has been the production of fragmentation, insecurity, and ephemeral uneven development within a highly unified global space economy of capital flows" (296). All of these—fragmentation, insecurity, and unevenness—could describe the direction Mombasa has taken in the last several decades. This process is intimately related to the building of socioeconomic "walls" that segregate and divide urban space along class as well as racial and ethnic lines (Caldeira 2000). I wish to demonstrate how these changes have affected Mombasa's handicrafts industry and especially the cooperatives that until recently were the most powerful players in Kenya's crafts industry. As has been the case with many industries in Kenya, from dairy to coffee, cooperatives were for decades the backbone of the crafts industry. But that changed through the late 1990s, when the cooperatives became the casualties of a "liberalized economy." Persistent struggle between traders and the government would culminate in the defunding of cooperatives, the realignment of patron-client networks, and eventually the demolition of kiosks in Mombasa and urban centers throughout Kenya.

This chapter begins by providing a background on the development of Kenya's tourism industry and crafts cooperatives with special attention to Mombasa. This sets the stage for the kiosk demolitions and the specific ethnoregional politics surrounding this period of change in the city's orientation to the tourism industry. Some of the stories in this chapter are optimistic and about survival. Others are about the alienation that so many tried to remedy using new digital technologies, which were first becoming accessible during this period.

CRAFTS, COOPERATIVES, AND COMPETITION

While Kamba woodcarving is a twentieth-century innovation, crafts and manufactured goods existed in East Africa well before the colonial period. Iron objects were vital to both pastoralists and agriculturalists long before the arrival of Europeans (Wandiba 1992:17). Kikuyu and Kamba speakers produced baskets called *viondo* (singular: *kiondo*) by weaving locally accessible fibers (Wandiba 1992:30, 32). Other important skills found in Kenya included the manufacture of salt and pottery, house building, woodworking, stone working, and leather working (Kitching 1980:13; Wandiba 1992). But while Kamba speakers of the pre-British era decorated and carved household items, were blacksmiths, and had the tools for carving, the style and production capacity of their artistry did not distinguish them from neighboring ethnolinguistic groups (Elkan 1958:314–15). In other words, before the colonial era, Kamba speakers living to the south and east of present-day Nairobi had not yet acquired the reputation as renowned wood-carvers that they would attain during the twentieth century. Walter Elkan, who published one of the only colonial-era studies of the East African wood-carving industry, noted that before the arrival of the British, "[casual] woodcarving was, in fact, widespread, if inconspicuous, in a belt of country between the coast and the Highlands" (1958:315).

Kenya's Kamba traders and artisans were in many respects unlikely candidates to develop and profit from commercial wood carving. While large-scale carving in precolonial Africa was practiced almost exclusively by communities living in heavily forested areas (Pruitt and Causey 1993:138), less than 2 percent of Kenya is covered by closed-canopy indigenous forest (Choge, Cunningham, and Ellery 2005:31). Further, much of the region from southeastern Machakos District stretching east to the town of Kitui, commonly known as Ukambani, has become increasingly arid and has been heavily deforested over the last century. It was, in fact, Ukambani's aridity and frequent droughts that made wood carving an attractive alternative to growing cash crops during the colonial period (Mount 1973:54).

In addition to having been blacksmiths during precolonial times, Kamba speakers were renowned elephant hunters and ivory traders and frequently traveled between the coast and the African interior as independent entrepreneurs dealing in commodities such as ivory, iron tools, and cloth (Kasfir 1999a:108–109; Munro 1975; Steinhart 2000). Kamba and Giriama men from the coast were also heavily recruited to serve in the British Carrier Corps during the First World War. The history of trade and entrepreneurship combined with recruitment into military service gave many Kamba speakers access to new ideas, information, and possibilities as they traveled broadly across eastern and southern Africa and as far as Europe at a time when few Africans were able to do so.

The man heralded by older carvers and previous researchers of Kenya's curio industry as the first Kamba wood-carver, Mutisya Munge, was "already renowned as a carver of ceremonial sticks before 1914" (Elkan 1958:314; see Jules-Rosette 1984:107; Miller 1975). Elkan postulated in 1958 that Munge had learned additional carving skills from members of the Zaramo community living in the hinterland of Dar es Salaam, where he was stationed during the First World War as a member of the East African Carrier Corps (1958:315).[2] Bennetta Jules-Rosette (1984:107) clarified that Mutisya Munge did not simply learn to carve from Zaramo artisans, but he also witnessed the potential revenue that could be made by selling carvings, as many Zaramo had begun doing before the First World War with the help of Lutheran missionaries (Elkan 1958:315).

After the war, Munge returned to his hometown of Wamunyu, located in Machakos District between the larger towns of Machakos and Kitui in the Ukambani region to the southeast of Nairobi. Under his tutelage, family members and others in the immediate Wamunyu area developed a unique style of wood carving that they sold to European settlers during the period between the world wars (Elkan 1958; Jules-Rosette 1984:107).[3] This was the period when European settlers began to enter Kenya in large numbers, becoming important consumers of Kenyan crafts and carvings, especially during the holidays such as Christmas (Elkan 1958:315). The Second World War brought a further increase in demand for wood carvings due to the rise in the number of British soldiers based in Kenya. This demand continued after the war, aided by the global rise in international tourism and expenditures on luxuries more generally (Elkan 1958:316).

The carvings initially made by the Wamunyu artisans and traders were not unique. Marshall Mount (1973:39) noted that in the mid-twentieth century, souvenir art could be found throughout sub-Saharan Africa, although production was concentrated in cities in countries like Kenya that either attracted large numbers of white tourists or had large settler populations.[4] What made the initial Kamba carvers and traders so successful was their quick recognition of colonial stereotypes of the East African highlands, where the settler population thrived. Unlike some parts of West and Central Africa, where there were precolonial traditions of bronze and wooden sculptures and masks, East Africa's masks, Maasai figurines, and animal carvings were shaped by colonial fantasies of Africa as a frontier inhabited by wild animals and "tribal" peoples. The Kamba did not sell their own culture to their colonizers. They capitalized on the assumptions that international travelers had of them and other peoples of East Africa, especially the Maasai.

In addition to tribalized caricatures of the Maasai, early Kamba wood carvings also prominently featured representative and naturalistic images of the animals of the East African savanna. Even before the carvings of Mutisya Munge, representational images of animals were typical in Kamba art. Describing Kamba art and carving prior to the First World War, Gerhard Lindblom (1920) wrote that although "no sculpture in wood or any other kind of ornamental wood carving is found" (366), the art the Kamba did produce contained representations that were "for the most part, reproductions from nature, and thus in the style of free imitative art. . . . The most important contribution to ornamental art is made, as one might expect, by the animal world, and by the animals in it" (357–58). As in precolonial times, the animals represented in Kamba wood carving are realistic representations of wild animals from the surrounding savanna rather than domesticated animals, like cattle or goats.

As Kenyan tourism grew following the Second World War, so did the profitability of handicrafts. Walter Elkan (1958) wrote of Kenyan handicrafts in the 1950s: "The Gusii make attractive stoneware, but it is bulky and fragile and therefore not easily exported; the Kikuyu and some of the Luhya make various sorts of baskets, but again they are almost impossible to pack" (317). He also mentioned that the "mats and fruit-plates made in Uganda" failed on the crafts market of the 1950s because they were "not distinctively African" (317). In contrast, the popular and economically successful Kamba carvings were described as an array of "salad-servers crowned by Masai or Nandi heads, figurines of warriors bearing spear and shield, and models of elephants and leopards" (314). The images produced by the Kamba clearly resonated best with the colonial and Western imaginations of the time.

Despite Kamba wood carving's early prominence and popularity with tourists and the government regulatory bodies, all of the other products mentioned by Elkan in 1958 are still sold regularly in Kenya through its crafts industry. Kisii (or Gusii) carvers of southwestern Kenya have been making soapstone utensils, bowls, and pipes since well before the colonial era (Kitching 1980:13; Miller 1975:25). As with Kamba wood carving, it was after the First World War that Kisii soapstone began to be developed and adapted to the local settler and tourist market as artisans learned to carve animals and modern European household items like candlesticks, ashtrays, and vases (Miller 1975:25). One of the first well-known Kisii carvers, Mzee Moseti Orina, began teaching carving as early as 1918 (Miller 1975:30). Networks for mass-producing soapstone carvings had consolidated by the end of the Second World War, when an Indian entrepreneur opened a wholesale and export shop in Kisii Town that dealt solely in soapstone products. By the 1950s Kisii soapstone could be purchased in most of East Africa's major towns and cities (Miller 1975:30).

Unlike the lush farmland of Kisii, the Ukambani region between Machakos and Kitui was dry, and the precarious state of Kamba agriculture made Kamba wood carving particularly popular among Kamba businesspeople and government officials. Following the Second World War, Kamba wood carving had become such a popular economic strategy and social pastime that Kamba men who were held in detention camps during the Mau Mau land-and-freedom movement of the early 1950s spent much of their free time carving (Kasfir 1999a:109).

In Kenya, from the 1950s through the 1990s, the colonial model of the cooperative society proved an important foundation for the development of indigenous African industries (Kanogo and Maxon 1992:372). Most of the first African cooperatives registered after the passing of the Co-operative Societies Ordinance of 1945 and the founding of a cooperative department under the Ministry of African Affairs were not initiated by Africans themselves but organized by the colonial administration (Kanogo and Maxon 1992:373–74). This was the case with the first Kamba wood-carving cooperatives. During the Second World War, the Machakos District Commissioner (DC) licensed Kamba traders to sell their carvings to tourists and soldiers outside of barracks and hotels in Nairobi (Elkan 1958:316).[5] As the demand for wood carvings increased rapidly through the 1950s, the DC and other administrators viewed the Kamba carvers as an important opportunity for indigenous African development. Expecting Africans to naturally cooperate, the British felt their primary job was to help Kenyans form cooperative industries that would connect to the larger economy. So in 1950, the colonial administration played a central role in organizing the original Akamba Industries Co-operative Society, which was officially registered in Nairobi on August 3 of that year.[6]

Initially, one government officer assisted in Nairobi while another officer helped from Wamunyu at the site of most of the carving (Elkan 1958:318). But after barely two years in existence, the cooperative society was deregistered by the Ministry of Co-operatives and Social Services and stopped receiving government support. This was at the suggestion of the cooperative officer, who felt that the cooperative was not working to the benefit of the group and was instead helping only some individual traders. This would prove to be a long-term problem within the wood-carving cooperatives.

From the earliest days of the original Wamunyu wood-carving cooperative, colonial officials perceived a lack of loyalty and witnessed cases of mismanagement and individual competition that challenged the group's sustainability. In a letter dated August 2, 1950, the Machakos District Co-operatives Officer remarked to the Registrar of Co-operatives in Nairobi that he thought the name "Akamba Industries" was most appropriate, since from his point of view, the carvers were organized as more of a "company" than a "co-operative."[7] In the same letter, he even suggested that it be registered as a "marketing society" rather than as a "co-operative" to avoid confusion. In October 1951, the Co-operative Inspector reported that "they have no manager, the old one having resigned, so the group does not know what exactly had been ordered and of what description."[8] He continued, pointing out the prominence of individual entrepreneurs doing private business inside the co-operative: "the committee too, is of a class of people who do more buying than carving: no better than a ring of buyers who are only interested in orders if they have the things themselves while the actual carver is so ignorant as to be unable to lead a Commercial life." He added, "Originally it was intended that actual carvers should be the members. Now, for the most part it consists of ex-carvers who have turned to petty traders." This last line powerfully illustrates the opinion of the colonial administration that the carvers themselves were not to become individually powerful entrepreneurs themselves. Rather, they were to remain carvers while European and Indian intermediaries handled business with the tourists and international buyers. The cooperative was to act as a way to set a base price for carvings within the market.

But the cooperative would never be able to maintain a monopoly, and attempts to give the cooperative a monopoly were repeatedly sabotaged from within. By February 1952, the Machakos District Rural Industries Officer was so fed up with the Kamba cooperative in Wamunyu that he officially remarked: "During its two years of trading there is reason to doubt if the society has at any time met an order in a satisfactory manner."[9] It was after visiting the Wamunyu cooperative and finding only a group of forty carvers working privately for an "educated" curio trader based in Nairobi that the Co-operative Inspector finally recommended the group's cancellation as a cooperative society.

Elkan (1958:318) pondered why, despite colonial efforts to bring the Kamba carvers into a cooperative group, they would not readily conform to the British model and work together. Of course, Kamba ethnic identity itself was a complex historical construct in which kinship plays a central role (Osborne 2014). The original carvers and traders had organized themselves through highly competitive family businesses. Elkan (1958) postulated that the failure was due to two factors: First was the distance between the urban center and the production networks in Wamunyu. Second, he viewed the social stratification already prominent among the Kamba as a hindrance to the formation of a cooperative society. "The division of profits created endless troubles," he wrote (318).

It is worth noting that Jules-Rosette (1984:108) found several carvers who attributed the initial cooperative's failure simply to "bad management." Either way, through the 1950s the wood-carving industry was primarily controlled by individual traders who, while actively drawing on complex production networks, still accumulated wealth and operated primarily as individuals and through family networks (Elkan 1958:318). Rather than cooperatives, the industry of the 1950s was organized around workshops, whose owners would supply wood to carvers and carefully control labor and the output of carvings for export or sale to tourists and European and South Asian clients.[10]

The 1952 collapse of the Wamunyu cooperative did not mean that there was a lack of business or industry development. This was a time when Kamba traders were rapidly spreading across Eastern and Southern Africa. The expansion of Kamba-speaking traders and hawkers of woodcarvings along the roadsides in the major trade centers such as Nairobi and Mombasa was a national spectacle and came initially with the blessing and support of the colonial government. After the deregistering of the Wamunyu cooperative, the Registrar of Co-operatives in Nairobi wrote to the Machakos DC recommending that, while they should continue trying to revive the society, "My idea would be . . . to allow the present hawking trade to go on. This type of trade which deals largely with the gullible tourist probably brings the maker a very good return."[11] This marked an important turning point in colonial policy on how to deal with African artisans. To the roadsides they were to go, in collusion with government administrators who also appreciated the profitability of exploiting gullible tourists.

By independence in 1963, wood carvings depicting the "tribal Maasai" and wild animals were being carried by Kamba-speaking traders "to every part of East and Central Africa, to the Rhodesias and the Sudan, the Congo, and, exceptionally, to England" (Elkan 1958:314). Always maintaining close ties with the town of Wamunyu, Kenya's Kamba-speaking carvers and traders would popularize the carvings through international exhibitions, such as the African Culture and Arts exhibit held in Minneapolis in 1967, organized by the African Development Corporation of New York, among others (Miller 1975:29). Kamba wood-carvers and curio traders were not alone among Africans pushing the limits of mobility under British colonial rule. But in Kenya they stood out through the late twentieth century as a success story of African entrepreneurship.

The economic success of Kamba wood carving came with a fair share of tension and compromise with precolonial and postcolonial governments, as well as a great deal of conflict within the cooperative societies. After independence in 1963, the government continued a dual policy of allowing hawkers to vend along the roadsides in major urban centers while encouraging wood-carvers to form cooperative societies designed to protect producers and keep profits out of the hands of intermediaries. Although Kenyans were initially slow to register their cooperatives, this would change in the 1960s, by necessity and because of relaxed government regulations and supervision that allowed profits to find their way to the government officials responsible for licensing and surveillance as well as to advantaged traders who came to dominate cooperative groups (Kanogo and Maxon 1992:374). The newfound attraction to the cooperative model was particularly evident among migrants from rural Kenya such as the earliest Kamba woodcarvers, the first of whom had arrived in Mombasa in the 1950s and 1960s in search of cheaper wood for carving and direct access to the local tourist market.[12]

Other than Mombasa, Nairobi was the major destination for carvers and Kenyans looking for a market for their crafts. During the 1960s and 1970s, the center of carving in Nairobi was on Quarry Road near Gikomba Market in Pumwani, where carvers could rent sheds from investors who supplied wood and agreed to purchase completed carvings (Miller 1975:27; Jules-Rosette 1984:118). In 1968 the Nairobi Handicraft Industrial Co-operative Society was formed. But despite some success, due largely to the high cost of rent and wood in the capital, the Nairobi carving cooperative was never able to reach the size of operation of Mombasa's Akamba Industry (Jules-Rosette 1984:122–23).

SPATIAL CONSOLIDATION IN MOMBASA

By the 1970s Kamba wood carving had become, along with Kisii soapstone, one of the dominant genres or "art movements" in Kenya (Miller 1975). Epitomized by the long-legged wooden giraffe, Kamba wood carving had become a global marketing phenomenon and one of the world's most commercially successful souvenir art products (Mount 1973:52). As Mount noted: "They can be purchased, in fact, in every East, Central, and South African city, and can be secured as readily in such cities as London and New York" (1973:52).

While the original market for both Kamba and Kisii carvings was in Nairobi among foreign settlers and missionaries (Miller 1975:25), the spatial organization of East Africa's artisan networks quickly shifted to the coast. Following the Second World War, Mombasa and coast resorts increasingly became popular holiday destinations for resident Europeans, particularly at Christmas and Easter (Sindiga 1999:227). Kamba carvers from the original carving centers near Machakos, Wamunyu, and Kitui were drawn by the tourist market and cheaper wood available from coastal forests (Choge, Cunningham, and Ellery 2005:38). By the late 1950s, many of the unemployed Kamba speakers who had moved to Mombasa had begun carving under the city's trees and selling directly to tourists who wandered the city's streets (Jules-Rosette 1984:109).

Independence in 1963 attracted more young Kamba men to Mombasa in search of employment and opportunity. Four carving communities would develop: at Mtongwe, Tudor Four, Magongo, and Kalahari.[13] When they could pay for licenses, the traders built small roadside stalls, or kiosks, along Salim (now Digo) Road and Kilindini Road (now Moi Avenue). Facing constant conflict with municipal authorities, the carvers slowly consolidated in the African residential estate of Tudor during the 1960s. Harm De Blij remarked in his 1968 urban planning outline of Mombasa: "Visitors to the

Tudor (African) residential development . . . will come upon a most unusual sight—literally mountains of wood shavings, upon and within which stand some modest huts" (76). The wood carvers, De Blij wrote, had "been at work for so long that the shavings form veritable mountains—on top of which they continue to work at their lucrative trade" (79). But the carvers had not actually been located there for long, and the pile of shavings spoke more to the amount of wood they were carving than the time they had spent at the site.

The initial Kamba cooperative in Mombasa, officially registered as the Akamba Handicrafts Industry Co-operative Society Ltd, was formed in Tudor on Mombasa Island in 1963 with open membership rules (Jules-Rosette 1984:112). For an annual fee of 100 Kenya shillings (about US$12 at the time; see Jules-Rosette 1984:112), carvers could gain cooperative membership and access to the work area. The cooperative itself took 15 percent from the sale of products through the cooperative, and carvers were encouraged to also sell privately, primarily from roadside kiosks in the central business district (Jules-Rosette 1984:113). This, however, did not sit well with those at the Ministry for Co-operatives and Social Services, who did not think the Kamba system fit for their ideal model of a production and marketing cooperative. They saw the small number of carvings being sold officially through the cooperative as problematic to its sustainability. The Mombasa Co-operative Officer initially even reported that the cooperative was "semiactive with no progress," due primarily to what he simply interpreted as "members' apathy."[14] In reality, the cooperative had been created by the carvers more to provide economic security and legitimacy rather than to actually function as a cooperative society as defined by the ministry.

Meanwhile and despite the Co-operative Ministry's views, many of the cooperative members with connections to roadside hawkers in downtown Mombasa were making significant profits, but in ways that were undesirable to the municipal government. As early as 1964, a government agent visiting the coast reported: "The number of curio hawkers continue to swell, and at times, they tend to obstruct traffic in the town. In Tudor area where curios are carved, the chopped up bits and pieces have piled up and overflowed to the extent of killing several trees through heat and lack of respiration in the roots."[15]

Then in early 1967, in one of many violent altercations, Mombasa Municipal Council *askaris* (security guards or police) burned down the sheds and stalls used by the Tudor carvers. A representative from the Department of Co-operative Development wrote to the Mombasa Municipal Council expressing his dismay on April 6, 1967: "I have received a delegation from the above society [Akamba Industry] that your Council has burnt their Carving shed in Tudor and that they are not having a place to carry out their business. . . . While I appreciate and respect the Council's decision to clean the Town it would have been wise for the Council to provide an alternative place so that this important Industry is not lost."[16]

With limited options, the members of the cooperative pooled their resources and in 1969 paid 45,000 shillings (about US$6,500 in 1969) for an 8.6-acre European-owned farm lying in the center of what was rapidly becoming a sprawling suburb of Mombasa known as Changamwe (Jules-Rosette 1984:114).[17] The investment in this location, along the highway from the airport to the city, would help make the Kamba cooperative the central economic and spatial hub of Kenya's wood carving industry. Entering the 1970s, the cooperative was operating from its own privately owned plot and was quickly growing. The 1971 annual report from the Ministry of Co-operatives and Social Services declared Akamba Industry the only successful independent African cooperative in Mombasa, with well over five hundred full-time members.[18]

Lacking a municipal curio market, roadside kiosks located in the downtown became the preferred way for cooperative members—both carvers and businesspeople—to directly access Mombasa's tourist market. These roadside stalls provided shade for hawkers, and the overhead was much less than for formal shops. But this sudden growth in roadside structures was alarming to municipal authorities. In June 1972, the Coast Provincial Commissioner wrote to Mombasa's Town Clerk:

Regarding carvers operating on Digo Road . . . I would like once again to bring to your council the growing tendency of allowing hawkers' licenses along the main roads in the town is most undesirable . . . advising you most strongly against continued licensing of hawking of food etc. on the highways. It is easy to build these shanties but a problem to get them out and it is, therefore, my concern that at this time of the year we have six months' period to put right what has been wrong. Let us see while renewing licenses for 1973 that particular effort is made to ensure that hawking licenses for vegetables, canteens, tea-rooms, carvings etc. are not renewed in 1973.[19]

The Kamba were the dominant ethnic group selling curios in Mombasa only until the Kisii began to arrive in the early 1970s. The first Kisii traders to sell in Mombasa set up stalls on Salim (now Digo) Road in downtown

Mombasa. Eventually, the majority of traders consolidated in Uhuru Gardens along Kilindini Road (now Moi Avenue), which connects Mombasa's central business district to the port. Other soapstone traders moved to a location near the colonial-era Manor Hotel, located along present-day Nyerere Avenue, where they did good business until the hotel was purchased and controversially demolished by a developer in 1996.

But few products could match the success of Kamba wood carving in terms of its rapid spread across Eastern and Southern Africa. As recently as 1978, the special Handicrafts Committee formed under the Kenya Export Transit Authority (KETA) lamented that Kisii carvers had not developed as quickly as Kamba carvers. In 1977, in a remark about the recent employment of Kisii carvers by African Heritage, a major curio outlet in Nairobi, it was noted that Kisii carvings lacked the "workmanship" of the Kamba carvings.[20]

But the soapstone business was different from the wood-carving business, due largely to the differences in the ethnoregional networks and the types of raw materials being carved. While wood for carving can be found in many different parts of East Africa and usually far from the sites of carving, soapstone can be found in only a single location and from a number of privately owned quarries in the small town of Tabaka in Kisii District to the southeast of Lake Victoria. Because soapstone quickly dries after extraction and becomes brittle and difficult to carve, most carving takes place near the quarries as soon as the stone leaves the ground. While wood is expensive, regulated, and quickly depleted, soapstone is cheap, can be mined by hand (although dangerously), and its supply as a raw material for carving has barely been tapped.

Judith Miller (1975:31) noted the low price of wholesale soapstone in 1975 and mentioned the profits that could be made when the carvings were sold at two to five times the cost of the raw material. But like the Kamba, individual Kisii traders were less interested in the redistributive elements of cooperative societies than the help they could provide in accessing raw materials and building economic legitimacy and stability. Mombasa's Kisii soapstone cooperative was modeled on a number of others, the first of which had been in Tabaka in Kisii District at the site of the quarries. Like the Kamba wood-carvers, the soapstone traders initially resisted the government's cooperative model, despite the significant government support the Kisii attracted. The first organized investment in the production of soapstone came in 1964 with a "soapstone manufacturing factory" built with money from the United States Agency for International Development (USAID; Miller 1975:31). While KETA and the government's Handicraft Unit wanted to bring the

Kisii carvers into the fold, they could gain full government support only if they formed cooperatives. Like the Kamba, the soapstone economy was organized around family networks, meaning that the ethnic-based cooperative development model had to be adapted to the industry that had already developed over significant time.

But despite the difficulty of getting all craft-producing communities and groups to form and register as cooperatives, by 1978 the Ministry of Co-operative Development estimated that 60–70 percent of full-time handicrafts artisans in Kenya had been organized into cooperative societies.[21] The Development Planning Division of the Ministry of Co-operative Development estimated the same year that 80,000–100,000 people in Kenya were employed in the production of handicrafts, although only 2,500–4,000 were estimated to be full-time artisans.[22] Mombasa's Akamba Industry was booming, and its 1,226 registered members made it "by far the largest society."[23] By 1981 the Mombasa cooperative had 1,720 members, with over 500 men working there regularly (Jules-Rosette 1984:114). These were "the glory years" I would hear so much about two decades later.

But the roadside hawkers' struggles with security and legitimacy continued through the 1980s and 1990s. Like the Fort Jesus Curio Group would do in the early 2000s, separate curio vendor and hawker organizations in downtown Mombasa pushed the municipal government to regulate and formalize their industry, but to little gain. In 1989, for instance, the Mombasa Municipal Council had a Kiosk Hawkers Working Sub-Committee, which recommended allotting a half-acre plot of Uhuru Gardens, a public park, to officially accommodate the six hundred curio vendors of Moi Avenue it had accounted for in its own survey.[24] No action was taken, however, and although members of the soapstone cooperative still moved their businesses into the park, they did so informally and remained in an insecure economic environment that the municipal government allowed to exist but could remove at any moment. They were licensed by the municipal council, but only to operate semilegally on road reserves without any secure access to commercial space and the market provided by international tourists.

PRIVATIZATION AND FRAGMENTATION

The economic downturn of the 1990s was long in the making. Despite fluctuations in the prices of many commodities on the global market, Kenya had remained politically and economically stable through the 1970s, relying on tourism, government investment in infrastructure, and the export of coffee, tea, pyrethrum, and other crops. But when Kenya's debt led to the implementation of structural adjustment and international creditors forced Kenya to cut costs, health care and education were immediately affected.[25] The primary effects of cutting funds for public services in order to repay debt and increase foreign exchange were that by the 1990s a large majority of the Kenyan population was unable to afford health care and education (UNDP 2002:6). As government expenditures on basic social services declined from 20 percent of total government spending in 1980 to 12.4 percent in 1997 (UNDP 2002:44), literacy, which had increased from 47 percent of the population in 1980 to 75 percent in 1994, sank to 70 percent by 1999 (UNDP 2002:7). Absolute poverty simultaneously increased from 44 percent of the population in 1992 to 52 percent by 1997 (UNDP 2002:7).

During the Cold War, Kenya's favorable image in the West combined with government incentives to attract foreign investment in the tourism sector (Kareithi 2003:6). But the rapid expansion of tourism in the 1970s and '80s was characterized by poor planning and haphazard development (Kareithi 2003:8). As has become clear in hindsight, important environmental and social issues were never factored into tourism planning (Akama 2002:7). The open policy resulted in an "unplanned and haphazard mushrooming of tourism and hospitality facilities" and an overall "tourism resource degradation" (Akama 2002:7; also see Ondicho 1999; Sindiga 1999).

Between 1990 to 1994, tourism generated more foreign exchange than coffee and tea combined, employing an estimated 120,000 Kenyans (Akama 1999:17). However, the political unrest of 1990 and 1991 and the U.S.-led Persian Gulf War had started shockwaves rippling through the tourism sector, and tourist arrivals to Kenya fell by 60 percent (Miller and Yeager 1994:149). The violence surrounding the 1992 Kenyan election continued the downturn in national tourism, evidenced by the drop in tourist arrivals by 114,000 that year alone (Redfern 1993:11). In response, tour companies participated in unregulated "price slashing," which did little to help the industry as beds remained empty, wages declined, and underemployment for tourism industry workers became the norm (Redfern 1993:11).

While the 1992 election violence hurt Kenya's image as a pristine and welcoming tourist destination, the Kaya Bombo killings in 1997 were particularly harmful because much of the fighting took place in close proximity to Mombasa's South Coast resort area. One of the many attacks took place at

Shelly Beach on September 5, 1997 (HRW 2002:62). A week later, raiders looted shops and killed several bystanders at the tourist junction of Ukunda (HRW 2002:62). The episode would eventually end in a firefight with police at the popular Diani Beach. The crash in tourism that followed was made even worse by the El Niño rains that year, which caused some of the worst flooding in forty years and damaged roads that would not be fixed for more than a decade (Wolf 2000:148). Other external factors that compounded the decline in tourism included the bombings of the U.S. embassies in Nairobi and nearby Dar es Salaam, Tanzania, in 1998[26] and the bombing of a tourist hotel just north of Mombasa and the firing of a missile at an Israeli passenger jet leaving Mombasa's Moi International Airport in November 2002.

From behind the counter of his shop in a beach hotel, a thirty-six-year-old vendor named Charles told me how all these events had affected the curio business: "Now there is no money. There are not even any customers" (author's interview, October 7, 2005, Mombasa). Charles was well-educated and had been employed to sell curios from the hotel shop since the early 1990s, a time when he said the industry was still profitable and offered upward mobility. But by the time of our conversation in 2005, he was simply grateful to still have a job. Charles did not actually rent the shop himself but was employed to manage the shop by a South Asian businessman who had moved with his family from Mombasa to London in the late 1990s. In 2005, Charles was still running the business for him in case Kenya's tourism industry rebounded.

I was at times surprised that even after the steady rise in international tourist arrivals beginning in 2004, Kenyans invested in the curio business remained very skeptical about the future of their businesses and the industry. By 2014, as tourism crashed again in the face of terrorist attacks and major travel advisories, it was clear that small traders' high profits in the 1970s and 1980s were a phenomenon of the past. The international tourists who had started returning to Kenya in large numbers in 2004[27] did not frequent Mombasa's downtown roadsides or public spaces as they had during the years when cruise ships had regularly emptied hundreds of tourists onto Moi Avenue.

As described earlier in this chapter, the first Kisii and Kamba traders had established their kiosks on Mombasa Island near the downtown because at the time tourists stayed in the city's central business district, walked down major thoroughfares from their cruise ships, and partied late into the night at Mombasa's several downtown hotels, clubs, and casinos. The Ministry of Lands and Settlement had claimed in 1974 that of the coast's thirty-two major hotels, twenty were in Mombasa.[28] Three years later, a July 1977 survey found that seventy-eight of the coast's ninety-nine licensed hotels were in Mombasa.[29] But after the insecurity of the 1990s, tourists were regularly escorted out of Mombasa by the new tourist police unit, mandated by their resorts to wear colored identification wristbands, and warned against buying from anyone not endorsed by the hotels' official guides. By 2013, almost no tourist bed-nights on the coast were spent in the city on Mombasa Island (Kenya 2014:211). For better or worse, tourism moved away from the city center through a combination of public opposition to tourists' behavior and rapidly dilapidating security, roads, and other infrastructure.[30]

Because tourists stayed within the confines of resorts and beach hotels, many of the once-popular downtown hotels and tourist venues—such as the Hard Rock Café, the massive Polana Hotel, and the popular Splendid Hotel—closed. Others were simply removed, like the nationally gazetted Manor Hotel on Nyerere Avenue, which was purchased and illegally demolished for commercial development. In the early 2000s, curio vendors were being squeezed off of Mombasa's roadsides and out of the tourist circuits, as both were redirected toward private networks located behind glass-topped or electrified walls and away from the city's public spaces. This shift was intimately related to the "city cleaning" and "economic cleanup" that would so violently affect my research participants.

DEMOLITIONS AND "CITY CLEANING"

The kiosks that were the focus of my 2001 study were only a few of the more than ten thousand that lined the roadsides of the four parliamentary constituencies into which Mombasa was divided at the time. Most of the land was officially reserved for use by the municipal council. When not in use, this public land had for decades been licensed to traders to generate revenue for the city and to aid in creating jobs. In an attempt to deal with the hundreds of thousands of Mombasa residents who lived below the absolute poverty line of US$1 per day (38.3% of Mombasa's population in 2000),[31] the council began in the late 1960s and 1970s selling business licenses to enterprising Kenyan men and women, including migrants from up-country and elsewhere on the coast. Yet the kiosks occupied an only vaguely legitimate economic space between structureless hawkers, who were frequently targeted by the municipal council for removal, and the formal commercial shops (*duka/*

maduka in Swahili) of colonial Mombasa. These formal shops required much greater overhead and were run mainly, although not exclusively, by traders of Arab or South Asian descent. The kiosk owners' and vendors' semilegal claim was risky and would eventually lead to removals and additional insecurity.

On December 22, 2001, and without warning, Shariff Nassir (Mvita MP)[32] led the demolition of the first 1,500 of Mombasa's kiosks from the protection of his personal limousine. Carried out by privately hired young men, the demolitions left the city looking like it was "in the throes of a civil war" (Mwajefa and Kwena 2001:6). Traders had to scramble without warning to find storage locations, such as Mombasa's post office, to temporarily deposit the stock from their small shops. Others arrived to find that everything on which they and their families had depended had been swept away, looted, or burned.

The demolitions illustrate how a politics of "city cleaning" was used for political gerrymandering and the manipulation of votes prior to the 2002 general election. Fighting for political survival, KANU's highest-ranking politicians, facing stiff competition from opposition leaders, allowed Nassir a free hand in destroying Mombasa's licensed roadside structures. Indeed, the demolition of Mombasa's kiosks made little sense from an urban planning standpoint. As one *Daily Nation* editorial made clear, "If it's a clean Mombasa you want, you don't start with the kiosks. You start with the garbage, which is everywhere" (Warigi 2001:8). But removing the kiosks was a very effective way of removing the poor from Mombasa's central business district and main thoroughfares. The political assumption was that removing Mombasa's kiosks would economically destabilize the opposition and largely migrant voting bloc while simultaneously drawing praise from the private sector, the formal tourism industry, and the high-capital South Asian investment community.

The underlying political motives were discussed openly in the press. For example, Gitau Warigi made these comments in a column in the *Daily Nation* (2001:8): "The timing of the demolitions is interesting. Voter registration begins in February, just a month away. The up-country folk living in Mombasa have never been great fans of Mr. Nassir, nor are they a reliable voting bloc for the *mama na baba* party [KANU]. Mr. Nassir and company have all along been itching for an opportunity to punish these elements. The city-status thing has provided them with the perfect excuse."

The official explanation for the demolitions was to qualify Mombasa for "city status," a level of political and economic specialization that until recently only Nairobi had held. In November 2001, a little over one month before the demolition of Mombasa's kiosks, Kenya's third-largest city, Kisumu, had its status upgraded to that of "city." This political move was widely viewed in the press as a way for President Moi and KANU to garner support from Kisumu politicians and residents. As Mombasa's demolitions began without warning just three days before Christmas of 2001, the official political explanation was that Mombasa could not officially become a city until the roadside kiosks were removed. While several municipal councilors publicly denounced the demolition of the licensed kiosks as "illegal," Nassir publicly took the lead, claiming that he was "flushing out drug dealers" (Mwajefa and Kwena 2001:6) and calling the kiosks, many of which had been in place for over thirty years, "dens for thugs, drug peddling, and chang'aa selling" (Mwajefa 2001a).[33]

Despite the rhetoric about illegality, licensed kiosks from which curios were sold were some of the first targeted in the demolitions since they were the most numerous in the central business district, especially along Nyerere and Moi Avenues. Looters quickly began stealing goods from kiosks as well as from the sidewalks surrounding the downtown post office, where wood and soapstone carvings and other items were being deposited in the absence of any safe storage location. "No notice. No warning. Nothing," one Kamba woman told me in 2006. Her kiosk had been located on Moi Avenue near the elephant tusks. "And nobody even stepped in to put a stop to it. The government was leading it, in fact" (author's interview, March 28, 2006, Mombasa).

On Wednesday December 26, 2001, demolition crews entered Changamwe constituency—home to large numbers of up-country migrants—where opposition MP Ramadan Kajembe threw himself to the ground in front of the bulldozers, forcing Nassir and his crew to temporarily skip over the area and continue toward the airport. When Nassir reached the Kamba wood-carving cooperative, he and his entourage were surrounded and violently attacked (*Nation* Team 2001a). Individuals called "hawkers" in the newspapers and who no doubt lived in the surrounding neighborhoods of Chaani and Magongo barricaded the road with burning tires, cutting off Mombasa from the airport. Armed with stones and other makeshift weapons, the people fiercely defended their livelihoods until the police escorting the demolition crew opened fire into the crowd. Nassir, leading the demolition team from his limousine, was badly injured in the melee by a stone that struck him in the head and had to be hospitalized. Many Kamba men would later half-joke to me that it he was really hospitalized because of the Kamba's famous "witchcraft" and that Nassir should never have made the mistake of attacking their livelihoods.

I received several e-mails from other people who knew they were about to lose their kiosks and their connection to the tourist market. I received this message from Davis on December 28, 2001:

> Now we are done. They just gave us a notice to vacate and move our stuff before the 31st of December. That is when they will demolish our kiosks. I am worried what to do next. You can imagine how much it cost me to have it, 75,000 Kenya shillings [US$1,000]. That is the money I have been working hard for many years to own that shop. Now it is going to be demolished in one day. I have already removed all my items from it, just staying at Fort Jesus doing nothing, waiting for the 31st to see my kiosk destroyed. Anyway, this is Kenya, and so now I am going back to square one, and I don't know where to start. This is part of life. So my friend, I keep my fingers crossed until the 31st.

Even after Mombasa was declared a city in President Moi's 2002 New Year's Day address (*Nation* Team 2002), the demolitions continued sporadically through January until the roadsides were almost entirely cleared. According to the *Daily Nation,* on January 14 alone, property worth millions of shillings (tens of thousands of dollars) was destroyed along with more than one thousand kiosks (Kithi 2002). Several kiosk owners who resisted were beaten and robbed by the demolition squad, many members of which were reportedly drunk.

In mid-February, continuing his cleanup of Mombasa, Nassir began the demolition of informal villages surrounding Mombasa, stating: "Slum dwellers will not be spared. Let them go back to their homes." In the first week of demolition, more than two thousand people had been left homeless (*Nation* Correspondents 2002). On February 26, 2002, Macharia Gaitho, Special Projects Editor for the *Daily Nation,* wrote a column entitled "Tribal Violence Looms at the Coast." Gaitho argued: "The kind of violence we are talking about is nothing less than ethnic cleansing. It is engineered with the evil aims of uprooting certain population groups from certain areas simply because they are deemed to hold contrary political views. If Mr. Nassir still insists on kicking 'foreigners' out of Mombasa, then he should do the decent thing and set an example by booking the first dhow to Oman. Was that not his ancestral home?"

As Nassir continued the demolitions, which had become flavored with uniquely coastal majimboist elements, the press openly criticized his actions.

The heightened ethnic tensions were a nightmare for migrant traders who had worked so hard to downplay and avoid such ethnic narratives and the accompanying insecurity. As the demolitions continued into 2002, another writer would conclude his short letter to a Nairobi newspaper by stating: "The minister seems to have struck a few birds with one stone, creating religious, political and social chaos in an otherwise quiet town. One can hardly wait for November 2002 for us to show those doddering old men where they belong."[34]

The kiosk and slum demolitions of 2001 and 2002 very clearly fit the historic model of violence accompanying land reform and the changing of patron-client networks in Kenya (Kanyinga 2000; Klopp 2000; Waaijenberg 1993). The image of shanty and kiosk demolitions had been a symbol of resistance to political hegemony during colonial times and in the early 1990s during the push for multiple political parties. Angelique Haugerud (1995:29) notes that demolitions such as the 1990 "shanty" demolitions in Nairobi were compared in popular music to colonial demolitions and outright removals, such as 1954's Operation Anvil. Images of bulldozers demolishing structures appeared at the same time on the covers of music cassettes labeled "seditious" by the Kenyan government (see Haugerud 1995:28–29). In a continuation of this historic pattern, between 2002 and 2007, towns in Kenya saw their roadsides cleared of traders and their kiosks, as images of running battles between police and roadside hawkers became regular front-page news.

In the end, Nassir emerged looking like "an enemy of the 'small' people's economic empowerment" (Ombongi 2005:318–19). Indeed, the demolitions marked the beginning of the end of Nassir's long political career, as they would be used against him in his 2002 reelection bid. Nassir protested that no one had attacked his political opponent, Najib Balala, for leading the cleanup of the Airport Road when he had been mayor of Mombasa in the late 1990s.

A businessman of Mombasa birth but Arab descent, Balala first had first risen to power as a nominated KANU councilor (later elected mayor) and chairman of the Coast Tourist Association who made good on his promises to beautify the city (Rakodi, Gatabaki-Kamau, and Devas 2000:161). Balala was popular among migrants as well as within the elite coastal business community (Ombongi 2005:306). During his brief stint as mayor, Balala gained support for improving garbage collection, paying council workers, and initiating successful public-private partnerships in the restoration of public parts of Mombasa that were falling into a state of disrepair (Ombongi 2005:307). Balala became a powerful ally of Mombasa's civil society, which was becoming "a popular mechanism of mobilising, agitating and bargaining with the increasingly repressive state" (Ombongi 2005:307). But like Nassir, Balala had built his political career largely at the expense of Mombasa's small-scale traders. He had denied licenses to curio traders working in downtown Mombasa (in 1998) and was also a primary supporter of the reorganization of tourist circuits so as to minimize the time visitors spent walking around the city center (Rakodi, Gatabaki-Kamau, and Devas 2000:161).

But in 2002, much to Nassir's consternation, Balala's actions as mayor in the late 1990s were remembered warmly while Nassir was tagged the enemy of the poor (Ombongi 2005:318–19). When Balala, an important member of Mwai Kibaki's newly formed National Rainbow Coalition (NARC), soundly defeated Nassir (16,000 to 2,000 votes), it was widely considered a humiliating loss for the seventy-eight-year-old politician who had dominated Mombasa politics for twenty-eight years (Mutonya 2002:12). But the damage had been done. As happy as the traders who were part of my research were that Nassir had lost the election, they had lost their livelihoods and were facing an increasingly precarious and competitive economic environment.

ECONOMIC FALLOUT

The demolitions created an interesting challenge for me because I could no longer rely on a particular area of roadside for locating my research participants. After the demolitions, nearly all absentee kiosk owners moved out of the curio business completely. With no interest to reinvest, Nyambuto, the one absentee landlord I interviewed, left the business and moved back to Kisii Town—near his hometown of Tabaka (the site of the quarries)—where he was working as a taxi driver the last time I saw him there, in 2006. One man and one woman, both of whom were Kikuyu and had owned their kiosks, also left the curio business entirely. While I was not able to follow up with the woman, the man in 2003 was selling vegetables in a market in Kisauni on Mombasa's North Coast. Two other Kikuyu women who had owned the kiosks in which they worked (Mama Wachira and Elizabeth) remained in the curio business by joining a "free mark," or shared shop, located in Old Town. Mama Wanjiru's daughter, Wanjiru, worked in the free mark for a short time before moving to the North Coast and renting a shop in a tourist hotel on Mombasa's North Coast. Mama Wanjiru also eventually left the free mark and found a site from which to sell fabrics and jewelry at Bamburi Beach to the north.

Of the three renters whose kiosks were demolished, Davis moved to Changamwe and became a full-time exporter, working primarily for a U.S.-based company. With the help of local Peace Corps volunteers, he had made contact with the company while working outside of Fort Jesus. He had used his knowledge of e-mail and the Internet to convince the company to hire him as their purchasing and export agent in Mombasa. Ronald, a Luo male in his late twenties with a college degree in accounting, moved out of the curio business. He sold clothes at Kongowea Market in Kisauni before marrying a German woman he met in Mombasa; they eventually moved to Germany. We still keep in touch regularly online through e-mail and Facebook, although he has not sold curios since the loss of his kiosk in January 2002. The third former renter, a Giriama man from the Takaungu area, returned to his farm in Kilifi District to sell palm wine. When I last saw him in 2005, he had returned to Mombasa, but had become very destitute and was making less than $1.00 per day selling firewood on Mombasa's North Coast.

Of the ten men who had been employed selling curios from the kiosks outside of Fort Jesus during my April 2001 census, the two Kisii brothers struggled but eventually found an opportunity to sell soapstone to tourists in the town of Watamu, well north of Mombasa and just south of Malindi. Two other men, one of Simon's brothers and Kazungu, found employment in two of the three shops outside of Fort Jesus that had not been removed. Simon's brother settled into the spot, where he continued to work through the writing of this book, while Kazungu left after two years of working for Njoroge to eventually work for a newly established curio exporter based in nearby Old Town.

Andrew and Simon joined Mama Wanjiru and Elizabeth in their free mark shop in Old Town. When their initial attempt failed, Andrew joined another free mark located on the same street, and Simon set up his own table as an informal hawker operating along the roadside outside of Fort Jesus. Another of Simon's brothers, David, found employment in a privately owned Old Town curio shop, which was run by a Maasai man in his early forties who had originally owned a kiosk along Moi Avenue before it was lost in the demolitions. Kahindi, who was Giriama, found work finishing and selling soapstone in Changamwe's Kisii Soapstone Co-operative, a connection made for him with help from his former boss, who was Kisii.

Simon's brother Omar, who had sold from a roadside table before the demolitions, remained as before, seemingly untouched by the demolitions due to his ability to pack up everything he sold on a daily basis. This informality gave him great mobility but less permanence and legitimacy. After the demolitions, his primary competition quickly changed from the kiosks to the formal shops and the free marks of Old Town.

During research in 2003 and 2005, it became clear that while the kiosk demolitions persuaded some to abandon Mombasa's curio industry, it also led to an influx of primarily Kamba, Kikuyu, and Kisii traders to Old Town. Most of these new arrivals had owned kiosks elsewhere in the city. The same type of cross-ethnic linkages of cooperation and employment continued as they had within the Fort Jesus Curio Group. As the following brief outline of traders' stories reveals, displaced traders tended to concentrate in the production cooperatives and markets in Changamwe, the remaining shops in Old Town, and the area immediately outside of Fort Jesus. This increased the competition outside of the fort even as the tourism industry continued to shift away from the city and toward the beaches and walled resorts.

THE NEW "OLD TOWN"

As the industry's spatial layout shifted, so too did the people participating in my research, which began spreading away from Fort Jesus and into Old Town, to Changamwe, and to the North Coast. I would eventually recruit nine primary research participants who had owned or worked in kiosks located along Moi and Nyerere Avenues just prior to the demolitions. Some had occupied their kiosks since the early 1970s, when Moi and Nyerere Avenues were spatially central to the tourism industry and curio trade. Of these nine, one moved into exporting and wholesaling from the Kisii Soapstone Co-operative in Changamwe. Another moved into exporting and selling wholesale from Changamwe's Magongo Market. Three former Moi Avenue kiosk owners, none of whom had ever done any exporting, moved their businesses to Old Town after the demolitions, where they each rented a large shop. Two other men found work in newly opened Old Town curio shops. Jimmy, the final Moi Avenue kiosk owner, briefly tried his luck in an Old Town free mark before eventually combining his stock with Jamal, a young Swahili man who owned one of the shops outside of Fort Jesus on museum land. Along with Omar's roadside table, the three shops built on museum land were the only curio enterprises outside the fort left untouched by the demolitions. They all quickly took advantage of the change.

Jamal was a young Muslim man from Old Town with a secondary school education, who had, along with his brother, inherited a shop on museum land just outside the entrance to Fort Jesus from a relative (author's interview, Oct. 24, 2005, Mombasa). Before the demolitions, Jamal had been struggling along with the other curio vendors but selling mainly shells and baskets. Like the other traders, he deeply resented the tactics of the large-scale Indian dealers and the way they would pay (or "bribe," *honga* in Swahili) buses and tour companies to bring customers. After the removal of the kiosks on Nkrumah Road and his primary competition, he joined with Jimmy, a Kisii trader in his mid-forties who had lost his shop on Moi Avenue during the wider demolitions. Combining stock meant Jamal felt comfortable selling a full variety of curios, including wood carvings, soapstone sculptures, beadwork, paintings, and even sunglasses, film, and music. Because Jimmy was Christian, Jamal had less hesitation about selling human and animal figures from the shop. Jamal had the location and Jimmy knew the curio business and had personal connections to the soapstone quarries in Tabaka.

By 2014, Jamal had shifted some of his capital into a small shop located within Fort Jesus itself, where he employed Simon's brother David to sell for him. The license to the museum was more expensive and he could rely only on paying visitors to the museum for customers, but the security inside the fort made it worthwhile.

David was one of the younger long-term participants in my study, and he always offered very keen insights. For example, this was his analysis of the demolitions: "So many of those people with kiosks were Mijikenda. When they say it was about chasing out up-country people, that was just an excuse. It was also about chasing out coastal people. It was about cleaning the city of the poor" (author's interview, February 10, 2006, Mombasa). According to David, the demolitions were especially difficult for people in the outlying areas of Mombasa, such as Magongo and Bamburi, where some people had turned portions of their kiosks into permanent residences. "The kiosks were an economic system that worked," he stressed. "We paid for licenses. We had to maintain our own kiosks."

Kazungu was another coastal Giriama trader with strong feelings about the demolitions and the broader restructuring of the economy. In his early thirties, he was from Kilifi to the north of Mombasa. With only a primary school education but significant experience in the curio business, he was able to find alternative employment in Old Town following the loss of the kiosk in which he was previously employed along with Andrew. He downplayed my suggestion in 2003 that there was any ethnic or religious cause to the demolitions. He stressed to me as he sat outside of Njoroge's shop, it was about *maskini na matajiri,* or "the rich and the poor." He returned the question to me: "Who owns the big shops that are now making money and getting the business?" While his entire life experience had been shaped by social inequalities that were all too familiar to him, he viewed the demolitions as having been primarily about class politics. I argued that class and ethnicity were inseparable in Kenya, but he replied that talking about "tribalism" (*ukabila*) was a distraction from the underlying issues (author's interview, July 11, 2003, Mombasa).

Kazungu found himself in an interesting situation since he self-identified as both Muslim and Christian and had Christian, Muslim, and Giriama names that he regularly used in different situations. Being Giriama, one of the larger Mijikenda subgroups, gave him social access and mobility on the Kenyan coast. Further, by being Muslim he could at times pass as Swahili if it meant endearing himself to or building upon genuine commonalities between himself and an employer or neighbor. As a non-Swahili coastal person, he had always found himself employed by non-Mijikenda traders who had superior access to education and capital.

Before the demolitions, Kazungu had been employed to sell from a shop split between himself and Andrew, who sold wood carvings while Kazungu sold soapstone. The demolition of the kiosks left both Kazungu and Andrew unemployed, but Kazungu had a significant advantage since he had nearby family who could support him while he looked for alternative employment. While Andrew was forced to move back to Kitui, where he had inherited a small family farm, Kazungu continued coming to Fort Jesus after the demolitions until he was finally hired by Njoroge, whose shop—built on museum land—had not been destroyed. In Njoroge's case, it was also worth investing in the extra labor since the removal of his primary competition, and Kazungu's job became enticing tourists who pulled up in safari vans outside the fort to step into the shop. "Looking is free!" Kazungu and others would regularly say.

After working for Njoroge for two years, Kazungu found employment with a Muslim woman who owned a rather Afropolitan-themed wholesale and export business dealing in soapstone carvings, fabrics, and handbags. College-educated and a proud member of an elite Mombasa family, she had entered the curio business in 1989 as a local buyer for an Indian-owned export company. She worked for both Indian- and British-owned exporting companies before finally opening her own business in 2005. The business relied on Kazungu and another long-term curio trader who was born and raised at the site of the quarries in Tabaka and who provided the small business with important connections and insider knowledge.

Kazungu's new Kisii partner was among the first traders from Tabaka to come to Mombasa in 1974. The demolition of his kiosk on Nyerere Avenue had devastated him. Like Davis and so many others, he no longer had a rural home in Kisii to which he could return. Like Kazungu, he was openly grateful to the local Swahili woman who had employed him, a "migrant from up-country" (albeit with important connections within the soapstone business).

Despite differences in ethnic background, education, and age, Kazungu and his new partners found themselves dependent upon one another. Many days we all sat together in the small shop on Old Town's Ndia Kuu Road, where they would kindly buy me cold soda and offer me their small fan as they watched me desperately try to cope with the Mombasa heat. They would tell me stories of their past and the way the curio business and the city had changed.

It should be no surprise that people operating in multiethnic environments that depend upon cross-ethnic linkages and collaboration blamed political elites rather than one another for their hardships. Simon's brother David clarified this perspective for me:

> The problem is these coastal politicians, these coastal leaders who blame it on the up-country people. OK. You will always have a difference between the coastal and the up-country people. But it's the Mijikenda who really have the problems, and they are from here. They have nothing. They sit on farms, and then will come here [Mombasa] and do anything. Look at me. When I started I made 800 shillings per month [about US$10]. Eight hundred per month. I had to pay 600 for a place to sleep. So what am I supposed to do with 200 shillings for a whole month?
>
> But the difference is this. The Mijikenda compete with the coastal upper class. But at the same time, they also compete with these up-country people. These are the two competitors for coastal people. But the thing is this. The up-country people bring productive competition. He will come and build a big house to rent to people. So that challenges you to build a bigger one. But don't destroy that house he's built; that's not development. But those are the tactics of these coastal leaders, these people who would rather use these tactics of destroying someone else's development rather than letting the competition take place in a way that might lead to development. And

they always use the Mijikenda. The youth. Those without education who will just follow. Even they [Mijikenda youth] were the ones who helped with the demolitions: "Clean our city, clean out the upcountry people." And where are they now? Homeless and in the streets. (Author's interview, February 10, 2006, Mombasa)

The tensions between traders and Mombasa's local government are not new. Neither is the insecure and risky economic environment that has been allowed to continue. Tensions are often made worse by the number of young unemployed men willing to take to the streets for politicians. But the vast majority of those struggling along the urban roadsides are trying to make enough money to eat that night and potentially get ahead in a business. The structural violence affecting these men and women have roots deep in the colonial past. The violence can manifest itself through demolitions or remain a more subtle aspect of the larger neoliberal trend toward privatized and sanitized spaces that exclude struggling businesspeople who have now lost even their right to be on the side of the road.

Since 2001, I have witnessed significant beautification in downtown Mombasa and on the island more generally. The traffic lights at the post office and other major intersections have been fixed, many new buildings have been constructed, old ones repainted, trees planted along some of the major thoroughfares, and roads repaved. But episodes of "city cleaning," "beautification," and kiosk and slum demolitions are acts of environmental injustice that, despite claims to being apolitical and about material beautification, function to maintain structures of inequality and further segregate the city and privatize and fragment urban space. City cleaning and beautification are never neutral processes just about a city's material realities. As my research participants stressed to me, Mombasa's kiosk demolitions were a product of politics and larger changes in the patron-client relations that controlled Mombasa's economy.

Even as tourist arrivals to Kenya began to break records in 2005 and 2006, many of the Mombasa curio traders I interviewed still found it difficult to turn a profit. The infrastructure for accessing the market had become exclusionary since the tourism slump of the 1990s and particularly after the removal of Mombasa's kiosks and the rerouting of tour circuits away from public locations. The tourists had also changed. Americans, Europeans, and Israelis, who were the big buyers of curios in the 1980s and 1990s, were no longer walking around the city in big groups as in the past. The 2003 U.S. invasion of Iraq compounded the Kenyan tourism industry's problems by increasing propaganda and fear against Muslims and ensuring the placement of the Kenyan coast on travel advisory lists from the U.S. and British governments. Even after the return of American, British, and other high-spending European tourists, Mombasa's security concerns meant that tourists were increasingly arriving on all-inclusive packages that left most of the profits with foreign agents and allowed tourists only a brief, often expensive bus tour of the city before returning to the confines of their hotels. This made life hard for the coast's local tourism operators and crafts traders, who relied on public spaces for connecting and meeting with clients. There was a need for a new type of mobility and connection, and digital technologies generated a great deal of optimism.

The significance of location to business and lifestyle in Mombasa was changing. In the days when a large proportion of Mombasa's crafts and carvings were being sold from the roadsides of the downtown, vendors operating outside of Fort Jesus told me that location was the crucial component to the curio business. Back when he still had a kiosk, Davis enjoyed telling me the keys to success in Kenya by quoting hotelier Conrad Hilton: "The three most important things in business are location, location, location." Following the demolitions, he would tell me, "Nobody wanted to move from Fort Jesus. We had the perfect location for this business" (author's interview, July 15, 2003, Mombasa). Ronald felt the same; as he had told me before the loss of his kiosk, "Even if I find a job, I'll continue in this place. I'll do it like part time" (author's interview April 27, 2001). The location for accessing tourists was simply too perfect. Many people compared the demolitions to the Kaya Bombo violence of 1997, particularly regarding the underlying ethnic tensions. However, Simon disagreed: "Kaya Bombo was bad, but the demolitions were worse. After Kaya Bombo, at least we still had a place to sell" (author's interview, Dec. 6, 2005, Mombasa).

By 2005, although many traders continued to emphasize the importance of location, the mindset had changed among many others. For example, once Davis moved permanently into the export business and away from a dependence on the local market, the value of location and urban access changed considerably. His cell phone and e-mail address had become his primary tools for accessing his customers and partners. After moving solely into exporting, Davis told me: "Everyone says that location is the most important thing, but now I'm not so sure that is true. For me, about the tourism industry in Mombasa, they will say it is all location, where the tourists are—around Fort Jesus, at the beach. But what I'm thinking of, it's not location. It's advertising" (author's interview, Oct. 10, 2005, Mombasa). The shifting strategies and aesthetics of the marketing and advertising of Kenyan crafts will be a primary theme throughout the rest of this book.

The historical relationship between curio vendors and the state described in this chapter raises serious questions about the long-term goals of the Kenyan government in promoting tourism and about the impact of tourism on Kenya (Sindiga 1999). Although tourism is economically important on the Kenyan coast, it has done little to develop the region as a whole. Similarly, because many facilities catering to tourists are foreign-owned and much of the income made through tourism is repatriated to non-African countries, tourism has, according to some analysts, only a "marginal positive effect" on Kenya (Alila and McCormick 1999:1). Sustainable tourism needs careful planning.

Amid the Kenyan government's shifts between laissez-faire and at times open hostility toward the small-business economy (such as kiosk demolitions without warning), those with social connections and capital persevered at the cost of the poor and the legitimacy of the government. As I will discuss in chapter 4, this reality would have a profound impact on the way struggling curio traders approached their businesses and viewed the Kenyan state's continued attempts at economic "cleanup" through increased oversight, taxation, and revenue collection.

FOUR

Negotiating Informality in Mombasa

DURING MY TIME SPENT CONDUCTING interviews and research outside of Fort Jesus, national politics were a regular topic of conversation. The hard-working Kenyans with whom I spent my time had hopeful expectations when President Mwai Kibaki's National Rainbow Coalition (NARC) won the 2002 election on an anticorruption platform of constitutional and economic reform. Kenya's digital age began with a new president, who for many represented a positive move toward transparency and development. But the hope for political reform was short-lived in Mombasa and many other parts of Kenya as Kibaki's first term as president was mired in repeated scandals and suspicions of corruption (see Wrong 2009).

At times I was surprised to hear nostalgic memories of the Moi era. As Simon told me, he respected Moi because he was not as well educated as other politicians and appreciated the importance of average Kenyans (author's interview, December 19, 2005, Mombasa). Simon had educated himself past standard 7, and he resented having fewer opportunities because of his limited formal education. He told me a story about Moi ordering his driver to stop his limousine in front of a roadside vendor so that he could buy some grilled maize. As the story went, Moi gave the roadside vendor a 1,000-shilling note for the 5-shilling piece of food, telling him to keep the change. For Simon, relating the story to me in 2005 from where he sat next to his roadside table topped with small carvings and beadwork, the anecdote demonstrated how Moi had appreciated "the average Kenyan" and had promoted the "informal," or *jua kali,* sector. But more than being about Moi, this nostalgic reflection was also a way of criticizing the Kibaki administration and its inconsistent efforts to tax and license roadside traders like Simon. He accepted that, lacking capital and alternative connections, had had to do his best to navigate the semilegal and semiformal roadside outside of Fort Jesus.

This chapter focuses on informal economic development in contemporary Kenya: formality versus informality, legality versus illegality, and taxation versus bribery. I am particularly interested in how the traders of Kenya's handicrafts industry, which developed in the 1960s and 1970s with significant government support, viewed themselves, often proudly, as members of Kenya's jua kali sector. This identification has emerged historically as a product of small-scale Kenyan traders' relationship to the Kenyan state. Simon's story, for example, was not so much about Moi's extra expenditure on grilled maize as about economic change and a past that had been better than the present. The story was his way of reflecting on how much harder life had become along Mombasa's roadsides for a wide variety of businesspeople working in many industries outside of crafts and tourism. Such perspectives have developed out of traders' lived experiences of national and local political change and the complex history explained in the last two chapters. The way that traders like Simon viewed the government powerfully shaped their decisions about whether they would work with or against official regulations. These experiences and views would also be powerful in uniting Mombasa against Kibaki's reelection in December 2007, when the opposition Orange Democratic Movement (ODM) would sweep all four of Mombasa's parliamentary and presidential elections.[1]

In 2002, not long after the demolitions of Mombasa's kiosks, Kibaki's NARC had defeated the much younger Uhuru Kenyatta, Moi's chosen successor, on a platform of implementing immediate economic reform, increasing revenue through tax collection, and strengthening anticorruption legislation.[2] There was almost unanimous sentiment among small-scale traders I interviewed that the rising taxes and license fees from the Kenya Revenue Authority (KRA) and the Mombasa Municipal Council were additional and hostile government incursions. However, this is not to suggest that the traders were against official recognition and formalization. To the contrary, what my research participants from numerous industries wanted was to be granted secure access to commercial space. These largely immobile traders desperately needed connections to market space and the formality that could make their livelihoods less risky and precarious.

While Kenyans working around the tourism industry tended to resent increases in taxes and license fees, there was little opposition to registering with the municipal council, forming organizations, wearing uniforms, or carrying licenses. Most of my research participants desired regulations that took into account existing systems of commercial access and tenure and did not place a financial burden on the traders themselves. This desire to formalize—also seen with the example of the Fort Jesus Curio Group—makes it difficult to romanticize the informal roadside traders as the antithesis of the state (Clark 1988:6). Summarizing a collection of studies of informal traders from around the world, Gracia Clark (1988) found that traders "value specific state relations that they feel improve enterprise survival and long-term profit level" (6). Indeed, it is quite common to see a voluntary push for formalization from the bottom (Nelson and Bruijn 2005). In opposition to strict neoliberal logic, there are mutual benefits to formalization and the role that governments can play in regulating the economy and reducing risk (Nelson and Bruijn 2005). Studies in Kenya have repeatedly shown how a lack of government support for formal organizations like cooperatives leaves traders in an unregulated and unstable economic environment where they have limited access to markets and almost no incentive to invest in businesses (Moyi 2003; Migiro 2006).

In this chapter, I am interested in how traders in numerous industries—from crafts to secondhand clothing—negotiated the economic instability and haphazard regulation of the 1990s and 2000s, particularly following the kiosk demolitions. While these largely immobile traders were finding new ways to use digital technologies to conduct business and communicate over long distances, they also recognized that new forms of mobility and new connections came with a host of new risks. More than mobility, they needed and were repeatedly denied secure, formal, and regulated connection to economic space.

KENYA'S INFORMAL (JUA KALI) SECTOR

When discussing small-scale traders' relationships with the state, it is common to discuss the boundary between ostensibly separate "formal" and "informal" sectors of the economy. This is particularly true in underdeveloped countries, where less time and fewer resources have typically been dedicated to creating and maintaining thriving, regulated "formal" economies. The first scholarly studies of the informal economy were conducted in Ghana and Kenya (Hart 1973; ILO 1972), sub-Saharan African countries whose cities were developing much more quickly than the formal economic sector and the government's abilities to develop adequate infrastructure. Anthropologist Keith Hart (1973) explored Ghana's informal economy to explain how the urban poor in Accra survived despite widespread unemployment. He argued that the majority of the population participated in an "informal economy," which was not recognized, regulated, or taxed by the state. In Hart's (1973) original model, the informal economy was one half of a dual economy of the formal and informal working symbiotically. Accordingly, an informal economy was an essential component of any national economy since it had to underwrite much of what the formal, state-sponsored economy attempted.

These working and often poor men and women have long made up the largest sector of employment creation in Kenya under the heading of the informal, jua kali, or microenterprise sector (Kenya 2005b:iii).[3] *Jua kali* means "harsh sun" in Swahili and was originally a spatial term used to refer to traders and craftspeople who lacked shelter and were left to work under the hot sun. By the late 1980s, the term had come to refer to businesses that functioned with minimal government regulation and oversight. *Jua kali* simultaneously became the economic identity of many traders who struggled daily in diverse economic circumstances.[4]

Jua kali traders who worked around the tourism industry had the important job of selling images of Kenya and representing the country to tourists and travelers. But they regularly found themselves in a particularly awkward economic environment. These traders were often migrants required to sell foreigners in a particular tourist destination from which they did not originally come. There was also regularly tension between them and the municipal authorities and local communities, making their role as cultural brokers even more precarious.

While Kenya's informal economy includes a wide array of production and service industries, Mombasa's related crafts and tourism industries demonstrate particularly well the complexity of formal and informal entanglements and the limited usefulness of the terms themselves. For example, although most crafts traders who participated in my research identified themselves as jua kali, they paid taxes, had government licenses, and worked from stalls and shops that had a semiformality and semilegality. The government has, in fact, long been involved in regulating and nurturing these industries.

As described in the last chapter, as early as the 1950s and 1960s, the Kenyan government was working through the Ministry of Co-operative Development and Social Services and the Ministry of Commerce and Industry to organize handicrafts producers and other artisans into formal cooperative organizations. Even before the 1972 ILO mission and the naming of Kenya's jua kali sector, studies in Kenya had already focused very specifically on Kenya's handicraft producers and had argued that the government had an important role to play in formalizing these traders to ensure that Kenyan producers might see a larger percentage of the industry's overall profits.[5] But ministries had questionable success making this work.

Through the 1970s, the ministry paid special attention to Kenya's handicrafts industry, and government agencies played a key role in organizing the various producer organizations into cooperative societies. In the late 1970s the Kenya Export Trade Authority (KETA) even organized a special Handicrafts Unit, which would eventually help develop the Kenya Crafts Co-operative Union (KCCU). The KCCU was an attempt if not to formalize then at least to provide some structure and protection for artisans.[6] These government bodies consistently recommended an increase in the Kenyan government's financial support for the handicrafts industry. For example, the Ministry of Co-operative Development's 1978 survey of "Handcraft Co-operatives" called for extensive technical assistance for cooperatives, the formation and support of a national crafts union, and a system of large, government-assisted loans for marketing and innovation.[7]

External advisers throughout these decades agreed that the only way to ensure that profits found their way to producers was through direct government assistance. However, by the late 1980s, organized government support for the industry had dwindled. As the concept of the "informal economy" gained a new strategic importance to the Kenyan government in the 1980s (King 1996), government aid was replaced with the official recognition that the industry operated beyond the responsibilities of the state. The global expansion of informal economies accompanied the accompanying expansion of a neoliberal, free-market approach to governance, as governments reduced spending and shifted away from the development-oriented, welfare-state model of the 1960s. As Colin Leys had recognized in the 1970s: "What stands out about the so-called informal sector is that most of what it covers is primarily *a system of very intense exploitation of labour*" (1975:266–67).

Hart (1992:215–16) later noted that his coining of the term *informal economy* was a reflection of the dominant Cold War ideology of the early 1970s. For many policy makers of the 1970s and 1980s who latched onto the idea, the informal economy represented the conceptual negation of Keynesian macroeconomics, which called for economic management by a strong welfare state (Hart 1992:217). As Hart (1992:216) put it, his initial coining was the product of a conceived "frozen opposition between the state and the market," which appealed to policy makers for its simplicity but obscured the struggle between citizens and bureaucracy by assuming the dominance of the latter. Labeling a massive sector of the economy as simply "informal," or jua kali, naturalized and even romanticized the problematic increase in unregulated small-scale businesses.

Not only did the Ministry of Co-operative Development and Social Services and the KCCU lose their funding and advisory assistance (following the reduction of funds from the Nordic Program, for example), but as is clear from reports made by local government officers from the 1960s through the 1980s, the quality of officials and their reports also declined. The result was the mushrooming of small-scale enterprises that lacked significant government support and internal coordination—precisely what advisors of the 1950s through the early 1970s stressed was needed for economic sustainability. Thus, the obstacles and risks that were being confronted by crafts traders struggling along Mombasa's roadsides were not new or inevitable, but rather the product of conscious political decisions. Their continued informality not only ensured that their connection to Mombasa's urban economy remained precarious, but it was also the root of their exploitation.

With the rapid rise in Kenya's population and increased migration of young Kenyans to urban centers through the 1970s and 1980s, the informal economy became critical for employment in Kenya and central to the national economy. Dorothy McCormick (1987) was one of the first to argue that the notion of an informal sector has several definitional problems in the case of urban Kenya. She suggested a continuum model, preferring to view businesses on a spectrum of varying formality. While her focus was much broader than just tourism or crafts, she still found that in many indigenous industries like handicrafts production, the line between formality and informality was rarely clear. This is true of small-scale Kenyan enterprises operating around the tourism industry more generally, many of which have been under the scrutiny and regulatory heavy hand of the Kenyan government since well before independence.

By the early 2000s, the Kibaki government chose to define Kenya's informal sector as "all small-scale activities that are not registered with the registrar of companies and generally use low level or no technology" (Kenya 2005b:78). But the traders and enterprises that are often lumped into the informal economy are *not* necessarily marked by a lack of interaction with the government or a lack of technology.

As I will discuss in this chapter, when government agencies intervene on behalf of traders—by vetting beach vendors or mandating that tour guides wear uniforms and carry licenses—this regulation and economic restructuring can be quite successful, be greatly appreciated by traders, and have the potential to increase the legitimacy of the state in the eyes of small-scale entrepreneurs and businesspeople. In this sense, formality, rationality, and legality can lead to the reduction of risk, secure access to economic and market space, and the acceptance of government regulation. There is, therefore, nothing inevitable about risk being the driving force within the global economy today. Rather, risks emerge when the necessity to manage risk is abandoned by governments and placed in the hands of individuals and personalized networks (Beck 2000). When informal economies and underground, semilegal industries are romanticized or accepted as the norm, traders are generally forced to work in precarious and risky environments, lacking legality and formal economic connections. As I will discuss further, this situation can result in a larger acceptance of bribery and other such informal relations that emerge as the government's legitimacy dwindles in the eyes of aspiring businesspeople.

PRESIDENT KIBAKI, THE ECONOMIST

At least partially because of his experience as a former minister of finance and his training as an economist, Mwai Kibaki's presidency was accompanied by unprecedented expectations of economic growth and renewed government emphasis on revenue collection and job creation. But it soon became apparent that most of the new jobs the government intended to create would, quite paradoxically, come from what had long been known as the informal sector and had more recently come to also be called the micro and small enterprise (MSE) sector. According to Sessional Paper No. 2 of 2005 (Kenya 2005b:iii), the majority of the 500,000 new jobs that the president had promised to create annually during election campaigns would come from the MSE sector.[8] While MSEs were defined as employing 1–50 workers (Kenya 2005b:5), the authors admitted that over 70 percent of MSEs included only one self-employed individual (Kenya 2005b:6).

Well before the 2002 election, there had been serious doubt about whether Kenya's small-scale traders would ever be able to amass enough capital to be considered an autonomous part of the national economy (McCormick 1987).

The 2005 sessional paper on the development of the MSE sector did not focus on limiting risk, securing land and market tenure, or giving loans or grants for firm growth, security, or development—all factors researchers had previously agreed needed to be addressed before MSEs would be able to grow effectively (see Ferrand 1996; King 1996; Macharia 1993; McCormick 1993). Rather, the authors of the 2005 sessional paper concluded very clearly that "the Government will intervene in the market only when there is a market failure" (2005b:39), making the continuation of a laissez-faire policy an explicitly stated goal. The government's job was to tax.

In the early years after his election in 1978, Moi had a reputation as a populist man of the people.[9] Several roadside traders who lacked significant formal education loved President Moi because, as Simon put it in 2006, "Moi understood the problems of the little guy. This NARC government, they do not understand Kenyans" (author's interview, February 4, 2006, Mombasa). He pointed to the fact that during Moi's presidency, the kiosks had been allowed to flourish while taxes and license fees were less than during Kibaki's first years in office. It had also been easier to simply bribe municipal officials to gain access to urban commercial space. At first, in the first year after Kibaki's election, several research participants including Simon told me they resented the loss of the old system, in which a "small something" (*kitu kidogo*, or "bribe") could secure a trader a place to sell in the city. But then very quickly and despite the hopes about Kibaki's anticorruption platform, the system along Mombasa's roadsides reverted back to how it had been before Kibaki's election, allowing some traders like Simon to remain informal and illegal. Other than everything being more expensive, there was an overwhelming sense by the later years of Kibaki's presidency that nothing had really changed (see Branch 2011)—except that for Simon, his connection to the market provided by international tourists was now more precarious than ever.

While many traders told me in 2001 that they usually could pay kitu kidogo to get out of having a license, many had stories about that one time when they were arrested for some type of licensing issue. Most accepted the system of small bribes, long in place along Kenya's roadsides, as natural and not something that the government should necessarily work to fix. This is not to say that traders, or even the average Kenyan citizen, saw a system of bribery as ideal or had much respect for Kenyan policemen or municipal *askaris*—a particular type of local police—who might accept bribes. However, underpaid officials who could be bribed played an important role in traders' daily routines. The ability to bribe officials decreased confrontation and enabled the roadside economy to function, albeit on the edge of the law. Andrew told me in 2005 that because his single business permit to sell curios from an Old Town free mark had risen to over 3,500 Kenya shillings (US$55) per year, it made more sense for him to go a year on 400–600 shillings (US$8–10) of bribes rather than purchase the license, which he could not afford (author's interview, October 18, 2005, Mombasa).

Although all Mombasa businesses were licensed by the year, it was not generally until late May and June that municipal askaris began circling on foot and asking to see licenses for the various shops. For curio vendors, it was convenient to have the first half of the year to accumulate the money necessary for licenses (1,000–4,000 shillings, or US$15–60), although by the time the askaris came looking, it was often the middle of the low tourism season, when most shopkeepers in Old Town were in debt, behind on rent, and so could still not afford the required licenses.

It was normal to bribe the *munispa,* as the municipal askaris were frequently called, with small amounts to get an informal extension of the license deadline. But even this system was confusing since there were different sets of askaris to check the licenses of the formal shops and to regulate those who sold from tables that were set up daily. I was told that these askaris were supposed to remove traders from the roadsides for operating without formal structures and trade licenses, but this would inevitably have led to confrontation unwanted by all parties.

The result was that the askaris who regulated the roadside traders collected an informal or unofficial "tax," which went to the askaris themselves but allowed vendors to remain on the roadsides. They had different ways of dealing with this "tax." Sometimes traders would pay 20 shillings (US$0.30) per day, and sometimes they even received receipts. But as Simon made clear, the money went directly *mfukoni,* "into the pockets," of the askaris. Yet Simon, a born-again Christian, insisted that the askaris were not bad or corrupt people and that they were just doing their jobs. He said they often sat and chatted a bit before taking whatever the traders could pull out of their pockets and moving on. He especially appreciated that it was nonconfrontational and friendly. The practice was naturalized with the oft-heard phrase "Everyone has to eat."

But the system did not always work out smoothly, particularly when the power of numbers upon which the traders relied was not present. Simon's brother Omar told me the story of how one day he had arrived to set up his roadside table outside of Fort Jesus around 8 o'clock in the morning as usual, well before most tour groups arrived at the fort. Although arriving early gave Omar a competitive edge, on this particular morning the munispa reached his location before any of his friends. He did not have even 50 shillings (US$.75 at the time) for a bribe and there was no one from whom he could borrow the money. To his chagrin, he was handcuffed and walked the short distance up Nkrumah Road to the police station, where he was held until the next morning when he went to court, after which Simon and another of his brothers came and paid the 1,500 shilling (US$22) fine with borrowed money. The judge also ordered him never to sell curios again, Omar told me, laughing from where he sat in the shade next to his roadside table. But his laughter did not suggest that he had enjoyed the experience. Rather, it reflected his view of how illegitimate and ineffective the local government's attempts at regulation were. And despite the joking and laughter, the presence of the munispa and the importance of licenses were very real. These important and expensive documents were usually kept locked in a safe, while the official receipt was framed and hung on the wall in case the munispa passed by.

For many successful traders, the steady increase in license fees was the biggest restraint to enterprise growth. Kiosk licenses had become much more expensive just prior to the demolitions. In 1999, licenses for kiosks had been issued for 1,000 shillings (US$15) per year.[10] But in 2000 and 2001 the licenses were 3,400 shillings (US$50), an increase of 240 percent just prior to the kiosks' unannounced removal. By 2005 the curio license reached 3,900 shillings (US$60) per year according to some receipts I saw. With additional fees and licenses, such as the 500-shilling license to sell shells, it often cost as much as 5,000 shillings (US$75) per year in licenses to legally operate a small curio business in Mombasa. It was a common opinion among my research participants that politicians would continue to raise the license fee until only the very rich were left running businesses.

Steadily increasing license fees compounded the financial constraints for all small businesspeople in Mombasa. By 2006, the Single Business Permit required of formal Mombasa businesses had risen to 4,250 shillings (US$65).[11] Such important and expensive licenses were usually kept locked in a safe, while the official receipt was framed and hung on the wall in case the munispa passed by. Maintaining a business also became harder in 2005 and 2006 because the KRA began requiring businesses to use an electronic tax register that calculated the 16-percent value added sales tax (VAT). Shop owners and local vendors resented having to turn over 16 percent of their sales to the government, the tax cutting directly into their slim profit margins.

It was usually not difficult to get curio vendors to talk about the effects of these taxes and fees on their businesses. As Jamal explained from his shop outside of Fort Jesus: "These are locally produced products and should not be taxed. They are not imports" (author's interview, October 24, 2005, Mombasa). Jamal was relatively well educated, having completed secondary school, and considered himself as having a good understanding of business regulations. This only furthered his frustration with the job the KRA was doing under Kibaki. In his words, it was "illegal" for the KRA to try to tax him. In Jamal's opinion, the government was determined to steal from his own meagre profits. Within a context where the government put little emphasis on legalization and instead privatized and commodified urban economic space, it was not surprising that many traders resented taxation more than bribery.

Not long after speaking with Jamal, another Old Town shop owner relayed similar opinions to me. He could not hide his disappointment in Kibaki's government. As he put it: "The government is not supposed to tax businesses that make less than 1 million shillings [US$14,200] per year, like mine. Now they want us to purchase these tax registers for 75,000 shillings [US$1,100]. Then in the papers today I saw that the ministers are receiving 5 million shillings [US$70,000] each to purchase a car. What an embarrassment our leaders are in this country (author's interview, October 24, 2005, Mombasa)."

He pulled out his receipt book, which had only one receipt in it. There were three items purchased: one for 200 shillings, one for 600 shillings, and one for 1,500 shillings. "That's about $35 worth of business," he explained. But that was all he had made in several days. He had made $35, and now the government wanted $5 of it. "How can I pay an additional tax on that? It is outrageous," he told me, echoing the opinions of many of Mombasa's shop owners.

While traders' biggest fear during my research of 2001 had been the upcoming 2002 election and the potential for violence, by 2006 traders' concerns had turned to the increased cost of overhead and the issue of electronic tax registers. The risks were coming less from ethnic tensions stirred up by politicians than from new taxation and licensing regimes.

"They want us to buy these tax registers for 80,000 or 100,000 shillings," said Andrew from his shop in Old Town in 2006. "The stuff that we have in this store might be worth 100,000 shillings, but that does not mean we have that money free to buy a tax register" (author's interview, August 12, 2006, Mombasa). Andrew, who had originally been employed selling curios from a kiosk outside of Fort Jesus, chronically lacked the capital needed to succeed in the crafts business. In his early thirties, he had a wife and two children who lived on a farm near Kitui, a half-day's bus ride away. It was difficult to make enough money to send home, particularly when the government was trying hard to increase its revenue collection out of his pockets. Paying taxes required costly equipment. Paying bribes did not. In this case, the art of connecting to urban market space had become rooted in the development of risky informal and often illegal personal relationships with municipal authorities.

Through 2007, the KRA continued its crackdown on traders who had not installed a register, arresting and charging violators with "defrauding the government" (*Nation* Correspondent 2007). Many of my research participants simply continued to operate without the electronic tax registers, bribing the munispa for an additional "extension" when necessary. Compliance from traders would come only when they felt a sense of trust in the government and when taxation seemed more progressive than bribery. Despite the early promise NARC and Kibaki had given to many Kenyans, after several years in office it was understandable why roadside traders remembered Moi and KANU so fondly.

Although Kibaki's administration received credit from the international media for turning Africa from the "hopeless continent" to the continent of "Africa Rising," economic growth alone did not mean the economy was moving in the right direction. For example, while there was a 24.5 percent increase in overall volume of trade in 2004, the Kenyan national trade deficit widened to nearly 150 billion shillings as a result of a continued faster growth in imports than in exports (Kenya 2005a:116). While GDP grew steadily between 2004 and 2007, only some sectors of the economy actually experienced growth. During the 2005–06 fiscal year, for instance, GDP grew by 5.8 percent (Wahome and Siringi 2006), but newspapers reported that the wealthiest 10 percent of the population continued to control nearly half (42 percent) of the country's wealth. As the divide between the rich and poor increased, the poorest 10 percent (over 3 million people) were left controlling less than 1 percent of the national wealth (Munene 2006).[12] As one editorial ("Growth of the Economy Is Laudable, But . . ." 2006) pointed out, a 5.8 percent growth rate meant nothing when the inflation rate during the same period was 10.3 percent. Many Kenyans expressed dismay when it was announced in 2006 that Kibaki's salary was being increased to US$528,000 per year, making him one of the best-paid presidents in the world ("Knocking Out the Lion's Teeth" 2006). "You know, they say this is economic growth, but what is that?" one Kamba vendor asked me from the doorway of his curio business in Mombasa's Old Town. "If Kenyans are still starving, that means nothing" (author's interview, November 8, 2005, Mombasa).

Despite Kibaki's statement in his early-2003 inaugural speech that corruption would no longer be a way of life in Kenya, *Africa Confidential* and other investigative sources reported that "within a year, graft was back up to the worst level of Daniel arap Moi's regime" ("Mwai's Muddle" 2005:7; Wrong 2009). By 2006, many Kenyans were convinced that Kibaki's government was at least as corrupt as that of his predecessor ("The Anti-Corruption Collapse" 2006). In February of that year, *Africa Confidential* ("The Hawks Are Circling" 2006) argued that Kibaki had been "fatally wounded" by his government's corruption scandals. The rumors of corruption in Kibaki's government would seriously hamper the legitimacy of some of the very progressive development initiatives put in place under his administration.

Despite attempts by government-aided bodies such as the Kenya Tourism Board (KTB) and the Tourism Trust Fund (TTF) to help small-scale traders through special development initiatives, none of my long-term research participants ever participated in these programs. For example, when I relayed to some of my participants that the government's TTF reportedly dispersed 225 million shillings (US$32.1 million) to tourism-related small-scale enterprises in 2005, the typical response was that the money must have "been eaten" or found its way into someone else's pockets. As the journalists covering the story reported (see Wandera 2006), it was basically impossible to find a single curio trader who had benefited from these grants and loans. No one seemed to know where the money had gone.

The question among Kenyans remained: if the tourism industry was growing, who was profiting? Some newspaper articles covering the issue began referring to "cartels" that had come to control the tourism industry by locking out small businesspeople (Wandera 2006). Paying off drivers and tour guides by ensuring them 10–20 percent commission had become so standard throughout Kenya that most traders who could not afford this investment or did not have personal connections with tour operators were denied business, whether on Mombasa's beaches, in Old Town, or in Nairobi. Again, the persistent informality meant that personal relationships and networks remained essential for a select few powerful individuals to maintain their connections and dominance. This was the reality for my research participants just as it was for Kenyans working in any number of industries or businesses.

Government agencies like the KTB were aiding not small-scale traders but large-scale and often international operators and investors. It was not hands-off market liberalism; it was at times highly selective corporate welfare and crony capitalism. The KTB and the government continued to stress international marketing and the promotion of all-inclusive packages to attract large numbers of tourists to the country. As a result, tax revenue from tourist entries increased, airlines did more business, East African Breweries' business boomed (with an estimated 16 percent of sales due to tourists), and several large hotel and tour-operator chains reported record profits (Wahome 2005). But at the same time, many long-term, small-scale vendors were pushed out.

The continued emphasis from the government planners was on large-scale projects aimed at international tourists and the Kenyan elite. This was particularly true at the coast, where the government's Vision 2030 called for the building and development of at least two "high class resort cities."[13] Kibaki's government continued to concentrate on international rather than Kenyan interests, as Tourism and Wildlife Minister Morris Dzoro announced in March 2007 that new international investors in tourism would be given tax holidays (Barasa 2007). Official policy had reached the point where international investors were allowed to operate tax-free while small-scale Kenyan traders were being taxed out of existence. Despite all the risks, for immobile and disadvantaged traders, the semilegal and precarious roadsides were a realistic alternative to regressive taxation and licensing regimes.

"FREE MARK" KENYA

After the demolition of Mombasa's kiosks in early 2002, the municipal council's suggestion to traders was to form a new type of shop, a "free mark," by getting a group of people who could not raise enough capital to rent a single formal shop to pool their resources and work cooperatively, dividing the rent and market space, and moving them off of the roadsides and into formal commercial space. This was very common around Kenya's urban centers in the early 2000s, as vendors of everything from clothing, electronics, and handicrafts were urged to formalize and move out of the harsh sun and into formal indoor, taxable shops. This model transformed parts of Mombasa's downtown. In Nairobi, Moi Avenue was particularly transformed by the free marks selling clothing, shoes, and other accessories. Kenyan writer Binyavanga Wainaina described the free mark craze and its origins in Nairobi's Uhuru (Freedom) Park, where a giant market called "Freemark" had been established around the year 2000, selling all types of goods from small, partitioned stalls

(Wainaina 2007). The free mark phenomenon of the early 2000s was adopted by displaced roadside vendors almost immediately as the best option after having lost their kiosks. For most, the roadside system had become untenable, and as much as anything, vendors wanted security. But while the name "free mark" was implicitly associated with freedom, it also meant traders were free to fend for and compete among themselves.

Many people with whom I spoke highlighted the class bias in the new system. In Simon's opinion, Mombasa's free marks primarily benefited landlords, who immediately profited after the demolitions forced traders off of municipal road reserves and into privately owned shop space. He protested that the money the kiosk owners had been paying regularly to the municipal council was now being paid to Old Town landlords, who in most cases belonged to different patron-client networks than those of the migrant curio traders. From a heritage perspective, however, it made sense to help the old Swahili families whose neighborhood had been radically changed by tourism and who had little left other than the bottom floors of their buildings as a means to make a living. In some cases, free marks would also provide what the kiosks had lacked: the security and formality sought by so many stakeholders in this economy.

Three months after the demolitions in early 2002, Simon, Mama Wanjiru and her daughter Wanjiru, Elizabeth, Mama Wachira, and Andrew decided to start their own free mark in Old Town along Ndia Kuu Road. To join, they each paid 2,000 shillings (US$30 in 2002). They also all made their own identification badges to avoid harassment from municipal askaris. The IDs were not legally necessary, but they voluntarily added this extra level of formality and protection from local youths and the munispa alike.

While the group made a promising start, and they kept me updated with regular e-mails beginning in early 2003, British Airways would cancel all flights to Kenya later that year due to terrorist warnings related to the invasion of Iraq. Seemingly unrelated to anything happening in Mombasa, the number of European and North American tourists plummeted amid flight cancellations and advisories. As soon as it started, the Ndia Kuu Road free mark crumbled. Many members, such as Wanjiru and her mother, no longer bothered going to work.

For Andrew, it was "terrible" (author's interview, October 10, 2005, Mombasa). He had to pay 1,550 shillings (US$22) every month to the landlord as his portion of the rent. In addition, he was also still competing against the other members of the free mark. While they shared the space and rent, they did not share profits. If the number of vendors in a single shop swelled to as many as twelve, or if family members or employees were present, the crowded sales environment stopped being friendly and welcoming. The curio free marks also tended to sell the same items on multiple shelves, making the crafts appear less distinctive. But few traders, especially those who had previously worked from a roadside kiosk, had enough capital to rent and occupy a full-sized roadside shop. Some found ways of surviving until 2014, but most of these had connections to a landlord or even more lucrative connections to an exporting company that regularly bought large quantities of goods. Otherwise, the economic level previously occupied by the kiosk-based economy was eliminated.

After the Ndia Kuu Road free mark folded, Andrew was forced to move back to his home near Kitui. He would, however, return to Mombasa in 2005, and join Elizabeth, Mama Wachira, and David in a new free mark. He complained to me that joining the free mark once again placed him into a crowded shop where the vendors all competed with one another in a small space that tourists were often afraid to enter (author's interview, October 24, 2005, Mombasa). He also mentioned that with their formalization, KRA agents had started telling the free marks they needed electronic tax registers to calculate and ensure that they were paying sales tax. There were many unanswered questions, such as how they would divide up the taxes in a free mark with multiple vendors. Who would pay what? Would they each need a separate register? But as the free mark members joked at the absurdity of the new requirement, the threats from the KRA continued.

As 2005 approached its end, the free mark's landlord, who they described simply as "an Arab," demanded three months' rent up front (30,000 shillings or US$450) if they wanted to stay in the shop entering 2006. Following the kiosk demolitions, larger numbers of would-be tenants were looking for commercial space, and landlords had no need to be lenient with tenants who could not pay rent. David, who had only been employed to work in the free mark by an older Maasai man who was rarely present, eventually left to work for Jamal directly outside of the fort. When Elizabeth and Andrew could not come up with their share of the rent, Mama Wachira was the one to push them out, coming up with the rent on her own and thereby making the shop solely hers.

Although this marked the end of their free mark, Elizabeth and Andrew were not entirely excluded. Mama Wachira was one of the older Kikuyu women who had served as a surrogate mother to many of the younger vendors (and to me) from the days at the kiosks. Even after she made the shop her own, she allowed Elizabeth and Andrew to continue to try their luck selling some small items. Elizabeth and Mama Wachira were both Kikuyu, and Mama Wachira told me quite openly that she had more of an obligation to Elizabeth than to Andrew.

Although they had all been friends since the 1990s, there was also constant tension. Elizabeth often expressed how unhappy she was with Mama Wachira, complaining to me that she was interested only in her own economic development and cared little if they had all worked together for a long time. But Mama Wachira was the single mother of an adopted child and was twenty years older than Elizabeth and Andrew, so she had reason to be concerned about her own survival. While she cared about how the others fared, she felt it her right to take over the shop as her own if she was the only one who could afford to pay the rent. The heightened competition just made it harder to deal with such moral and ethical dilemmas.[14]

It was hard as a researcher to watch vendors who were research participants slowly fall out of the business and into abject poverty and ill health, as was the case both after the demolitions and after the collapse of many of the Old Town free marks. Andrew began to regularly show me sores that broke out on his body before asking for money to get the needed shot at the hospital. He was not alone. I did not ask people to identify their affliction, sparing traders like him the discomfort of admitting they had a disease like HIV or another common ailment such as a chronic bowel problem or tuberculosis. Yet such health problems frequently kept traders away from work and limited their productivity, especially in times when people could not afford basic health care, clean water, and sufficient food. Although I generally did not pay research participants for interviews, I started a habit of helping people pay for medical expenses and "promoting" vendors by giving them some badly needed business, even if just worth a few dollars.

Through 2006, record-breaking numbers of tourists arrived every day through the airports, but few of them bought from the vendors in Old Town and outside of Fort Jesus. Some participants in my research became noticeably thin and sickly. Others simply disappeared for weeks at a time, seeking out alternative livelihoods selling secondhand clothing or vegetables in more formalized municipal markets. But these industries were also overcrowded and struggling to adapt to the new markets and economic organization in the city. The goals of many traders changed from trying to "outlast the rest" to trying to "get out as soon as possible." For those with a rural home, it was

competition amongst themselves.?

important to know how much money would be needed to get home as a last resort. For those without a rural home, something in Mombasa had to give. There was no other option.

Referring to the free mark before its eventual dissolution, Andrew explained to me in 2005: "There is no security in the group. Because of the insecurity, people need to just all look out for themselves. If some kind of a cooperative forms, like the one at Fort Jesus [the original Fort Jesus Curio Group], then that cooperative is destroyed with kiosk demolitions. If people aren't all ready to just fend for themselves, they don't have a chance" (author's interview, October 24, 2005, Mombasa). From Andrew's cynical but realistic perspective, doing business individually was not a preferred strategy but a last resort for which traders had to be prepared in this new economic environment. Without the cooperatives and associations that had previously provided security and ensured access to a market for their goods, the curio vendors and traders had few options besides working on their own.

TRADERS, ARTISANS, FORMALIZATION, AND MOBILITY

While certain government initiatives in Mombasa have proven harmful to small businesspeople, I found that there was always a genuine desire for regulation and formalization that was *fair*—not from the perspective of the Western consumer of a Kenyan-made product, but from the perspective of the Kenyans working in the industry itself. Not all state-sponsored initiatives were resisted, and many were great successes. These stories are often lacking. As with the case of Kenya's free marks, the success or failure of any model or intervention depends on a broad array of contextual variables. The next two examples have been chosen to demonstrate just how complicated and yet successful this negotiation can be.

Case 1: The Fort Jesus Tour Guides

In May 2005, the National Museums of Kenya hired Mohamed, a young, ambitious, and dynamic college graduate from Mombasa's Old Town to serve as Fort Jesus's new public relations officer. One of Mohamed's early tasks was to monitor the tour guides operating outside of the fort on the museum's behalf. In his first month on the job he called a meeting for all guides and mandated that they create their own organization with an elected chairman and that they give Mohamed a complete list of all official guides. The job was challenging, and Mohamed, with whom I regularly met, updated me on the progress. Many of the tour guides were over thirty years old and had started working as guides in the 1980s when there were more tourists, fewer visitors came on all-inclusive packages, and there was a steady demand for local tour guides. With the national economic decline and the crash in tourism by the 1990s, many of the tour guides had started openly using if not selling hard drugs (most problematic being heroin) outside of the fort.

As Mohamed complained to me, "How can I have people who are supposed to be tour guides dozing off on heroin right there in front of the fort on that bench like this [making a wobbly movement]?"[15] When he first took the job, he had met with several large tour operators who had stopped bringing tourists to the fort simply because of the bad impression given by the local tour guides, particularly as they ran up to approaching buses, clawing at the windows and fighting for customers. "In this era," he said, referring to the insecurity and travel advisories in coastal Kenya, "you simply cannot do that. It scares the tourists."

The first step was to mandate that the guides all wear a simple uniform of a collared white shirt with black pants. After a month, half of the guides had readily complied. But the others continued to resist Mohamed's attempts at formalization and professionalization, not respecting his authority and continuing to dress as they wished. In distress, he went to officers at the Ministry of Tourism office in Mombasa, who liked his idea and drafted a letter for him to give to the tour guides. The letter directed the guides to wear the uniforms and name tags and to always carry licenses issued by the municipal council. Qualifications and training were left to the tour guide organization itself, which would be formally approached should there be problems with individual guides. If they did not comply, the tourist police unit at Fort Jesus could be used as a policing mechanism. The letter gave the guides until October 1, 2005, to comply.

This KTB response was a great help but also created an ethical challenge for Mohamed, who wondered what he would do if the guides did not comply. He had grown up with many of those men. "They are children of Old Town," he told me. "I can't fire them. They grew up here. They live here. This is what they do."

When the tourist police started arresting the guides who had not complied, he simply asked, "What else could I do?" Going through formal police channels was a risk of its own, but by late October 2005, the tour guides association was turning to Mohamed to help police their own ranks and differentiate between the legitimate guides and those who were involved in illegal activity. He received several formal letters from the newly elected chairman of the tour guides association asking for help in regulating the guides. The more professional guides readily wore the uniforms and carried their licenses, wanting to secure and maintain the jobs upon which their families depended. Many of the guides were very proud professionals with an incredible depth of knowledge about Mombasa's history. When these more professional guides began coming to Mohamed for help—in their neat black pants and white, collared shirts—it was, in his words, "a major coup."

A smart, funny, and extremely ethical man, Mohamed was, in my opinion, very successful at making the tourist experience outside the fort more formal and professional. While he would eventually take new, higher-paying jobs, the precedent he set (which still holds today) demonstrates that people working in informal economies will readily formalize if given the opportunity and if they see the formalization as beneficial to them.

Case 2: The North Coast Curio Vendors

The North Coast beach vendors provide an example similar to that of the Fort Jesus tour guides. The vendors on the beaches of the North Coast had not been directly affected by the kiosk demolitions, although they had been hurt both by the drop in tourist arrivals beginning in the early 1990s and by the negative views of the increasing number of beach operators and guides (often simply called "beach boys") held by many tourists, hotel owners, and Mombasa residents. Large numbers of men and women who had lost their kiosks had also moved to the beaches to sell their crafts, increasing the number of vendors and the overall competition.

The vetting of the beach operators by the Ministry of Tourism began officially in 2003 in the first months after Kibaki's NARC won the 2002 general election.[16] While the beach operators were in direct economic competition with the guides and shop owners located inside the hotels, the government (specifically the Kenya Tourist Police, the Ministry of Tourism and Wildlife, and the Coast Provincial Administration) decided to license the beach vendors instead. They could have easily removed them, which would have made the hotel owners much happier. But instead they chose to formalize and regulate the small businesspeople.

The first wave of formalization came through a mandate that all legal curio vendors and tour guides wear their name tags, licenses, and uniforms while working. A group of mainly Kamba curio vendors with whom I spoke during the height of the 2005 high tourism season said they welcomed these regulations for giving them permanence (author's group interview, November 8, 2005, Bamburi Beach).[17] While there was a strong suspicion among the beach vendors that the government intended to eventually remove them, traders whom I interviewed appreciated whatever legality and protection they could get, even if only in the short term. Most of them are still there in their faded yellow shirts at the time of writing.

There had previously been a series of organizations, such as the Bamburi Beach Association. But after the vetting of the vendors and the implementation of the new regulations, all coastal organizations from the Tanzanian border to Malindi were combined into the Coast Beach Curio Operators Association at the end of 2004. As I was told, the new rules that came with the reorganization were also important because they helped differentiate between vendors who were deemed legitimate and the unlicensed tour guides, drug dealers, and female and male sex workers, or "beach boys." As the former secretary of the Bamburi Beach Association told me in 2005: "It is a good system now because with the shirts and IDs, we can police ourselves. If someone is selling curios and is not a member, we will chase them away. You cannot sell *bangi* [marijuana], cocaine, or do any illegal activity, which is good for all of us" (author's interview, November 8, 2005, Bamburi Beach). He stressed to me that the new organization was about gaining trust and legitimacy for curio vendors in the eyes of tourists, hotel owners, and the police.

As another Kamba trader operating outside of Nyali Beach Hotel told me a month later: "The regulations are better, to everyone's advantage" (author's interview, December 22, 2005, Nyali Beach). He had formerly belonged to a smaller curio organization, "but then we didn't have IDs from the Ministry of Tourism," he said in comparison. He showed me his ID, which was also marked with "Nyali Beach Hotel"; he and several others were the only vendors permitted to do business outside of that hotel. "As long as we work from 8:00 A.M. to 6:00 P.M. regularly, they let us stay here," he told me. "In fact, one of the reasons they let us stay here is that we provide security for the hotel," he added. In case there was an incident, he pointed out that they all had name tags, so anyone officially licensed could be sought out and dealt with individually while the rest were allowed to remain.

To this day, the case remains a successful example of regulation and formalization. But this is not to suggest that all traders were in favor of these regulations. Many traders and beach vendors would find jobs in exporting or wholesaling so as to avoid the wind, uncertainty, and sun of the beach. While the regulations were protective for some vendors, they also allowed the tourist police unit to harass other Kenyans who were not carrying IDs or wearing the appropriate uniform. This was particularly the case with young women who, if they were not involved in sex work when they arrived at the beach, had often been charged with such a crime by the time they were released from jail. On multiple occasions during my stay in Kenya from September 2005 to August 2006, I received phone calls from female friends and research participants asking me to retrieve them from the local police station, where they were being held on charges of prostitution for having been a female Kenyan walking alone on Bamburi Beach without an official license. Such charges—hardly legally defendable—were attempts to solicit bribes, usually from people like me who would come to the rescue. Complications with the police could be avoided by becoming licensed as a crafts vendor, the licenses themselves giving access to an important space for making international connections.

DANGEROUS CONNECTIONS

Many of the informal socioeconomic connections that developed in Kenya's cooperatives outside of Fort Jesus and along Mombasa's North Coast beaches came with all types of new risks. Long before the digital age, some crafts vendors—women and men—quite strategically supplemented their incomes and sought out new international business connections by dating tourists and other travelers (see Meiu 2011). They were easy to meet, and tourists often approached first, readily offering to pay for drinks, dinner, and sometimes more. But young women were in a particularly vulnerable position. While cell phones and social media mean that Kenyans can more easily carry on lasting relationships with the tourists they meet, becoming more intimately connected or traveling overseas with international foreigners can be genuinely dangerous. But despite considering the consequences, many young Kenyan decided to try their luck.

Maria was an exceptionally attractive young woman in her late teens when she took over her mother's shop near Bamburi Beach on Mombasa's North

Coast in 1999 to sell curios and crafts to tourists (author's interview, October 31, 2005, Mombasa). She insisted to me in 2005 that her goal all along had been to meet a white man who would marry her. She was the first of five children and grew up in the same Mombasa household as two of her mother's younger sisters. Both of her aunts frequented local tourism venues and dated white men while she was growing up. Maria would often meet these wealthy and exotic foreigners when they visited her Mombasa home. As she told me, "So many of my birthdays when I was young, I celebrated with *wazungu* [whites] and I felt so special." One of her aunts, who Maria said worked briefly as a model, married a Swiss man and was living in Switzerland at the time of my research.

When she decided that she would not be going to high school, she dropped out of school in standard 8 and took over her mother's business near the beach. Her parents were upset with her for leaving school, but her mother finally told her that if she wanted a white man, she could go and work in the family shop at the beach. But Maria was very shy. After flirting with men for several years and never becoming intimately involved with anyone, her aunt's Swiss husband decided to take Maria to Switzerland to find her a job and a husband. Or that is what he told her. She could not have been more excited, bragging to me in a 2003 e-mail about her new opportunity.

But during her first week in Switzerland, her uncle brought her to one of his friend's houses, where she was shown pornography and left alone with the friend, who she said was in his forties or fifties (she was twenty-one). When he went to take a shower, Maria opened the door and ran away. After she returned to her uncle's house, he was furious and took her to a strip club in a casino, where she was given alcohol and made to audition as an exotic dancer. The club owner was apparently delighted and told her that she could start working right away. Later that night, she slipped out of her uncle's house for good.

The first day she met a man from Senegal, to whom she spoke because he was the only other black person she saw. As it turned out, he was what she called simply a gangster, or *jambazi* in Swahili. "He helped people with passports," she said. "He burned their old ones so they could stay in Swiss," as she put it. He also sold drugs. But because she felt he respected her, she stayed with him for several months. According to her, they fell in love. When she told me the story in my Mombasa living room two years later, she pulled out pictures of the two of them that she still carried with her.

Their relationship in Switzerland ended abruptly. One day when she was unknowingly wearing a jacket of his in which he had sewn a large quantity of cannabis, she was stopped by a policeman with a drug-sniffing dog outside of their apartment. Her boyfriend saw her and, fearing she would be arrested, called her uncle. But Maria, not knowing there were drugs in the jacket, talked her way out of being arrested and arrived home unharmed. Her uncle, however, had already been called, and when he arrived, there was a violent altercation. In the end Maria was taken directly to the airport. Furious, her uncle returned her to Kenya with nothing but a single 1,000-shilling note (US$15) and the shameful story her uncle broadcast about her running away to live with a drug dealer. His wife—Maria's aunt—had remained silent the whole time, she said. "All she did was cook and clean," Maria complained, as she explained that, unbeknownst to the rest of the family, her aunt was living in complete fear of her husband.

When I saw Maria in 2005 for the first time in years, she had given birth to a mixed-race daughter a year earlier and was living with friends on the North Coast. While she still sold crafts to tourists, she and her friends made most of their income from tourists they met and dated on the North Coast. She was no longer the shy eighteen-year-old I had met in 2001.

Despite having been trafficked for sex by her own uncle, her family viewed Maria as an embarrassment and a failure. She returned to Mombasa's beaches daily to sell crafts and meet tourists. But the men she met (about whom she often told me) offered her very little money. Her goal was to find someone to marry her and take care of her for good. But most foreign men were only interested in spending a night with her and then giving her a little extra "taxi fare" to get home the next morning. She told me in 2005 that her strategy had become to wait for a tourist to mention money or try to pay her before she would begin to protest. She would question a man's intentions and insist that she did not have sex for money and that she was genuinely attracted to him. She would use the guilt and confusion this generated among half-drunk white tourists to ideally generate a longer-lasting relationship that could lead to something more than just a one-night stand. This was her art of connection, and for many years such strategies were how she and hundreds of other young men and women survived on the North Coast.

When her daughter was born with an unknown white father, Maria's family finally completely cut ties with her. She was scorned, and by 2005 looked anorexic, convinced that white men only dated skinny women and that her only hope for a future would be to marry a white tourist. She had attempted to bleach her skin, which left her color patchy, and she was embarrassed to be seen in Mombasa away from the tourist venues. There was very little I could do for her besides pay for some of her daughter's medical needs and try to convince her to eat and stay out of nightclubs and in her crafts business, which she continued operating for many years as a daytime way of meeting foreign men.

Maria's experiences were difficult, especially because she was one of my first Kenyan friends whose family and friends I also knew quite well. When she allowed me to interview her about her experiences in Switzerland, she openly admitted that she wanted other young women to learn from her story. The more I spent time on Mombasa's North Coast, the more I realized how many young women like Maria had moved there to "try their luck" around the tourism industry after having been abused or ostracized by their families. Such women are in desperate need of legal services and protections. She is only one of several women I knew in Mombasa who had been trafficked to Europe for sex at some time in their lives. While human trafficking and gender violence was not an expressed focus of my research, like sex tourism, it has become an unavoidable issue in the shadows of Mombasa's tourism industry. Despite all the promise of making new international connections and even traveling abroad, women like Maria found themselves having to support children while inhabiting cramped mud houses in Mombasa's informal settlements, having been denied important international as well as local family connections while living without running water or electricity within walking distance of lavish tourist hotels.

LOVE AND LOATHING IN MOMBASA

Because my specified goal for being on the North Coast was to investigate the impact of cell phones and Internet access on small businesses and entrepreneurs working in the shadow of Kenya's coastal tourism industry, I felt obligated to also explore the economic informality that characterized the experiences of tour guides, taxi drivers, and young Kenyans looking for personal and sexual relationships with tourists. Their experiences provided fascinating parallels to the stories of my primary research participants.

As Kenya's tourism industry fell on hard times in the late 1990s, many nightclubs and discos originally intended for tourists opened their doors to average Kenyans in order to sustain their businesses. During time spent in Mombasa, I often found myself one of only a handful of white men or women in "international" nightclubs jammed primarily with hundreds of formally employed Kenyans. I had largely avoided the nightclubs and tourist venues during earlier trips, when I was barely in my twenties and had a strong desire to differentiate myself from white tourists. I felt very uncomfortable in Mombasa's nightclubs, which I found to be heavily sexualized and difficult to socially navigate.

But during later trips I would go to many of these nightclubs either with Kenyan friends or visitors from abroad. I only really felt comfortable doing this once I spoke Swahili well enough to manage the unpredictable situations that often accompany a night out in Mombasa. The mixture and blending found in Mombasa's nightlife proved illuminating. In the tourist venues, Kenyan men were in many ways the opposite of the German, British, and Italian tourists, despite the fact that they frequented the same venues and sought the same pleasures. Whereas international tourists tended to wear shorts, T-shirts, go unshaven, and yet still, almost inadvertently, wear name-brand sandals, watches, and other accessories, Kenyan men were in a different position and under different pressures. I found middle-aged Kenyan men to be more comfortably intoxicated, often with bulging potbellies, wire-rimmed glasses, gold watches and wedding rings, cigarette cases, carefully shaved heads, dress shirts, and polished shoes. I spent many evenings sipping Tusker with friends like Davis while playing pool or sitting in the back shadows of tourist establishments, marveling at the odd fashion juxtaposition of cologne-wearing Kenyan men in starched shirts and suits and sunburned tourists in tank tops and cut-offs.

Being younger than most tourists, I generally found that the only other people my age were the young Kenyans who were working around the tourism industry. Many of the young Kenyan women I met in the North Coast venues said they were on the coast just for a few months, "visiting relatives," "staying with a sister," or "changing scenery." While such stories helped women avoid talking about being involved with sex work, the stories were also often true. There was a very fine line between sex work and the leisurely lifestyle promoted by the tourism industry and used to entice tourists, including Kenyans. In places like Mtwapa, Shanzu, and Bombalulu—all small settlements on the coast north of Mombasa—small and cheap apartment buildings were densely occupied with young women who had come to the coast from Nairobi to "try their luck." Many had saved money and would try to fund the party lifestyle as long as they could. These women had no pimps, and some of them had quite a bit of money. They were simply being modern, independent, and successful by being tourists in their own country. They ate fast food and watched MTV and the latest American romantic comedies at home on their DVD players (along with a lot of Nollywood films) to learn about the latest styles. Having relationships with overseas pleasure seekers further authenticated the leisure lifestyle.

There was no denying the exhilaration that came from daily living and working in such international and multilingual spaces. A remarkable number of women explained to me that they continued living in Mombasa because, as they put it, "Hii maisha imekolea" (I'm addicted to this lifestyle, or This life has consumed me—grammatically incorrect Swahili). Most of the women I knew were realists who knew they were boxed in socially. The North Coast and Mtwapa in many ways represented a last resort. Even if they had legitimate blame to place on abusive family members or socioeconomic factors for their predicaments, they usually admitted they had also made personal choices that revolved around modernity and lifestyle. Underneath the wigs, the makeup, the skin bleach, and the accents was the denial we all shared that it was all a sad game. But we just kept on dancing. In Kenya, a frequent toast has long been "Maisha matamu na marefu" (To a long and sweet life). The regular toast of the North Coast was "Maisha mafupi na matamu" (To a life that is short and sweet).

On a Friday night in March 2006, I was woken up by a text message from Lucy, a young woman I knew from one of the popular hangouts near the public beach on the North Coast. At 3 A.M. she wanted to know if I could get up and pay to release her and a friend from Bamburi Police Station. That night there had been a major police raid, or *msako,* on the North Coast, which usually involved police locking up all young Kenyan women who happened to be in public around a nightclub at a particular time in the early morning. I knew the msako scenario and had heard many stories, but there was little I could do at that time of day. I apologized, rolled back under my mosquito net, and went to sleep.

When I called Lucy the next morning, she and her friend had already been released. They had used their phones to bribe the police. Their phones had become a type of currency that could be used for trading and bartering a variety of goods, including sex (also see Molony 2008). Luckily they could keep their SIM cards, so they still had their contacts, and Lucy was able to slip hers into a friend's extra phone. She was back in network within an hour of leaving the police station, and she had plenty to share of her opinion of Kenyan police. She and her friend had immediately purchased *miraa* (a mild stimulant) and gone to the beach to go swimming after being released. I was told that because I had not gone to release them, drinks were on me.

According to Lucy, plain-clothes police officers were standing along the road next to the *matatu* bus stop outside the nightclub and were stopping and arresting women as they were boarding the minibuses. At the police station they were put into cells that were so full there was not enough room for anyone to sit down. I suggested that Lucy and her friend's outfits might have had something to do with their being targeted, but she swore that even older women who were there with dates were also arrested. "It was just an msako," Lucy told me. "That's just how it is."

But the two women said that even though they had been arrested before, this time it was very different. In the past, the police had always taken their shoes, valuables, and more importantly, their cell phones. They said that men, many of them white, very quickly started appearing at the station to release various women, who the police would call by name when they had been paid for. The opening offer from the police to each person arrested was 3,000 shillings (US$50) if they had cash on them. If someone came to release one of the women, it would cost 5,000 shillings (US$75). By the next morning the price was down to 1,800 shillings (US$30). At this point, Lucy and her friend were able to barter by arguing that their phones were each worth the 1,800 shillings.

While I cannot clearly follow the pathways of the money on the North Coast, the police have given new meaning to the word *cell* phone. They can eat their piece of the tourism cake while still being gracious to tourists—just lock up young Kenyan women around tourist areas at 2 A.M. on a Saturday morning, put them in cells with their cell phones, and see what money walks through the door.

At the same time, as with the crafts traders I studied, cell phones were revolutionizing young men's and young women's abilities to operate independent of nightclubs and the defined North Coast circuits. The Nakumatt grocery store in Nyali, for example, became a major meeting place, where an initial encounter in the soda aisle need only end with the exchange of phone numbers. The domestic aesthetic of Nakumatt provided an extreme contrast to Tembo Disco just a few hundred yards up the road. Meeting at a major supermarket helped make a Kenyan there to meet foreigners look and feel less like someone at work.

The way cell phones and e-mail have been breaking North Coast women's dependence upon access to nightclubs, beaches, and hotels directly parallels the experience of art traders and their use of the same technologies to become independent of the beaches and urban roadsides to vend and export their wares. As the art vendors leave the competitive urban roadsides for the Internet cafés and the export business, so too the young men and women of the North Coast have a new mobility and socially mediated capacity to create new international connections. Not surprisingly, it is almost rare now to find a nightclub or tourist venue that does not have wireless Internet or an Internet café nearby or even inside the larger facility.

The experiences of Lucy and Maria demonstrate the risky nature of "trying your luck" and making new informal international connections in the shadow of Mombasa's tourism industry. As with Kenya's curio industry, there was a widening digital and socioeconomic divide on the North Coast that was a product of the economic informality that had been allowed to thrive for decades. As the opportunities within this informality have changed with access to new digital technologies, the lucky and educated can move online and become independent escorts or simply "online singles," a twenty-first-century version of mail-order brides. But is this a good thing?

In August 2006 I found an advertising sticker on the monitor of my computer in an Internet café in Mombasa for www.AfrikaDating.com. It said, "Completely Free Dating Service Connecting Kenya to the World!" When I decided to go to the site, the main page confronted me with this illuminating block of text:

The ladies who go to Willy's Internet Cafe in Shanzu, Mombasa . . . have been asking if the site actually works. Well—Palesa from South Africa told us she had met the right person on AfrikaDating, and was making wedding arrangements. Bina from Germany met her true love in Ghana on AfrikaDating. Chris from Tanzania met Precious from the USA and is shifting to America. He said: "I think this was meant to be my meeting point for the love of my life whom I will always treasure and regard as my wife. It's so interesting that this site is all free and it has made me have my future queen. Certainly we will be glad to share our success story with you whenever you will want to have it posted. I wish you all the best on this site we treasure so much. GOD BLESS YOU SO ABUNDANTLY!!" (Cheers, Chris). . . . And yes, a number of our Jungu [rather derogatory Kenyan slang term for *white*] visitors have already made the trip to Africa to see their friends (and more) they met here. This is just a little of what we do know has happened thanks to AfrikaDating, as we don't push so much for testimonials. So, ladies from Shanzu, it does work and it's still free. You'll only have to pay Willy (and his boss) to use their services! And if you find someone, do tell us!

Reading this immediately made me smile to myself, knowing the type of young Kenyan men and women who might turn to such dating sites with optimistic hope. Many North Coast women are struggling to be recognized as independent businesswomen and to be able to date foreigners as an "online single" rather than a "sex worker" or "prostitute." But despite the agency that such well-educated and intelligent young Kenyans have to use their multilingualism and new technological literacy to pull themselves out of poverty, they are still very vulnerable actors with structurally limited opportunities. The stories I have shared demonstrate what I will continue to discuss further in the next chapter—that investing in international networks can have its drawbacks and be downright dangerous.

FIVE

New Mobilities, New Risks

Now as we have this Internet, most Kenyans are learning they have the ability to go to the Internet. You know, they sense the Internet they can use to sell their items. And there they find buyers for their items. Actually, you know, the connection, it was the problem.

DAVIS, MOMBASA
(Author's Interview, October 10, 2005)

We used to deal with a lot of risk, you know. And now, because of M-PESA, you don't have to, and if I trust you, I can send you the money, get me that something. Immediately you will see that the money is in your account. Or let's say something has happened to you and you don't have any money. You can call your friend and tell him, "I'm stuck here, please send whatever you can." If he can, he will send it to you, to your phone, and then I can return the money later.

DAVIS, NAIROBI
(Author's Interview, June 4, 2014)

ECONOMIC INFORMALITY AND POLITICAL INSECURITY create risky and precarious economic environments that push traders competing in such environments to seek new opportunities and connections. While cell phones and other new digital technologies can help struggling businesspeople overcome their immobility and lack of access to urban economic space, new forms of connection come with a host of new risks. The previous chapters have discussed the reasons why traders who participated in my research were increasingly working independently and without clear coordination with government departments following the demolitions of Mombasa's roadside kiosks. At this time, many successful traders who ran large workshops and enterprises simply abandoned the economic insecurity and high rents of the cities in exchange for spatial flexibility and a greater reliance on cell phones and Internet access. This allowed connected intermediaries to avoid the most competitive markets, as the business moved almost completely out of the tumultuous public and downtown spaces and to the suburbs and estates where it had developed over decades.

One example is a successful, middle-aged, Nairobi-based trader who ran a family export business with his wife. He and his wife, both Kikuyu, had sold their crafts for wholesale prices along with hundreds of others from Nairobi's Maasai Market since the 1990s. But as the market fees and the competition increased steadily, they shifted primarily into exporting. As artisans, they gathered banana fibers from their one-acre farm and other neighboring farms, located fifteen kilometers outside of Nairobi just past Runda. They then employed local children to help them cheaply make banana fiber products for export by pasting the fibers onto wire frames. Using Internet cafés and cell phones, the husband-and-wife team managed their local supply-and-export business without having to deal with the competition and rising license fees and overhead of the city's crowded curio markets. The businessman explained this to me one sunny day in May 2006 just after they had made the transition. They were definitely ahead of the curve, and he was bragging of their success.

We were in a parking lot in Nairobi, standing next to his Peugeot, which was packed, even on the roof, with banana-fiber Christmas trees destined for France. "There are too many markets," he told me, referring to Nairobi's four weekly curio markets (author's interview, May 18, 2006, Nairobi). He explained that as a result "too many people in this business are trying to make just a few shillings per day. There used to be so many vendors down in town. But most are gone and the shops don't do well. The customers go to the markets like the ones here in Westlands, which these days sell mostly at wholesale price. The business is really now in exporting."

I questioned him more on this spatial shift from the downtown. He responded: "Most of the older folks who used to be doing this business have moved out to the estates. That's where the real business is going on now. Out in the estates. Not here in town." When I asked if that shift was enabled by cell phones and the Internet, he responded: "Absolutely. The business has completely changed."

Although some businesspeople I met were able to use their artistic skills, education, or personal connections to develop new internationally connected enterprises, most were excluded and structurally demobilized. Even for the most talented and lucky, technological literacy and the math and English skills acquired from a formal education became crucial to being a successful long-distance businessperson, so those with less education and limited access to capital had difficulty competing. This was a major issue for Davis, who lacked a formal education. He had worked in the crafts business since the early 1990s and had many connections to craftspeople and carvers. But like the carvers, he had great difficulty maintaining relevance in international networks. Davis explained what was needed for success in twenty-first-century:

> If you go to the carvers, none of them will ever tell you that he will one day be a seller. Maybe when there were kiosks. But if you go to the big shop owners, [and] you ask them, "How did you come into this business?" he would say he did some kind of finishing school and then came to invest in this business. For the producer to do well, they need the government to come in and come up with some kind of sponsor or marketing for promoting this tourism and trade. (Author's interview, September 23, 2005, Mombasa)

Davis doubted that carvers and artisans would ever become wealthy or famous from the multimillion-dollar crafts industry. The actual producers were relegated to the ranks of the disadvantaged and exploited like they are in any number of global industries, be it textiles or agriculture. However, I also found that artisan-exporters—those who could produce and sell—were some of the most economically successful businesspeople. Before his business collapsed in 2007 and 2008, Davis had himself been a painter, applying colors and polish to soapstone items that he sold from his kiosk outside of Fort Jesus. He regularly claimed that he had a moral upper hand because he had worked his way up from the ranks of the artisans (although he had never been a carver or cooperative member). He used these claims to promote his brand and argue that he was ethically connected to the actual production networks, even if this was only a vague reflection of the reality of his business. At the same time, Davis would often brag about the fact that he had succeeded despite never completing primary school. His well-educated competitors, he would argue, had never been artists themselves. Such self-representations contained hints of the NGO aesthetics and marketing of marginality that was becoming central to the crafts industry's marketing and self-promotion.

Always thinking ahead, Davis turned to the Internet, e-mail, and mobile phones to expand his business after the loss of his kiosk. With the help of local Peace Corps volunteers, he soon had his own website and had left the hazards of the city to work from his own house in a migrant neighborhood closer to Mombasa's airport, seaport, and crafts cooperatives. By 2003, while so many of his former colleagues struggled in Old Town's new free marks, Davis thought he had finally found a new and more secure way to buy and sell the wide variety of bags, sandals, beadwork, and carvings that he could order by the truckload and ship through the port by the container. With his business card adorned with not just his Mombasa P.O. box but also his e-mail address, phone number, and the explicit claim that he was an ethical businessperson, he was no longer dependent on tourist arrivals and Mombasa's local tourism industry.

As Daniel Miller and Don Slater (2000) found of Trinidadians in the 1990s, many Kenyans like Davis took almost "naturally" to cell phones and the Internet, which gave a sense of mobility, modernity, and the possibility of making international connections well beyond East Africa. Davis's hope was to "jump scales" (Smith 1993) beyond Mombasa's local politics and economy and into the global crafts business. In 2005 Davis explained to me: "Now as we have this Internet, most Kenyans are learning they have the ability to go to the Internet. You know, they sense the Internet they can use to sell their items. And there they find buyers for their items. Actually, you know, the connection, it was the problem" (author's interview, September 23, 2005).

For three years Davis had made several hundred dollars in profits every month. His story seemed a clear illustration of the importance of new connections in urban Kenya—especially if these connections were with wealthy foreigners. But in a dramatic reversal of fortunes, by 2007 Davis could not afford his website, which he had struggled to update and maintain on his own, and he had stopped receiving orders from his American and British customers. His major buyer in the United States, who had even supplied him with his own ATM card and business cards, told him they had enough of the carvings, beadwork, and handmade goods he exported. His primary American employers informed him that their Florida-based company would no longer be needing orders from Davis. The economy was in decline, the dollar was weak, and with fewer Americans traveling and spending money on small souvenirs, the company was cutting back on orders from their overseas suppliers. With no orders and no income, Davis was suddenly stranded, ejected from the international networks in which he had briefly been a major actor.

Like many other Kenyans whose businesses had briefly expanded in the early 2000s, ten years later Davis was left asking what he had done wrong. He had bridged the digital divide and connected to international business networks. But the informal connections to the global economy upon which he had become dependent had never been stable or secure. When Davis's role in the commodity chain stopped being profitable for his employers (or when his claim to being connected to artisans was revealed to be untrue), he was cut out of the business altogether.

Davis's and others' stories illustrate that privatization and deregulation of the economy—especially telecommunications—do not necessarily lead to widespread socioeconomic development, poverty alleviation, or business creation, as is often suggested in the development literature and implied by corporate marketing. For example, a 2005 *Economist* cover story titled "The Real Digital Divide" argued that if governments would simply "open their telecoms markets, . . . firms and customers, on their own and even in the poorest countries, will close the divide themselves." Arguments like the *Economist*'s ignore situational complexity and the need for policy tailored to individual cases. The for-profit sale of new technologies on the open market in Kenya has perpetuated various types of often violent "friction" and "structures and processes not just of connection but also of disconnection" (Ferguson 2002:141; Tsing 2005; Bruijn and van Dijk 2012). Rather than a story of new global motion and mobility, the lived reality of global interconnection today is characterized by discontinuity, immobility, awkwardness, and the fear and uncertainty that accompany these characteristics (Tsing 2005).

Davis's story sheds light on the disconnect between the economic mobility promised by corporate marketing of new digital technologies and the experiences of physical mobility (or immobility) that define the lived experiences of so many in urban Kenya. The dual emergence of digital hype and mobility hype (or the "digital-mobile") has been a fundamental aspect of neoliberal globalization in Kenya, with all of its contradictions. Among my research participants, I found a distinct disconnect between their lived realities of exhaustion and struggle and the marketing hype surrounding new digital technologies. The corporate marketing of powerful companies like Safaricom and Airtel plays on dreams of wealth and physical mobility. They ensure that cell phones are "accessible symbols of the rapid flows associated with globalization, even if they do not in themselves significantly increase the odds of physical mobility" (McIntosh 2010:344).

The idea that technology leads to greater speed and accessibility to social connections is a powerful ideological construct that has influenced development literature through the neoliberal frame of ICT4D, or information and communication technologies for development.[1] Discourses of freedom and liberalism were, maybe not surprisingly, central to the marketing of digital technologies in Kenya. As Celtel's chief executive officer explained in 2007: "Communication is about freedom." ("Celtel Raises the Stakes" 2007). Large corporations have for decades claimed the technologies they provided and the new digital communication networks they made possible were going to eventually "set us free" (McChesney 2000:5). But as Robert McChesney (2000:7) pointed out more than a decade ago, this "Web utopianism" was "based not just on a belief in the magic of technology, but, more importantly, on a belief in capitalism as a fair, rational, and democratic mechanism." For example, government-owned Telkom Kenya was privatized under the assumption that deregulation would attract international investment, increase market competition, *and* create the best possible scenario for Kenyan citizen-consumers. But making the provision of digital technologies the job of multinational companies removed the responsibility to manage risk from the Kenyan state and placed it upon these same citizen-consumers and their personal networks. In many cases, small-scale Kenyan-owned enterprises were left operating with minimal insurance and legal protections beyond informal social and ethnic networks.

Others who have studied long-distance East African traders' use of mobile phones have described how digital technologies can become an excellent means of managing the risks inherent in long-distance trade and travel in East Africa (Molony 2009b). In Tanzania, Thomas Molony (2009a, 2009b) found that because of the many risks inherent in long-distance trade, trust itself was a major requirement for making the cell phone useful within long-distance networks. Risk and precariousness are important factors for the exploration of various types of mobility and immobility and how these experiences are shaped by the power of neoliberalism and political-economic changes. Not only has Kenya, the birthplace of M-PESA money transfers (Maurer 2012), been at the forefront of Africa's technological revolution over the past decade, but it is also well-known for its dangerous roads and urban transportation system. While there is a "need for speed" in urban Kenya today (Carrier 2005), that speed (especially on the roadways) comes with significant dangers (Mutongi 2006). Services like M-PESA have been successful not simply for "banking the unbanked" (Maurer 2012). As I will discuss later in this chapter, mobile money has become particularly popular because it has made expensive, dangerous, and time-consuming physical travel unnecessary. I agree with Molony's (2009b) assertion that mobile phones are greatly valued as "travel-saving technologies." I will build upon this idea in this chapter, arguing that they are also risk-saving technologies, especially because they allow Kenyans to avoid the dangers of travel.

The comparison of Davis and Simon that I develop later in the chapter is meant to demonstrate how mobility can lead to new types of confinements and forms of exploitation. Both of these men took risks as they pursued various economic strategies and invested in very different social networks. Their stories help demonstrate how the types of risk—both physical and in the form of potential disconnections from important global networks—shape their strategies for jumping scales or staying local and balancing the precarious and often fuzzy boundary between economic formality and informality in Mombasa. My goal is to draw attention to risk and insecurity as central to the lived experiences of mobility and the digital-power divide in much of the world today.

DIGITAL(LY DIVIDED) KENYA

Beginning in the mid-1990s, the Kenyan government came under intense pressure from the International Monetary Fund, World Bank, and wealthy private investors to sell off its stake in its telecommunications sector, which was dominated by the state-owned corporation Telkom Kenya and the highly politicized regulatory body, the Communications Commission of Kenya. Even the government accepted that Kenya's mobile telephony market badly needed an economic jolt, as the waiting time for the connection of a landline had increased from 5.6 years in 1997 to 9.6 years in 1999 (Chowdhury and Wolf 2003:5). This well-known reality prompted various jokes in urban Kenya about the "line for a line."

Although Kenya's was the most substantial market for mobile phones in East Africa, the only service provider, Safaricom, had the highest charges in the region ("Phone Sects" 1999). This changed when a large stake in the company was sold to Britain's Vodafone in late 1999 to help generate capital for upgrading and investment (although the Kenyan government still controls a large share of the company). Once a second company (initially named Kencel and later Celtel, then Zain, and then Airtel), was officially licensed, prices decreased and the market grew. The number of subscribers increased dramatically from 20,000 in September 2000 to over 400,000 by July 2001 (Kenya 2002:109). By 2004 the number of mobile phone connections had grown to roughly 1.5 million (Kenya 2005a:214). When I first set foot in

Kenya in January 2001, cell phones were rare and highly prized possessions. By the time I returned in June 2003, it seemed like everyone in urban Kenya owned or at least had access to one. By 2013, 75 percent of Kenyans had regular access to mobile phones (Kenya 2014:7), and the country of just over 40 million people had 26 million mobile money subscribers (Kenya 2014:232).

Despite the dramatic expansion in access to digital technologies, liberalization of African telecom sectors has been slow and highly politicized (Muiruri 2007; Wilson and Wong 2007). Privatization and hands-off liberalization succeeded in creating "two Kenyas," divided between the connected urban elite and the excluded on the marginalized periphery. In one of the first studies of digital technologies conducted in Kenya, Eliud Moyi (2003) found that up to 40 percent of small enterprises could not capitalize on new digital technologies because of poor access to electricity and other basic necessities. Studies of digital technologies and enterprise development in Kenya have come to the same conclusion: that new technologies do not overcome but tend to reproduce existing inequalities (Chowdhury 2006; Migiro 2006; Moyi 2003). As my data show, by no means does access to new technologies necessarily lead to poverty alleviation or economic development (also see Burrell 2012; Horst and Miller 2006; Molony 2008). Rather, economic mobility and success is rooted in many other factors, particularly the ability to mobilize ethnic and family networks and the related ability to understand and negotiate semilegality and informality.

But digital technologies have become central to the mobilization of social networks and the negotiation of economic change. Well beyond just the realm of business development, they have become an important part of the broader social landscape. While much of the ICT4D literature has indeed largely been hype, digital technologies have still brought about concrete social effects on the ground, or a "technological charisma" (Mazzarella 2010:784). As early as 2001, friends in Mombasa would talk about the upcoming generation and their affinity for new technologies, calling them *ma-dot-com*. Despite their typically slow speed, cybercafés sprang up around most urban centers in Kenya and became important hubs for experiencing a new type of mobility and imagination. *Digital* and *analog* were commonly used in jokes to refer to being "modern/online" or "backward/offline." Mombasa's cybercafés were not unlike those in Ghana described by Jenna Burrell (2012) as being decorated with images of well-known international locations or places about which Internet users could fantasize while surfing the Internet and imaginatively "realizing migratory aspirations" (Burrell and

Anderson 2008:203). Indeed, my local cybercafé for much of the time lived in Mombasa was named Istanbul and was largely decorated with images from Turkey and the Middle East—places with which Mombasa and East Africa have long historical relationships.

As cell phones and digital technology became a part of everyday life and conversation in Kenya, it is important to note the difference between digital technologies' widespread use for social networking and the early emphasis placed on business creation and expansion (Donner 2006). During research conducted in 2005 and 2006, I found that of my eighty-four research participants who were involved in the Kenyan crafts business, thirty (36 percent) worked regularly in exporting or in trading Kenyan handicrafts internationally. Maybe not surprisingly, all of those thirty used either a cell phone or e-mail in their export businesses. At the same time, the fifty-four research participants who were not exporting were not using e-mail or cell phones at all for business. This does not mean that they lacked access to technologies or that they did not want to jump scales into international networks. Rather, while some privileged parties were profitably expanding their businesses and enjoying the flexibility allowed by going digital, a majority could not find ways to make the services and their new digital connections work for their businesses. Meanwhile, everyone was spending large sums of money, helping fuel record-breaking profits for companies like Safaricom.

Throughout East Africa, cybercafés have long been famous for their slow connection speed (Mwesige 2004:98). But compared to Internet cafés, where thirty minutes cost only around 30 Kenya shillings (US$0.40 in 2005), cell phones were very expensive, with one minute costing as much as 50 shillings (US$0.73 in 2005) during prime times (depending on the calling plan or tariff). While Internet speeds and costs have decreased dramatically in the last ten years, during a crucial period of economic transition, these technologies were prohibitively expensive for many small businesspeople. One Mombasa shopkeeper I interviewed in 2005 told me seriously: "You know, maintaining a mobile phone is more expensive than maintaining a car. Sometimes you can use 2,000–3,000 shillings per day [US$30–45 in 2005]. Other people use only 100 shillings per day [US$1.20]. That is still 3,000 per month [US$45] when your salary is just 5,000 per month [US$75]. It is ridiculous" (author's interview, Oct. 7, 2005, Mombasa).

It was during this critical period that the advantaged few made their move to solidify their roles as intermediary traders of Kenyan carvings and crafts. Even many of those who had early experiences of success would soon find themselves outcompeted by traders and business administrators who could better accumulate the capital necessary to win over the small yet potentially lucrative international market. While some small businesses were able to jump scales around local impediments like roadside demolitions and dangerous and time-consuming long-distance travel, many of those same scale-jumpers would falter with time. This reality demonstrates both the importance of a longitudinal perspective and the genuine danger of confusing macro-level expansion with the actual long-term effects on small-scale businesses (Matthews 2007:818).

A comparison of the stories of the two traders Davis and Simon will help us explore how individuals balance various types of digital and analog mobilities while weighing the accompanying risks. I argue that economic success comes not purely from access to capital and connections, but how one can use access to finance and social capital to manage risk and insecurity.

DAVIS AND THE GLOBAL HANDICRAFTS BUSINESS

Born in Western Kenya in the early 1970s, Davis moved to Mombasa in 1991 at the age of sixteen. He originally started working at the kiosks while employed as a domestic servant, or "houseboy," for an Indian businessman living in Mombasa's Old Town. Every day he would pass the vendors outside of Fort Jesus, some of whom spoke Kisii. He had never actually lived in or even near Kisii District, but his mother had been from Kisii Town, and Davis had learned the Kisii language as a child. After much hesitation, he asked a Kisii vendor who had empty shelf space if he could "try his luck" selling a few chess sets. Since the soapstone came primarily from the small town of Tabaka near Kisii Town, Davis could use his language skills to buy chess sets cheaply from the wholesalers working from Mombasa's Kisii Soapstone Co-operative. In the early 1990s, the tourism and crafts industries were still somewhat lucrative along Mombasa's roadsides. After several years of learning the trade, Davis finally saved enough capital (US$1,000) to move entirely into his own kiosk as a renter and later the owner.

While selling such crafts in the late 1990s Davis met the small but well-connected community of Peace Corps volunteers based in Mombasa. As tourist arrivals declined, Davis worked to maintain a valuable socioeconomic relationship with the American volunteers. He became a primary crafts dealer for Peace Corps members visiting Mombasa and the coast from elsewhere in the country, and he benefited substantially from their business and advice. A Peace Corps member introduced Davis to e-mail in late 2000 and helped him set up his website, although he could afford to maintain the initial site for only one year. Another Peace Corps member would later open a business in the United States selling "ethically imported crafts." Davis was employed as the "authorized" Kenyan buyer (as per his business card). It is worth noting that such haphazard or "lucky" connections came from informal international organizations rather than a formal Kenyan political or legal structure. It was also typical for these business connections to be made during serendipitous face-to-face meetings.

When I began my research in the early 2000s, very few of my research participants had ever learned formally about computers, cell phones, or even business management. A few like Davis had learned from friends and relatives or from tourists, visiting students, volunteers, or missionaries. But like Davis, those who knew tended to keep this knowledge to themselves since monopolizing such information allowed them to potentially operate as small-scale tycoons. As Davis told me in 2005: "I guess most of the people who are here, you will find out they are not really very well connected with the Internet. Mostly they are isolated. But you work it alone. That's very nice. You go and work it alone."

A multiethnic urban Kenyan who had lived in three of the country's major cities, Davis enjoyed working it alone. Living independently and with no relatives in Mombasa, he had no dependents to hold him back. His independence gave him the mobility that others with burdensome kin networks lacked. Because of his strong ties to wealthy foreigners, going it alone in Kenya seemed a good strategy, even if it meant depending upon an expensive cell phone, very slow Internet access, and international buyers he rarely saw in person. Despite the risk, he had hope that new apps, social media, and tools like "mobile money" would help him maintain his long-distance business connections.

Davis's daily life was always in motion. In 2005 and 2006, as an art exporter with American and British clients who placed regular orders, Davis woke up every dawn and was frequently on his cell phone and in and out of carving cooperatives, wholesale markets, and Internet cafés until the evening hours when the roads and small paths near his house in the Mombasa suburb of Changamwe were too unsafe to risk passage. Since the loss of his downtown kiosk in 2002, Davis had removed himself from the inconsistent regulation and police presence around the tourist hotels and beaches. He had opted for the largely up-country-migrant neighborhoods of Changamwe, which were close to the cooperatives, the airport, and the seaport but far from the main tourism circuits.

But despite his connections, his life was extremely stressful, and he was deeply suspicious of most of the other Kenyans with whom he worked. One morning in 2006, while still working regularly with his U.S. employers, Davis woke me up with a phone call, frantically complaining that he had no friends and that he had almost been killed for 350 shillings (US$5). He said he had been drinking beer the night before in a local bar near his home. He owed 650 shillings (US$9), so he paid with a 1,000-shilling (US$15) note, which was the only money he had. When the barkeeper denied him change, he demanded his 350 shillings. Instead, everyone in the bar turned on him. He told me that he was convinced the others in the bar thought they would be able to get some of the change the barkeeper was denying him. "They were going to kill me," he insisted. He was saved by a group of Kamba craftsmen who suddenly entered the bar and intervened on Davis's behalf.

"Why was there not a fight?" I asked him.

He replied simply, "*Kabila* [ethnicity/tribe]. They are all Kambas, and I am a Kisii. Nobody could stop them but other Kambas, because they were Kambas that were going to kill me. And those carvers, they depend on me for business, so they had to save me."

He stressed that while his government identification card said he was from Kisii, he had no connection to the other Kisii families who came from Kisii District. Many people, in fact, thought he was Kikuyu. He was glad that in the end, the barkeeper, while still refusing to give him his change, gave him three beers and told him to never come back. He gave the beers to the carvers who had pulled him out of the bar. But the stress was relentless, and he quickly switched bars to a place run by a friend who was Meru—the same ethnic community as Davis's girlfriend—and who Davis thought would protect him. This was the situation in which Davis, a Kenyan "individual," found himself, "working it alone."

While idealized by some traders and enabled by telecommunications, working it alone was the source of significant insecurity and stress. Working it alone also left Davis with a very limited support network when his employer stopped sending him orders in 2007. In the coming years, social media would expand, and mobile money would revolutionize business transactions. But despite becoming quite active on Facebook and other social media, Davis has spent nearly ten years without any regular international clients, struggling in vain to find new overseas buyers or some other form of consistent employment. In a Kenya with few formal salaried jobs, working as an informal agent was still the best Davis could hope for. Such a livelihood gave him flexibility in his daily routine but left him with no job security.

Simon offers an interesting contrast to Davis. Both men were in their mid-twenties when I began my research in Mombasa. They were two of the first participants in my study to invest large amounts of money (around five shillings, or US$0.07, per minute) into learning how to use a mouse and type on a keyboard. Before the kiosk demolitions, Simon had earned a salary of 1,000 shillings (US$20) per month selling soapstone from several kiosks neighboring Davis's. In December 2000 Simon met a pair of British missionaries visiting Fort Jesus for the day. After striking up a friendly conversation, Simon asked them about computers and the Internet. He had first heard about computers in primary school in the early 1990s and had always wanted to use one. The missionaries took Simon to an Internet café, helped him open his first e-mail account, and taught him the basics of how to use a computer and check his e-mail. After about a month of regular checking, he had acquired enough computer literacy to communicate comfortably.

Simon would later meet several American students and tourists with whom he exchanged e-mail addresses and contact information. This was essential for him to expand his social networks and practice e-mailing. While Simon had never left Kenya's Coast Province, with an e-mail account he could communicate with people from other parts of the world and dream about the economic and social mobility he had never known.

Unlike Davis, Simon was raised on a farm fifteen kilometers west of Mombasa and was from the coast. He was ethnically Duruma, one of the nine subgroups of the coastal Mijikenda, and he needed only 200 shillings (US$3) to take a bus to his father's farm, which he often described as "just dust." There he would have food and a place to stay with relatives. But for him, Mombasa was a place of connection and potential wealth.

Although having a family home only a few hours from Mombasa gave him flexibility typical of many coastal Mijikenda, he lacked capital, a primary school certificate, and any hope of formal employment beyond day labor. He did not have young American friends in the Peace Corps nor the knowledge of websites and mobile phones to fall back upon. Simon's Kenyan networks, however, were geographically closer than Davis's. As someone from the coast, Simon also had a certain advantage when it came to claiming ethnic belonging, which was central to negotiating the often murky boundary between economic formality and informality along Mombasa's roadsides (see the last two sections of chapter 2).

Immediately following the kiosk demolitions, Simon purchased a mobile phone, but it was a very cheap model, and when it broke, he never replaced it. For a few years he kept the mobile phone line and the SIM card, which he would carry in his pocket in a plastic bag to prevent it from getting wet. He was one my few research participants who did not trust new digital technologies and decided to spend his money on other things. He preferred to do all business in person, was afraid of scams, and told me as recently as 2014, "phones are all about lies" (author's interview, June 12, 2014, Mombasa).

It has become quite common in Kenya to be in a restaurant and hear someone say on their phone, "I am stuck in traffic; I will be there in five minutes," or to be in a bus and hear someone say, "I am just walking up the pathway now." Kenya has terrible traffic jams, and you can never quite trust even your best friends when they tell you by phone or text message where they are or how soon they will arrive (I do not think this is unique to Kenya). One newspaper cartoon from 2006 depicted this phenomenon with a man in a bar ordering Picana and "*sembe* brown" (boiled maize meal, a diet staple) while telling someone on his phone that he was stuck in traffic. For Simon, at least, phones were not to be trusted.

Weighing his options and the risks and costs entailed, in 2005 Simon decided to do something Davis would never have dared: set up a small table daily outside of Fort Jesus. He referred to the fort as his office and his location on the map. Simon preferred to do business face-to-face, and it was essential to find access to commercial space near the Old Town tourist circuit. He stressed the importance of being a regular at that important location, even if it meant sometimes sleeping in the park outside the fort. Whereas Davis felt unwelcome in Old Town because he was from western Kenya, Fort Jesus was an ideal spot for Simon, who was from the coast and could target tourists directly as they headed down Old Town's main tourist avenue.

But working from the roadside was tricky following the kiosks demolitions. A non-Muslim, Simon often dealt with harassment from young Muslim men from Old Town, which he could usually deflect by arguing that he was from the coast and needed a place for business. This was a technique

Davis could not have used. Similarly, when police would tell Simon to vacate his semilegal location, he would often slip them some "small money" and argue that he was from the coast and needed somewhere to go. The police, who might have put Davis in jail until he left the city for another part of Kenya, would work with Simon, who in turn thanked them and often remarked to me that if he could not have bribed the police, he would not have remained doing business outside the fort. While Davis was investing heavily in his exporting business and the maintenance of overseas connections, Simon's advantage was rooted in his social, ethnopolitical, and family networks that gave him direct face-to-face connection to his clients and customers. These connections provided enough security and benefit to make his risky informal and semilegal business worthwhile.

For Simon, jumping scales into exporting and a deeper dependence upon foreigners was not worth the risk. It was, at least, not the best use of his capital. He did not need a phone to do business if he could be found outside of Fort Jesus daily. Further, having only a very small number of carvings and beadwork pieces set up on a small table made him quite physically mobile. If he ever had to pack up and go home due to pressure from police or local teenagers, he could do so in a matter of minutes and be on his way.

In his study of long-distance Tanzanian tomato and potato wholesalers, Thomas Molony (2009b:105) asked if it was possible to continue doing business without a mobile phone. He concluded that yes, it was possible, but in addition to charisma and contacts, it required a great deal of traveling or access to physical locations where business could be conducted face-to-face. Using his charisma and social capital, Simon was able to make the roadsides outside of Fort Jesus his office and thereby continue to conduct face-to-face business. For Simon, as long as he could continue to have a place to erect his table every morning—albeit illegally—he could maintain a connection to Mombasa's crafts business without a phone.

SIMON'S HOUSE IN KWA NG'OMBE

In early 2005, Simon began saving the small profits he would make every day and set aside a little bit to eventually buy a small plot of land in an area of Changamwe called Kwa Ng'ombe. Kwa Ng'ombe was an informal settlement located on government land, partially beneath electric lines and separated from nearby neighborhoods by the railroad tracks connecting Mombasa to

Nairobi. While the land could not legally be privately owned, in 2004 Simon's older brother Omar had paid the local chief (a political administrator) in that area of Changamwe a relatively small sum of money (essentially a bribe) for the rights to build a mud hut on a plot in Kwa Ng'ombe. Simon soon decided to do the same. The chief in question, also Mijikenda, had built a reputation for helping other Mijikenda living in Changamwe with the acquisition of plots for the development of informal settlements of primarily coastal people (as opposed to migrants from central or western Kenya like Davis). That the land belonged to the government and could not legally be sold seemed an afterthought to Simon, who carefully typed and printed his own title deed in a local cybercafé and brought it to the chief, whom he would henceforth refer to as his "good friend." For 1,500 shillings (US$200), the chief signed the title deed, which Simon proudly showed me. In Simon's mind, the small plot of land was his.

Although he still traveled throughout Mombasa on a daily basis, Kwa Ng'ombe had a certain pull for Simon, who was slowly able to make a place for himself in the community. He regularly invited me out to see his progress. The roughly two hundred people living in Kwa Ng'ombe were almost all from various Mijikenda subgroups, and almost all spoke a similar dialect in addition to standard Swahili. The only informal local leaders were the pastor of the small mud church built in the center of Kwa Ng'ombe and the *mzee wa mtaa,* a local elder and political representative. Despite being a semilegal settlement, it did have representation in local politics. Simon quickly befriended both men. Although two of his brothers were Muslim, Simon soon became an assistant to the pastor. He would dedicate much of his free time to teaching other younger men about Christianity in the very ethnically and religiously diverse community located literally across the railroad tracks and under the power lines.

Both Simon's house and his small table outside of Fort Jesus occupied public land from which certain authorities could remove him legally and without notice. His strategy was, therefore, inherently risky. But he retained an impression of formality and legality by slipping money to the munispa and by printing his own title deed, in both cases pragmatically using his ethnoregional identity as a coastal person for leverage. Like many other roadside traders, Simon preferred a system of informality and semilegality over what he saw as the regressive overtaxation of his former colleagues who were still struggling in Old Town's free marks (see chapter 4).

Simon slowly saved the profits from his small roadside business and by the end of 2006 had constructed an eight-room mud structure with a roof

FIGURE 10. Tudor Creek from Kwa Ng'ombe. Photo by author, 2006.

thatched of palm fronds on his plot in Kwa Ng'ombe. He immediately started renting rooms to young women who worked in the nearby garment factories, which lined the main road out of Mombasa to Nairobi just a quarter mile from Kwa Ng'ombe. We spent many afternoons eating lunch from the shade of his house, enjoying the cool breeze and the view (figure 10)—a rarity in Changamwe. Despite the factories and smokestacks just a short distance away, the steep and rocky valleys that lined Tudor Creek were heavily cultivated with maize, papaya, coconut palms, and mango trees. Kwa Ng'ombe was like a lush rural village nestled secretly amid the realities of the global economy.

Both Davis and Simon took risks as they pursued various economic strategies and invested in very different social networks. As downtown Mombasa was slowly "cleaned" of the informal economy, young men and women with fewer economic opportunities were reoriented toward the periphery of the city, to areas like Changamwe and Kwa Ng'ombe. A new social space was emerging in the bars, barbershops, hair salons, revivalist churches, and Internet cafés on the city's margins (see Hansen and Vaa 2004:13; Weiss 2002; Burrell 2012). Simon would eventually become an assistant pastor in the church in Kwa Ng'ombe, whereas Davis found himself frequenting cyber-cafés and bars, disdaining the Pentecostalism that so attracted Simon.

Simon complained when family members soon moved into four of the eight rooms in his house, but this arrangement only gave him more social status within both Kwa Ng'ombe and his family. Although his walls were mud and his roof was thatched with palm fronds, he invested in a cement foundation for his house to give it more permanence. The corners of the building were also later supported with concrete, further ensuring the structure's formality. A few years later, he again expanded his moneymaking and formality by purchasing a pipe to run water to his house from the church on top of the hill at the center of Kwa Ng'ombe.

While Simon's tap and meter became a way for him to make money by selling water, the water and housing he provided were important services not being supplied by the government or the nearby industries. He was also informally subsidizing the production of clothing in Mombasa's garment factories and export-processing zones by providing cheap housing and water to the young women who worked in them, over on the "formal" side of the railroad tracks. I could not help noting that tourists who purchased carvings and jewelry from him outside of Fort Jesus were also subsidizing the cost of some of the new clothing they would purchase after returning to their home countries.

THE INFORMALITY OF EXPORTING

Kenyan businesspeople who had lost their kiosks in the demolitions attempted a variety of strategies in the following years that were enabled by digital technologies and the further integration of East African economies. A common option, especially for Kamba traders who had lost their kiosks, was to carry Kamba carvings to sell to Tanzanian shop owners in places like Lunga Lunga, Tanga, Dar es Salaam, and Arusha in exchange for Makonde carvings, batiks from Zimbabwe, and bowls from Malawi. Other migrants had the option (or were forced) to move home to their farms or family in rural Kenya. During a 2006 visit to Tabaka and the soapstone quarries, I found that dozens, if not hundreds, of men who had once worked in Mombasa selling soapstone had returned to Tabaka and Kisii Town to continue wholesaling soapstone or to try something different altogether. Many such regional traders had tried their luck in Tanzania and Mombasa but had gone home because all the other big regional markets for curios were glutted with traders and hindered by over-production that drove down the price of the products. One such businessman told me from his shop in Kisii Town: "We used to have local markets like Nairobi and Mombasa. But we got exploited there, wanting for money. And we need to live. We started to work at a loss. Now we have just come back here" (author's interview, May 19, 2006).

During my first day in Kisii Town in 2006, I happened to find Nyambuto standing next to his new Toyota station-wagon taxi, which was parked outside the entrance to my hotel. Nyambuto had been Simon's initial employer outside of Fort Jesus, where he had owned several kiosks in addition to those he had built on Moi Avenue. His role in the curio industry had since changed, and his primary job was now ferrying soapstone back and forth between the quarries in Tabaka and the bus stations and wholesale shops in nearby Kisii Town. He was happy to not be directly invested in the soapstone business, telling me that the demolitions were the type of *ujinga* (stupidity) that should show a researcher like me the direction in which the crafts business was headed.

Rural family or a "home" outside of the city was an important support mechanism for urban curio traders. There were few alternatives for individuals like Davis or for coastal people who lacked rural or up-country connections. Even in the migrant neighborhoods of cities like Mombasa, ethnic networks were still important to economic organization. A lack of clear regulation and licensing for exporting also made it difficult for someone striking out on their own to compete in the crafts market.

But despite the competition and risks, many of those with the capital and connections were able to successfully work around the cooperatives and profitably jump into the full-time export industry. This often required moving to a cheaper location outside of the downtown. On the one hand, moving one's business to a suburb such as Changamwe was economically sensible and meant paying lower rent than on Mombasa Island. It also meant being closer to both the seaport and airport. But traders had to consider the risk of distancing themselves from the local market and becoming overly dependent upon connections with overseas buyers.

The new distance enabled by the regularity of this new long-distance communication also created a space of potential illusion, or "lies," as Simon simply put it. More than anything, exporters were cautious of any additional intermediaries, agents, or regulations cutting into their profit margins. The most essential and despised intermediary for curio exporters was the clearing-and-forwarding agent, an individual who did little more than sign forms and supply the correct licenses for exporting. Such agents were needed, however, for any international shipment leaving Kenya. Dealing with clearing-and-forwarding agents could be avoided only by shipping through the post office.

The post office was an efficient option for small items like books but not for large shipments since the rates quickly rose with weight, and the maximum for any individual package was only 20 kilograms. The next option was the airport, which in 2006 charged US$3 per kilogram but for a minimum of 100 kilograms, meaning that US$300 was the minimum price for a shipment. That did not include the agent's fee, which could be in the hundreds of dollars. For large shipments in the tons, it was efficient to ship only through the seaport and by the container, a steel box of either 20 or 40 feet in length. Shipping by the container, as Davis had done for several years, could be very profitable. But it also required a major international client who had a market for such a quantity of arts and crafts and the services of a clearing-and-forwarding agent.

Competing for minimal profits, exporters were particularly disdainful of clearing-and-forwarding agents. One soapstone exporter explained: "We lose a lot of money to them, but there is not much that they do—just stamp some documents. There are some times they come to you with stories. They used to charge more, but now it has gone down because I've been able to catch the little things they do to add weight, or they'll write down something that isn't there" (author's interview, September 24, 2005, Mombasa).

Clearing-and-forwarding agents were often also blamed for factors outside of their hands. The soapstone exporter quoted above complained to me that his agent had tried to cheat him again by charging 22,000 shillings (US$300) to ship a 77-kilo shipment of soapstone through the airport. Although I knew that was the regular rate, he was doubtful and upset, mainly because the soapstone itself had cost him only 20,000 shillings (US$280). He protested to me that the agent must have still been pocketing some of the money. But the real problem in this case, as for many curio exporters, was that the heavy soapstone was cheaper to purchase wholesale than it was to ship.

Despite the suspicions, clearing-and-forwarding agents were essential for exporting handicrafts from Kenya. As one exporter told me, it was nearly impossible for someone like him to get his own clearing-and-forwarding license, which requires taking a special course (author's interview, November 23, 2005, Mombasa). Even with the license, he admitted, the job requires buying one's way into the favor of taxation officials and others at the airport and seaport. Like all exporters, he inevitably submitted to turning a portion of his profit over to the agents.

It puzzled me that several exporters continued to use the same agent, even after repeatedly complaining to me about his corruption and cheating. There were larger and more formal companies, but they either handled much larger orders or were unknown to my research participants. On one occasion Davis told me that it could cause genuine trouble for his business if he did not use his regular agent, who was also Kisii and who he called a "tribalist" for pushing his business on him and other Kisii soapstone exporters because of their ethnic connection. In such cases, traders needed to seriously weigh the costs and benefits of specific connections and associations and whether exporting was even a profitable endeavor.

Vendors like Simon, who could maintain access to the local market in Mombasa, were understandably wary of exporting and a continued reliance on expensive digital technologies. Other successful local curio vendors, like Njoroge outside of Fort Jesus, were also wary of moving into exporting. Because his shop was situated on museum rather than municipal land, it had not been touched during the demolitions. He had even seen an increase in profits with the decreased competition outside the fort, and he had been able to hire employees like Kazungu. He had thought a lot about exporting because he had a social connection through a relative who had married a German man and was living in Europe. But he said he decided there would be very little profit (author's interview, October 18, 2005, Mombasa).

Sitting relaxed in the shade next to his shop outside of Fort Jesus, Njoroge told me that exporters had ruined the local market by putting the highest quality products on the international market and exposing potential tourists to Kenya's unique crafts before they ever even set foot in Kenya or Africa. He said that tourists regularly told him that they could find everything in his shop in their home country. He was always trying to find what was unique. For him, exporters were part of the reason why the local curio business was declining. Because his shop had one of the best locations in Mombasa, he wanted to avoid any possibility of further compromising the local crafts market.

Njoroge was not alone in blaming exporters for ruining the local market for crafts among tourists. Many exporters, including the chairman of Mombasa's Kisii Soapstone Co-operative, reflected on this issue during interviews. But in the case of the chairman, he still made most of his money from exporting. The trick, he told me, had become to keep his products hidden and secret so that they remained unique and were not copied. He could then guarantee his overseas buyers that they would be able to sell unique new items from their shops in Europe and North America. This nurtured innovation and experimentation, for which soapstone was an excellent medium. I found workshops from Mombasa to the site of the quarries in Tabaka that had hired special artisans whose sole job was to develop new styles and models that could later be photographed and e-mailed to overseas customers. As several exporters would remark to me over the course of my research, the most valuable items were no longer the antique-looking or "tribal" products but rather *new* items that buyers had never seen before (for photos of such items, see chapter 7).

Despite the promises for jumping scales into the global crafts business, for individuals like Davis and Simon, the overall impact of new communication technologies like cell phones has been rather ambiguous. "Although mobile phones are associated with change in the direction of modernity in places like Kenya," Janet McIntosh writes, "the technology can also serve as an embodiment of disappointment or danger as well as a means of reinforcing customary life" (2010:337). In Kenya as in the United States, when individuals become dependent upon cell phones and Internet access for work and leisure, their life becomes, in the words of Mark Deuze, "completely contingent with the fickle and unpredictable nature of the contemporary global economy for which risks no one but themselves is expected to take personal responsibility" (2007:12).

The comparison of Davis and Simon demonstrates how traders balance various types of mobility for economic success based on the inherent risks associated with these strategies. The cases of Davis and Simon draw attention to risk and insecurity as central to the lived experiences of mobility and the digital-power divide in much of the world today. On the one hand, Davis felt strongly that investing in overseas networks and moving into exporting would have the most promise. This opinion was influenced by both corporate marketing as well as his lack of solid and trustworthy social networks in Mombasa, ethnic or otherwise. Simon, on the other hand, lacked Davis's capital and overseas connections. But he had an array of local social and ethnic connections in Mombasa that, while a gamble, proved quite profitable. While Davis's cell phone and Internet literacy gave him a certain type of mobility, without a support network or business connections, he was left in poverty.

Whether one chooses to expand into international networks or invest in local ones, there are unique and often unforeseeable risks. Placing these risks at the center of mobilities studies helps push beyond ideological constructs like the digital-mobile and focus on the lived experiences of inequality and exploitation that new mobilities are making possible.

M-PESA, "MOBILE MONEY," AND RISK

When I returned to Kenya in 2014 after having been away for several years, most of the patterns I had previously identified were still in place. Rampant inequality, competition, and precariousness continued to characterize the lives of small businesspeople. Digital technologies were as central and essential to daily practices as ever. Over a beer I had just bought him in a Nairobi restaurant, one young man who described himself as an "urban hustler" brought me up to date: "Digital technologies have grown a lot in Kenya. We came from phone booths until now everyone has a cell phone. You can find anyone, anywhere, anytime, anyplace. These days there is even M-PESA [mobile money]. You can send money and you don't even have to be there physically. You can have businesses, or you can have transactions, all through M-PESA."

Although M-PESA has been available in Kenya since 2007, many Americans and Europeans are still unfamiliar with the system. To open an M-PESA account or to withdraw funds, a customer needs to provide three items: a Safaricom SIM card, an official form of identification (a Kenyan ID or an international passport), and a personal identification number (PIN). If I were to, for example, arrive in Kenya on an international flight with only a few dollars and a phone, I could quickly and cheaply purchase a SIM card (figure 11), place it into my phone, register my M-PESA account for free, and call any friend in Kenya to ask them to send me up to 70,000 shillings (US$700 in 2015). After the instantaneous transfer (assuming I could find someone willing to send me money), I would receive a text saying that I had received the money. With my ID and my PIN, I could collect cash from an agent. My account balance would be automatically updated, and I would be notified by text message. It is a very easy and efficient system to use.

While there have been fears of fraud and the use of M-PESA in money laundering, most of the long-term research participants with whom I spoke raved about the safety that comes with using M-PESA. As one man explained: "They give you a PIN. You know, even if somebody steals your phone or takes it, there's nothing they can do with it."

FIGURE 11. A typical M-PESA advertisement, announcing that this shop owner is an M-PESA agent who can put cash into your account, give you cash from your account, and do SIM-card registration and replacement. Photo by author, 2014.

"The best thing about M-PESA," explained another businessman, "is that you don't have to carry cash. If you need to withdraw money it is very easy. You see everywhere: M-PESA, M-PESA."

Cellular phones and the new applications they enable have, in the minds of many analysts, revolutionized the ways that Kenyans communicate, exchange information, conduct business, manage livelihoods, pay for things, and bank their profits. But M-PESA has accomplished much more than simply "banking the unbanked." In fact, most (but not all) of my research participants had bank accounts in addition to M-PESA. One struggling businessman in his forties told me how he uses M-PESA:

> So let's say I have cash. The first thing I do, instead of going to the bank and putting it in the bank, I put it in my phone [via an agent]. I think even now the banks are being hurt by it. And then you can use M-PESA for actually an account. Some banks, they have access for M-PESA to transact your money directly from your account to M-PESA. Let's say now you pay me some money, like 20,000 or whatever. Instead of risking walking with it, I put it in M-PESA directly [via an agent]. It is very accurate actually. Safaricom is

like a bank. That is what they are coming to. They are their own bank now. (Author's interview, June 4, 2014, Nairobi)

M-PESA was originally the idea of Nick Hughes and Susie Lonie, both of whom worked for London-based Vodafone, a partial owner of Safaricom. The original idea was to create a mobile money transfer system that would allow borrowers to repay microfinance loans more easily. When they approached the Central Bank of Kenya (CBK), the country's banking regulator, which was aware of the underdevelopment of Kenya's banking sector, it was open to the idea of mobile money transfers. The United Kingdom's Department for International Development (DfID) supplied seed money for early experimentation with M-PESA, and the program was put in place in 2007.

But Safaricom and Vodafone soon realized that in Kenya M-PESA could be used for much more than simply repaying microcredit loans. There was a desperate need for more reliable and cheaper ways for transferring money, both within Kenya and from abroad. Kenyans I interviewed doing business between Mombasa and Nairobi had to buy goods using cash, which either had to be delivered in person or cleverly sent. I knew many Mombasa-based businesspeople who would spend an entire twenty-four hours traveling to Nairobi and back just to pay for a shipment of products. The shipping of the goods was not the problem, and that would take place later. It was the payment that was the challenge. Some people I knew would use a trusted employee of a bus company as an intermediary. On one occasion, I witnessed a Mombasa-based businessperson tape an envelope with cash to the inside of a large box, which he then filled with newspaper to dissuade someone from searching it and finding the money.

Safaricom's marketing strategy was also central to M-PESA's success. As cell phone companies began functioning as banks, it was essential that they hold the trust of their customers—few of whom trusted the formal banking system. The initial marketing strategy invited the public to "send money home," clearly identifying the need of many Kenyans to remit money from urban centers and foreign countries to rural homes without having to travel on dangerous roads in person with cash. One particular ad featured a young Kenyan man in typical middle-class clothing holding a cell phone with an arc of money crossing to an older woman on a farm with a huge smile, clearly happy to receive the money so quickly.

Safaricom claims that because all transactions have a mobile footprint, it can easily monitor transactions for fraud or money laundering. Safaricom has, unlike the government or the formal commercial banks, succeeded in creating a sense of trust and transparency at a time when such values are increasingly valued. According to a 2010 Gates Foundation study, 98 percent of M-PESA users said that the service was safer and faster than other options for transferring money, and 96 percent said it was more convenient and cheaper (Mas and Radcliffe 2010).

M-PESA's success in Kenya has clearly been related to its ability to make everyday financial transactions more secure and to allow Kenyans to quickly transfer money without having to travel in person. Especially following the post-election violence of early 2008—when digital technologies were desperately needed for opening lines of communication and passing along reliable information—Kenyans increasingly adopted new services that allowed them to better manage the risks and challenges of the new economic and communicative environment. Several years before the 2008 violence, Safaricom had introduced its *sambaza* system, which allowed Safaricom subscribers to send phone credit to one another free of charge. Along with M-PESA, such services broke customers' dependence upon face-to-face transactions for purchasing everything from phone credit to African masks. According to the government's economic reports, in 2013 alone Kenyans transferred over US$9 billion (914 billion shillings) through mobile money services (Kenya 2014:232). M-PESA is both an important part of the economy and an important financial tool.

With M-PESA, the percentage a customer pays decreases the more money that is sent. In 2015, the fees ranged from one Kenya shilling (US$0.01) for transactions up to 1,000 shillings (US$10) to 110 shillings (US$1.10) for transactions between 15,001 shillings (US$150) and 70,000 shillings (US$700; the maximum that can be transferred). Daily transfers are capped at 140,000 shillings (US$1,400). These fees are much less than those charged by Western Union and commercial banks. The agents are not paid by customers, but receive a flat payment from Safaricom for every transaction they conduct (Kenyan Safaricom agents are estimated to make about US$70/month). The fee paid by the customer for each transaction goes directly to Safaricom from the customer's M-PESA account at the time of the transaction.

It is significant that M-PESA—an app originally designed to help farmers more easily repay microfinance loans—was quickly utilized by Kenyans for other practical purposes. Still, we should be wary of M-PESA's conceptual roots in the development narratives of "microinformality," or informal economic development through the more recently reformulated ideas of the micro and small enterprise (MSE) sector and microcredit (Elyachar 2002). Such narratives, which are central to the rationale behind microfinance banks, frame the discussion of African development around the need for increased access to avenues to finance and foreign investment. Although access to credit was a problem for many of my research participants, access to credit was almost meaningless if traders did not have access to stable economic environments where there was an incentive to invest. Further, the new banking applications associated with M-PESA place much of the onus of risk management onto individual customers, few of whom have training in financial management. This again raises questions about the economic benefits of and underlying motives behind a system of microinformality that had become so pervasive around Mombasa.

In 2012, Safaricom launched M-Shwari, an application that enables Safaricom users to access a savings account and to take small loans. Deemed "revolutionary" by Safaricom, M-Shwari works through M-PESA but is a product of the Commercial Bank of Africa. Unfortunately, M-Shwari also caused many of my research participants to go into debt. One man complained: "Oooh! It has bankrupted me. It gives you a loan, then you pay it within a month. If you don't pay it within a month, they send you a warning. If you don't pay it within that second month, they send you another warning. But me I've been blocked! I can't get M-Shwari anymore. I still have an outstanding loan [laughing]. I'm a very stubborn guy. . . . I have a loan of 2,000 [shillings], but you can get as much as 75,000 from M-Shwari" (author's interview, June 7, 2014, Nairobi).

For all the promise of transferring money and accessing new financial services, many Kenyans immediately took loans that they could not possibly repay, putting people into debt. When I first arrived in Kenya in 2015, I immediately sent Davis a few hundred shillings of phone credit via Safaricom's sambaza service to let him know I had arrived in Nairobi. But I heard nothing from him for a whole day. When I eventually called him, he apologized and explained that he was so in debt to Safaricom that the company had simply "eaten" the credit I had sent him. But he thanked me for helping him pay down his debt. As Davis explained with a laugh, "This is Kenya. If you are not in debt, you are not a real Kenyan."

While M-PESA has been heralded for banking the unbanked, financial education among the Kenyan businesspeople targeted by these products is minimal, and there is an increasing potential for companies like Safaricom to become predatory. Responsibility is firmly placed upon the individual customers. One Mombasa businessman told me in 2014 that what Safaricom has succeeded in doing with M-PESA is to put all of the liability on the individual customer. "They are passing that liability and risk back to you," he explained. Safaricom ensures that the financial transaction is secure. But from that point, all financial responsibility is placed on the individual customer.

It is also important to remember that Safaricom and Vodafone are for-profit companies. "At Safaricom, they are making money, and a lot of it," the man who had been blocked by M-Shwari told me in 2014. "Because, you know, if you put your money in a bank, you are given interest. With M-PESA, you are actually paying them. So who's fooling who?" (author's interview, June 7, 2014, Nairobi).

There are important lessons to be learned about the Africa Rising narrative from Safaricom's and Vodafone's success with M-PESA. The poor offer little return to commercial banks that generate profits from the interest they make loaning and investing depositors' money. M-PESA's success has revealed the value of using mobile tech to make financial services accessible to the poor. Because M-PESA generates revenue for Safaricom through usage and not the interest made from accounts, including the poor has become profitable. In other words, the global financial industry has found new ways to extend itself into even marginalized Kenyan traders' daily lives and finances.

As Kenya is continually referred to as the "Silicon Savannah," researchers and analysts must ask about the technopolitics of new digital technologies and apps like M-PESA. Development has continued to be uneven in Kenya. Mobile money, with its credit, lending, and development angles, plays a role in enabling certain individuals and their networks. For them, M-PESA has become a trusted anchor for risk management and a sense of security. However, in an economy characterized by informality, new digital financial apps have also brought new risks, namely of becoming entangled in micro-credit schemes and falling into debt to cellular providers.

SIX

Crafting Ethical Connection and Transparency in Coastal Kenya

DURING AN INTERVIEW IN MOMBASA in October 2005, Peter, a successful Kenyan exporter of Fair Trade wood carvings, referred to his cell phone as his "best friend" (author's interview, October 26, 2005, Mombasa). He did not know how to use a computer or e-mail, but that mattered less as long as his best friend was on a lanyard around his neck. I liked to ask such traders what they would do if they ever lost their phone. "I would immediately buy another," Peter told me. "I would close this entire shop to keep my mobile."

Peter was actually on the verge of doing just that. He had recently been accused of being a witch (*mchawi* in Swahili) by several former colleagues from the Akamba Handicraft Industry Co-operative Society. The cooperative was located less than a half-mile down the road from Peter's new shop in Magongo Market (see map 3). Officially a cooperative member since the 1970s, Peter had left to compete with his former colleagues as an independent businessman. As a result, he and others like him were seen by many in the cooperative as having knowingly hurt the cooperative's business.

The accusation, like many other such accusations of "witchcraft" or sorcery found in African market cultures, allowed cooperative members to highlight the few in the business who were accumulating wealth while defining what counted as appropriate and ethical business practices (also see Geschiere 1997; Smith 2008). The accusation was just one part of a larger debate over what constituted ethical business practices in the age of cell phones, Internet access, and continued economic informality and change. At the same time that Kenya's crafts industry was becoming heavily involved in ethical branding, changes in the nature of the business were necessitating a rethinking of business ethics on the ground. At the core of the accusation was a claim about ethics and morality. The networks of patronage and reciprocity central to Kenya's economy are, in the words of Angelique Haugerud (1995), "a terrain of cultural and moral debate, as material stakes and other circumstances shift" (110). The emergence of the cell phone and Internet access at a time when cooperatives were adapting slowly and receiving less formal assistance set the stage for a shift not just in stakes and circumstances but morality and business ethics.

Some Western readers might be surprised to learn that a Kenya Fair Trade exporter had been accused of witchcraft due to his business practices and that those business practices had been enabled by the new digital technologies that are so visually central to the Africa Rising narrative. Yet the cell phone around Peter's neck was a central vector for the witchcraft of which Peter was accused. If we take the accusation to have been fundamentally about highlighting what the accusers saw as the immorality of Peter's new business practices, then although packaged as witchcraft in a uniquely African form (see Geschiere 1997), the accusation itself targeted not an African but a very Western neoliberal witchcraft. The accusation highlights the very same business practices that are enabled by the Africa Rising narrative. But clever traders and exporters like Peter continue to deploy and represent images of the Africa Rising narrative through their businesses in a way that obscures what their competitors find to be unethical about their business practices.

As certain crafty traders have gained a comparative advantage, the moral debate over clientage and reciprocity has emerged with a fury, as exemplified by witchcraft accusations and market burnings. More specifically, traders and cooperative members have become actively engaged in a negotiation over what constitutes ethical development of an industry often branded as Fair Trade but rooted in exploited labor and fierce competition. While Peter has maintained certain business connections since the 1970s, their nature and "social life" have changed (Bruijn and van Dijk 2012). An inherently illusory notion of transparency has become a valuable tool to Peter's negotiation of the changing nature of the business. New digital technologies have becoming important tools for successfully balancing visibility and invisibility, or revelation and obfuscation. With fewer face-to-face transactions with overseas clients and customers, clever branding on business cards and websites had helped to make business development appear fair or ethical while remaining rooted in the exploitation of carvers and craftspeople and the exclusion of competitors.[1]

The situation was framed by the economic changes outlined in previous chapters. My research participants' experiences have been shaped by the neoliberal narratives central to both ICT4D and microinformality.[2] We can see the combined influence of these development narratives in the policies of President Mwai Kibaki (2002–2012). As discussed in chapter 4, Kibaki's presidency was initially accompanied by expectations of economic growth and a renewed government emphasis on revenue collection and job creation. The majority of the president's promised 500,000 new jobs were to come from the MSE (micro and small enterprise) sector (Kenya 2005b:iii). But despite the increasing role of MSEs in development literature since the 1990s, aid agencies' rhetoric about the importance of microenterprises and credit schemes does not always materialize as support for programs (Hansen and Vaa 2004:17). The enterprises and cooperatives I studied received almost no state support even though the "informal" or "microenterprise" economies were supposed to be the sources of the new jobs that the government intended to create.

The Kenyan government significantly cut support for cooperatives just when it could have played a major role in helping them move online and remain competitive, both within Kenya and internationally. The coordinator of the Kenya Gatsby Trust, an NGO dedicated to helping small-scale Kenyan traders in business expansion and wealth creation, urged the government to enhance business training for traders and artisans such as carpenters and wood-carvers. He argued that such craftspeople and artisans did not lack skill but rather business sense and the ability to access and use the Internet. The Gatsby Trust coordinator told the *Coast Express* in 2006 that the Ministry of Trade and Industry could easily set up a website for displaying products to overseas buyers, a point of market access that many traders lacked (Buluku 2005). The article quoted him as saying: "[A] majority of these traders are missing excellent opportunities for their products because they do not have any access to a website that can highlight their merchandise." Consistent with my own findings, he claimed that because traders mainly worked independently and without clear coordination with government departments, they were left at a disadvantage in terms of their products' overall sales and promotions.

But the new informalization did not bother well-connected exporters and intermediaries like Peter, who could make the most of this new economic environment to leave his old colleagues and competitors behind. He was left with the responsibility of maintaining the perception of ethical connection only to artisans and producers. More than just a symbol of global connectivity and Africa Rising, the cell phone hanging from Peter's neck helped him to juggle visibility and invisibility—revelation and obfuscation—through the production of an illusion of intimacy and the notion of transparency (Archambault 2013:88; Molony 2009a).

While we live in a "transparency-obsessed world" in which "the freedom of the rational individual is often presented as good in itself" (Hetherington 2012:242), transparency remains a fundamentally "political technology" that is rooted in negotiating imbalances of power (Ballestero 2012:160). The broader ideal of ICT4D has always been fundamentally ideological, with the idea of transparency at the center of the hype (Mazzarella 2010:784). As I explained in chapter 1, I find it useful to think of transparency in two senses: first, to be transparent is to be ethical, and second, to be transparent is also to be invisible. I highlight in this chapter the role of transparency within economic competition, as ideas of transparency are strategically deployed in a way that can both erase and conjure up realities of digital modernity and ethical citizenship. The examples I use help to show how transparency can shine a selective light on marketable realities while simultaneously obscuring realities inconvenient to marketing crafts. This maintenance of perceptions allows for a unique "race to the bottom" by businesspeople to find and organize the most exploitable artisans (the handicapped, single mothers, homeless children) into workshops and artisan organizations that explicitly market the marginality of the producers through NGO aesthetics and ethical branding. There is an art to this.

In the following sections I will discuss many of the challenges that have faced cooperatives and innovative Kenyan traders as they have struggled to adapt to the changing economy. I conclude with a discussion of how ostensibly ethical businesspeople negotiate the tension between competition and innovation. But first, I will explore the old ways information was produced and exchanged before the digital age, including the place of the cooperative society in this history.

COOPERATIVES AND COMPETITION

As discussed earlier, Kenyans from the inland began migrating to Mombasa to work in the crafts industry beginning in the 1950s and '60s. With substantial state assistance and insistence, cooperatives like Mombasa's Kamba wood-carving and Kisii soapstone cooperatives became the foundation of Kenya's carvings industry during the 1970s and '80s. Despite the communal ideal of the cooperative industry, struggles within Kenya's handicraft cooperatives are as old as the cooperative organizations themselves (see chapter 3). It took just a few years for the Ministry of Co-operative Development (in May 1967) to start raising questions about the "cooperative element" of Mombasa's wood-carving cooperative.[3] The ministry found in 1978 that "only a fraction of the carvings produced by the members appears to be marketed through the societies."[4] The same authors noted that 90 percent of the wood carvings produced in Kenya's three woodcarving cooperatives were bought directly by private dealers who bypassed the cooperatives. This competition and tendency toward circumvention was a reality with which the cooperative administration had to constantly struggle, usually with support from the Ministry of Co-operatives and Social Services. Even at the peak of international and government support for handicrafts in the early 1980s, an adviser to the government's Handicraft Unit remarked: "It is puzzling that the loyalty of the primary societies and their members is more to private middlemen than to their own organization and that they obviously are prepared to put its continued existence into jeopardy."[5]

Some of these struggles can be explained by the paternalistic nature of the Kenyan government at this time (Muthuma 2012). Government agencies were often directly involved in cooperative management, which curtailed the cooperatives' financial autonomy and limited learning and innovation. Government agents working with the cooperatives have also historically viewed the development of Kenyan artisans and carvers from cooperative members into independently powerful intermediaries and traders as a problem rather than as a key organizational component of the industry (see chapter 3).

But despite the government's long-standing disapproval of the way the crafts cooperatives functioned "cooperatively," many long-term cooperative members I interviewed highlighted the benefits of being associated with the cooperative. Thousands of Kamba-speaking men from rural Eastern Province remain active in carving at Akamba Industry, finding a market through the cooperative's showroom or wholesale shops. Before the number of members in Akamba Industry began to grow rapidly in the mid-1990s, it was relatively easy for migrant farmers from Ukambani to gain cooperative membership as carvers. Potential members had to go through a trial period of several months and then pass a carving test before gaining full membership. But this was not considered a difficult complication for men who had been carving since they were children. In addition to help with sales, the cooperative continues to help urban carvers gain access to wood for carving (figure 12), which often comes from distant areas of Kenya and Tanzania. The cooperative also has a

FIGURE 12. Inside the wood-carving cooperative, logs lie next to the carving sheds. Photo by author, 2014.

kiln, which is important for drying certain types of wood (especially neem, which is roughly 80 percent of the wood carved since the early 2000s). Many older members I interviewed had stories of the profitable years in the 1970s and '80s, when the cooperative's profits allowed poorly educated carvers to make a living and educate their siblings and children.

But things changed when cooperative membership was capped at 2,400 in the 1990s (author's interview, head of records and book, September 26, 2005, Mombasa). It became difficult for anyone without a personal connection to access the cooperative. Young men of Kamba and other ethnic backgrounds working near the cooperative regularly told me that the only way to become a member was to wait for someone to die. Memberships could also be bought and sold, but buying one of these valuable memberships could cost as much as several hundred if not several thousands of dollars. I knew several younger Kamba men who were based in Changamwe and did not bother with the cooperative. They told me from their small sheds in nearby Chaani that their chances of gaining membership or even small jobs in the cooperative were so small that it was simply not worth it. There were too many people and not enough business. They would often say things like "There is no more room" or "It's mostly old men there at Akamba anyway" (author's interview, unemployed man in his early 20s, September 23, 2005, Mombasa).

Throughout the early years of Kenya's digital age, the crafts cooperatives largely remained offline. In late 2005, while I was in the middle of an intensive survey of Changamwe's handicrafts exporters, Akamba Industry did not have Internet access on site or even a website of its own. The head of records and books told me that a computer would have helped him tremendously since the nearly fifty-year-old cooperative's records were still all on paper (author's interview, September 26, 2005, Mombasa). The cooperative's head of exports, who was in his mid-twenties, told me they had had a website for a short time, but it was no longer operational due to the expense and what he described as a lack of will by older cooperative members to invest in such endeavors (author's interview, September 26, 2005). The cooperative had been promised a computer by a charitable organization, but he forgot which one and nothing had ever materialized. Relying on outside assistance was not helping them.

The head of exports was responsible for all outside communication with major customers. But he did so through a local Internet café or by phone, giving him no advantage over the many other traders in Mombasa who had access to the same technologies and facilities. He resented the fact that as he sat in one of Mombasa's crowded and slow Internet cafés, many of the men and women around him were receiving orders and sending e-mails to his and the cooperative's former customers. While the competition was not new, the cooperative was losing its spatial importance and centrality to the industry as international buyers suddenly had dozens of options for sourcing their crafts and carvings.

Many of these new enterprises and workshops had their own e-mail addresses and carefully constructed websites, which were created and maintained by independent, digitally empowered intermediaries and exporters who were balancing intimacy and distance in more innovative ways than the cooperatives. For aspiring entrepreneurs, the new business model hinged on their ability to maintain a trusting and transparent connection with customers by representing themselves and their enterprises as ethical and well-connected to needy artisans and craftspeople. This was often achieved with the help of Fair Trade labels or by printing a catchphrase like "ethical exporter" on business cards. Because most communication took place over long distances and not in person, these labels were rarely questioned by Western importers and buyers who no longer had to visit producers in person to place orders. Very quickly, the dozens of new enterprises that sprang up in Changamwe were attracting the cooperatives' old customers.

At the time of my interviews in September 2005, Akamba Industry had only one order to fill. The order itself, sent via e-mail, provided little colored pictures next to each item to ensure accuracy. The Fair Trade labels were to be applied in Kenya before the products were boxed up and shipped "so that they can go straight on the shelves once they reach their destination," I was told. "But this order is only for three hundred pieces," the head of exports explained to me. "We have almost three thousand carvers here. These days, people are carving more for fun or to pass time than to meet a customer's order" (author's interview, September 26, 2005, Mombasa).

For many traders, carvers, and finishers in Akamba Industry, Mombasa's wood-carving cooperative was no longer a viable economic option as the number of men and women regularly seeking employment there soared as high as several thousand. Unemployment peaked as orders were few and overproduction reduced the value and quality of the carvings produced. Because the cooperative had difficulty coming online and streamlining market access for its members, through 2005 and 2006, those men and women who could use their own e-mail accounts and cell phones were suddenly operating at the same economic scale as the cooperative societies.

From a buyer's perspective, traders like Peter, located in Magongo Market, could offer goods for lower prices. There were enough small enterprises in the market for an exporter or overseas buyer to do business with several different people before settling on someone dependable. By 2006, several exporters I knew looked down on those who bought from the cooperative's wholesale shop as naïve (*mafala*) for not going instead to Magongo Market to get the lowest price.

When Magongo Curio Market first opened to crafts traders beginning in the late 1990s, many of the more business-minded cooperative members with enough capital to do so had made the move. By 2006, over one hundred traders were selling from within the market. Of these, best estimates showed that 80 percent had previously worked in the cooperative. Nearly all of them worked from a wooden structure with an e-mail address or a cell phone number written above the entrance. Traders who had moved from the cooperative to Magongo Market all cited heightened competition within the cooperative as the reason for their move, and cell phones as the primary tool that enabled them to leave the cooperative behind. Although they did not all meet with success, cell phones and Internet access helped break Kenyan intermediaries' spatial dependence on the cooperative as well as its near monopoly on the marketing of Kenyan wood carvings.

The logic of the move to Magongo Market by an entrepreneurial cooperative member like Peter was understandable. In 2005, a 22-percent commission on items sold in the cooperative's main showroom for tourists paid for the salaries of the cooperative's staff members and for water and electricity (author's interview, September 26, 2005, Mombasa). The wholesale shop, designed for local traders and exporters, had a 6 percent commission. The cooperative's wholesale shop was generally considered a good way for carvers to sell large quantities of items to local shop owners.[6] By not selling through the cooperative, the Magongo Market traders were denying the larger community of carvers and artisans significant revenue and driving the cost of carvings down throughout the industry. By selling from Magongo Market, just up the street, wholesalers and exporters could offer a lower price than even the cooperative's wholesale shop and they could bypass the cooperative's rules and seniority.

It is no coincidence that there was an exodus of cooperative members to Magongo Market at the same time that traders like Davis were abandoning the hassles of the city for the flexibility of the suburbs. Lacking government programs and unable to cope with the glut of young carvers and traders entering the cooperative, a small minority of connected and savvy businesspeople like Peter abandoned the competition and the old rules to work independently from Magongo Market. Many of his old colleagues from the cooperative were furious with him and accused him (along with many others) of being responsible for the practices that were hurting the cooperative and the rest of the industry. The accusation itself came in the form of calling Peter a witch, although Peter laughed at the "backwardness" of the cooperative members' resorting to such traditional means of policing the economy. Few of Peter's European or North American clients would question the ethics of his business practices. With a big smile on his face and his cell phone on a lanyard around his neck, Peter almost belonged on the cover of the next *Time* or *Economist* special issue on Africa Rising.

The Kamba had an interesting power and presence in Changamwe. As an ethnic community, they largely comprised poor or middle-class farming families, and many were labeled *washamba* ("backward" or "country bumpkin") in Mombasa. Many Kamba men and women I knew looked to urban life as a way of countering these stereotypes by pursuing economic modernity in the city. Kenya had experienced a historical baby boom from the 1970s through the early 1980s, a time when Kenya may have had the world's highest annual rate of natural population increase (Miller and Yeager 1994:62). Most of the young Kamba men working in the crafts business whom I met during my research were between the ages of fifteen and thirty-five and had been born during this period of historic population growth. They had remarkably similar stories, to which I could often personally connect. I was also of their generation, and while I came from an entirely different background, I found many connections between the struggles and perspectives of my Kenyan friends and those of America's Generation X and Millennials. Most importantly, people felt trapped in a global economy that was controlled by their parents' generation but that had—despite all the hype about new technology—fewer and fewer options for the younger generation.

Generational politics among the Kamba also played a role in the ethical considerations that accompanied new economic strategies. The situations and attitudes of these younger Kamba men and women were very different from those of their parents. Generational differences have long played a major role in the politics of the Kamba wood-carving cooperative. The patrilineal clans of the original members had provided the basis for organization through the 1970s, and the traditional Kamba ruling pattern of gerontocracy was initially maintained through the cooperative's central committee (Jules-Rosette 1984:115). Complaints that the cooperative is dominated by "old men" have continued through the present day, as younger traders and artisans increasingly pursue free-market ideals of development. They tend to stress the innovation nurtured by individual competition rather than the social safety net, the cooperative industry, of their parents' generation.

New digital technologies, which were marketed directly to young Kenyan businesspeople, allowed the younger generation of entrepreneurs to compete with long-established traders. But many got lost in the competition, and few were able to ultimately claim economic success. Many older traders who had been in the industry for decades claimed that the problem was an influx of young entrepreneurs who just wanted to get rich. These young people pointed a finger at the older and more-established carvers and exporters, blaming them for their lack of innovation and initiative. Most of the successful exporters I knew actually came from the older generation and had long-established international contacts. But they often preferred to remain silent or invisible, to keep their business practices and contacts secret, and to understandably avoid or downplay ethical debates taking place around the cooperative and the related accusations.

For James Smith (2008:4–6), the concept of development (*maendeleo*) in Kenya is not just a spatiotemporal reference but "implies inventiveness" and is a way that Kenyans discuss the manifestation of their "creative energy" for the public good. Debates around ethical development practices and the public good, therefore, are also debates about creativity and innovation. Significantly, many exporters I interviewed argued that creativity and innovation—and therefore development—were precisely what the cooperatives lacked, thus hindering the cooperatives' development. The young entrepreneurial class knew their tactics, which they described as "innovative," could raise ethical questions (people were familiar with the accusations), but they argued that these tactics were necessary for the public good and, therefore, development.

While the exporters I knew were always looking for new motifs and items to sell, cooperative members often carved or decorated the same few items they had been carving for decades. Carvers in the cooperative often wondered why their items, which had been popular in the 1970s and '80s, were no longer selling. In turn, exporters and independent traders often accused the carvers of being backward. Successful exporters not only invested in innovation and creating new products and artistic motifs, but they also were careful to keep new motifs secret. They had found that they could add value by guaranteeing customers that specific items were not being mass-produced elsewhere. But this also meant that secrecy had become an important strategy within a formerly cooperative business.

The innovation and creativity of marginalized traders has long been an important if rarely studied component of noncorporate globalization. Mombasa's crafts exporters allow us to, as James Ferguson (2004) has suggested, "conceive, theoretically and politically, of a 'grassroots' that would be not local, communal, and authentic, but worldly, well-connected, and opportunistic" (394). Kenya's art traders were culture brokers, forced to navigate the inequalities of the global economic system and find ways to creatively represent themselves and adapt their craft to correspond to shifting global understandings of Africa. It is no coincidence that it was during the transition from cooperative to neoliberal development model that the Fair Trade sticker and other such labels emerged as a primary tool of the savvy Kenyan exporter who was often fed up with the mismanagement or lack of innovation in the cooperatives.

Cooperatives, Fair Trade stickers, and new digital technologies all can help to produce a sense of transparency and trust over long distances. This is particularly important within an industry that is experiencing intense competition and the reshaping of its underlying moral economy. The Kenyan crafts trade has long relied on a performance similar to the mystification and exotification central to most tourism branding (see Bruner 2001; Kasfir 2004; MacCannell 1976; Steiner 1994). Labels and brands lend legitimacy and authenticity to traders who have long been competing with South Asian and European exporters' superior financial capital and the moral superiority of established cooperatives. Fair Trade's ethical philosophy involves connecting craftspeople and producers directly to Western importers, thus bypassing intermediaries (Reichman 2008:108).[7] The label signals to overseas buyers that the exporter, his or her business practices, and the commodity chain of which he or she is a part are transparent and easily understandable. In producing a sense of transparency, the Fair Trade sticker not only gives Fair Trade businesspeople the moral upper hand in the larger competition, but it also makes them invisible. The Fair Trade sticker is just one of a series of linguistic and symbolic cues that function to maintain fleeting notions of transparent and trusting long-distance connection within the minds of everyone in the network. This is the art of connection. Clever labeling and branding tactics—which include removing all of the original labeling placed on products by the actual producers—were essential for exporters and intermediaries like Peter and Davis to maintain their jobs and positions within the commodity chain.

The imagery used in Kenyan crafts enterprises' labeling and branding reflects the Africa Rising narrative and at times an Afropolitan aesthetic through symbols of modernity and global connection. Among the business-card-bearing exporters I interviewed, there was little evidence of traditional or ethnic labels in the marketing of their crafts or in the names of their individual (rather than communal) enterprises. Rather, business cards were adorned with titles such as "Modern Handicrafts," "Stone Arts: Local and International," or simply "Global Crafts," as these traders found more value in representing themselves as modern, innovative, and connected.

As discussed in earlier chapters, the businesspeople who participated in my research were operating within an extremely insecure and risky political and economic environment. Kenyan art that showed the nation to be modern and changing represented Kenya as welcoming to tourists without playing on labels, brands, and symbols that were often politically sensitive. It appealed to tourists on their own terms, as modern or worldly with a global identity, and not tribal nor traditional in either a cultural or an economic sense. Ethnic symbolism can undeniably still add value to certain commodities within the global marketplace (Comaroff and Comaroff 2009). But I found that ethnic tension in Kenya was one of many reasons for crafts producers and traders to downplay the ethnic or "tribal" symbolism of their products—despite the realities of ethnic difference and the importance of ethnoregional and linguistic networks for maintaining a business and communicating with one's buyers and suppliers. The industry was rooted in ethnic networks, but many individual traders downplayed the ethnic imagery of what they sold just as they put Fair Trade labels on items consciously sourced through exploitative channels.

A Fair Trade exporter I had known for several years interjected during a 2008 conversation about the state of the crafts industry: "You do know this is a business that is based on exploitation, right?" The realities of Kenya's free-market integration into the global economy meant that exporters and intermediaries were living a number of different contradictions and were forced to make difficult ethical decisions every day. If an exporter was slow to adapt, his competitors could and would quickly cut him out of the business. This competition necessitated taking risks and could even lead to accusations, social ostracism, and falling into poverty. To survive and remain relevant, individual entrepreneurs with personal connections were generally under more pressure and, therefore, much quicker than the cooperatives to start using new digital technologies for business transactions and keeping up appearances. This allowed crafty exporters to offer buyers better prices while remaining transparent.

It was difficult for exporters to balance their ethical responsibilities with the needs of their personal businesses. Many exporters had conflicting responsibilities. But much of this conflict was brushed aside by those in power, who saw the changes the industry was experiencing as the inevitable results of "progress" and the market "freedom" introduced by digital communication technologies. This was always an easy assessment when an individual was making money. As the chairman of Mombasa's Kisii Soapstone Co-operative told me in 2005, openly and while surrounded by other cooperative members: "I go and I check [my personal e-mail], and I have an order. I go to a clearing agent; I get like 4 million shillings [US$50,000]; I clear a few crates. I go and I pay the carvers and everyone, and I make maybe 200,000–250,000 myself [US$3,250]. It can be a good business" (author's interview, September 23, 2005, Mombasa).

The chairman was referring specifically to business that he did individually rather than as the head of the cooperative society. He was explaining to me that one of the hardest parts of his job was finding the carvers and artisans to produce enough carvings on credit for him so that he could ship the several tons of stone to his overseas buyers prior to payment. Avoiding other cooperative members (and his potential competitors), the credit came from the carvers in Tabaka. It was essential that he keep them satisfied and in his trust even though he was based in Mombasa (primarily so that he could deal with the person he viewed as most troublesome with the business: the clearing-and-forwarding agent). He could work from Mombasa only because of his personal connections to the soapstone quarries in Tabaka and because his cell phone allowed him to communicate directly with people at the quarries daily.

The chairman's extended family did much of the carving for him, so his personal kin network was essential to making his business work. His eventual profit of US$3,250—a large sum by Kenyan standards—would have to be redistributed to maintain a moral contract with family members and the dozens of other producers, finishers, miners, transporters, and agents that handled the stone from the time it came out of the ground until the time it was shipped. But he was able to personally negotiate the terms of each of these relationships within his own private network. Unlike the cooperative, his family network was organized around ethical obligations and reciprocity rather than any type of collective bargaining, unionizing, or cooperative organizing by the carvers.

Maybe most importantly for international buyers of handicrafts, since the chairman was not selling or sourcing the carvings through the cooperative, he could offer a much lower price while still increasing his profit. Rather than redistributing this profit through the Changamwe-based soapstone cooperative, he would personally determine how the profits would be redistributed throughout his own personal networks. Despite his position as cooperative chairman, his real economic power came from these personal networks.

To avoid the midday sun, we were crouching down in one of the few shaded sections of Mombasa's Kisii soapstone cooperative, located in a part of Mombasa's Changamwe constituency called Chaani. The chairman was apparently not worried about telling me or having other cooperative members hear how he operated his private business while also serving as the business manager for the group. Everyone seemed to know one another's business.

But one of the more successful long-term soapstone dealers told me in 2005 that the biggest problem with the society was "corruption" (author's interview, September 26, 2005, Mombasa). "The administration" he explained, "had problems with corruption," carefully choosing his words in English and appearing somewhat uncomfortable with the topic. "You see," he continued, "we each do our business. And the cooperative is supposed to be attracting buyers here to this cooperative. Then they get an order, and then they are supposed to distribute it out, like ten here, ten here, ten here. But instead almost all the business is done individually now. With our e-mail accounts, we can all work independently."

This independence meant that cooperative members had no incentive to invest their time and money into the products they sold through the group. To demonstrate, he pulled a life-size carved apple from a shelf in his small market stall in the cooperative. He said he had carved and polished it the night before out of boredom. Like many of the traders and exporters, he had learned to carve as a young boy but had left the trade behind because he could make much more money selling the products in wholesale quantity rather than making them individually. But he had spent extra time carving and polishing the apple he was holding in his Mombasa shop, located on the opposite side of the country from Kisii and the quarries. Perfectly shaped, it was polished bright and glassy smooth, showing pink speckles and lines running through the stone. After allowing me to examine the apple for a moment, he pulled down a much larger intricate sculpture of interconnected abstract human forms, which had not been polished like the apple. As complex as the second piece was, the stone had a dull color and was not as attractive as the apple, which glistened in my hand. He continued:

> There is no comparison. The apple is just finished. Beautiful. Polished. But I cannot just go and use one entire piece of sandpaper on each one of these sculptures. That one piece of sandpaper, that will cost me 50 shillings. And the cost of transport to town to get that sandpaper, that is another 50 shillings. It is just not worth it. If the cooperative wants ten pieces of a certain type, I won't polish them nicely. But with my own customers, it's entirely different. I would spend the money on the sandpaper. You have to work to stay on top. You have to spend the extra money to finish the product perfectly. (Author's interview, September 26, 2005)

He laughed, "Many exporters think the American or European dealers will do the *msasa* [finishing, polishing]. But they do not. They take them straight out of the box and put them on the shelves." In a hushed voice, switching from English to Swahili, he said, "Hii ndiyo siri kubwa ya hii biashara" (This is a big secret of this business).

This code shift not only indexed his awareness of the ethical problem with his business practices, but he was also pointing out the new reality of the business: that buying through an individual trader like him, despite the ethical dilemma, will get you a better product for a cheaper price. There was direct incentive for innovative businesspeople to compete with the cooperatives by selling private customers high-quality carvings while supplying the cooperative with those that were lower quality or simply unfinished. But there was, as his shift from English to Swahili reveals, also an awareness of the larger controversy surrounding such business practices.

As the new advantages enabled individual businesspeople to bypass the group, organizations like the Kisii soapstone cooperative ceased to operate as cooperatives at all, particularly on the level of marketing and sales. The cooperative label remained and continued to fit the Kenyan government's understanding of a legible organization and to attract some international clientele and donors in a way similar to Fair Trade labels. But cooperative members were still forced to depend on themselves, and the loyalty of the cooperative's own administration was frequently compromised by conflicts of interest.

Through 2008, although the Kisii soapstone cooperative remained an important location for the trade in soapstone in Mombasa (even after a destructive and targeted fire in April 2006), it functioned primarily as a private wholesale market frequented by Mombasa's shop owners, exporters, and beach vendors, and was unable to attract tour groups or develop a social safety net. By 2014, only a few stalls remained, the rest of the space being occupied by newly built housing and shops selling other goods to residents of the surrounding neighborhood of Chaani. Some of those who remain are still optimistic about the cooperative model and still speak nostalgically about the boom years of the 1980s and '90s when the cooperative was located in Uhuru Gardens near Moi Avenue's elephant tusks.

EXPORTING, TRANSPARENCY, AND
MARKETING MARGINALITY

While Changamwe's Akamba Industry was facing stiff competition from individual businessmen like Peter, who had shifted to exporting privately from Magongo Market, other workshops and production groups were coming online. Aid-based NGOs have been in a particularly good position to move into the crafts business because they are adept at writing grants for aid and using people in disadvantaged economic situations to attract funding (or in the case of crafts, to increase the price of a commodity). This marketing strategy often involves making producers' marginality explicit.

For example, all crafts sold through one American distributor were labeled with a large tag that read: "The artisan communities we mentor thrive on profits generated by their own skills, and in turn foster sustainable creative solutions to instability in regions once plagued by poverty." This type of ethical branding not only plays on the assumption of Kenya and Africa as areas plagued by poverty and insecurity, but gives people the sense of helping by buying a product. The consumer now feels a special connection with a producer they have just helped, even though they have no idea who this producer actually is.

One label I found attached to Kenyan carvings being sold at Busch Gardens in Tampa, Florida, read simply: "Your purchase has helped the Artisans, their families and their community. A portion of the proceeds have been donated directly to the local community. THANK YOU FOR YOUR SUPPORT" (capitalized in the original).

It is worth noting that this type of marketing was not being imposed upon the industry only by white Western importers and vendors (although that did take place). Kenyan exporters were also quick to learn and take advice from their Western partners, many of whom had worked in the NGO or non-profit sector at one time. If Kenyan crafts start to adopt an NGO aesthetic that reflects Peace Corps volunteers' view of African development, that is because Peace Corps volunteers have been actively helping Kenyans develop international crafts businesses for decades. The intermediaries who actually conduct the global crafts trade have learned from NGOs that have found success rationalizing their interventions under the guise of transparency. Martin Webb (2012) has argued that these NGOs use transparency activism to produce "an 'ethical scene' in which their poor clients are encouraged to understand themselves as potentially empowered citizens of a nation wounded by corruption and bad governance" (206). During the time of my research, I witnessed many crafts organizations emerge by producing an "ethical scene" characterized by what I call NGO aesthetics. This complex of symbols consists of a variety of labels and brands that strategically use transparency to ethically brand products as made by marginalized groups of people who are being empowered through the crafts business. These symbols also often reflect the symbolism of microinformality, the digital-mobile, and the other neoliberal elements of the Africa Rising narrative.

Take Nairobi's Mango Workshop as an example. The workshop opened in 1982 with ten mentally handicapped young adults from a Nairobi special needs school. While such children had few options in Nairobi, they were able to accomplish simple, repetitive tasks like making jewelry or beadwork. A new director took over in 2000, making use of his college degree in accounting and his experience working at the workshop since 1994. He explained to me in 2005, "I pulled the workshop up from nothing through honesty and transparency" (author's interview, November 13, 2005, Nairobi).

He told me that when he took over, none of the staff had been paid in seventeen months. His main job was to find customers and generate cash flow. At the time of our interview, almost all of the workshop's main customers were Alternative Trade– or Fair Trade–certified importers in Germany and the United States. The director explained that such companies were willing to pay more "to support artisans." In 2005 alone, a U.S. importer had given them US$25,000 of business, for which the director was deeply grateful. Such contracts allowed him to plan ahead, stop applying for funds from charitable organizations, and bring ten more mentally handicapped men and women into the workshop.

Mango Workshop would probably have not continued to exist had it not been for computers and the initiative of the director to move all communications and marketing online. In 2004 the director had even had a computer with e-mail installed in his office. He called this an essential step for communicating directly with his customers and outcompeting other such workshops. As he explained, "I have never been there to England or America. I don't know what it is like there, or what people want there. I rely on these people to tell me what colors. They will send me a template, a color sample, even through e-mail, and I will develop that color, or several colors, and send them back" (author's interview, November 13, 2005).

He had initially depended upon Nairobi's slow downtown Internet cafés, but he had problems with buyers who wanted very fast replies. "Especially the British," he said, would start worrying and calling on the phone if they had not received a reply to an e-mail within a few hours. He finally invested in installing Internet directly into his office, a practice that was just becoming affordable for small Kenyan businesses.

"Before e-mail," he told me, "it could take two weeks for us to send an invoice and then you never knew if you sent the right thing. Sometimes it would take five months to fill an order. That has all improved by having e-mail in my office." At the time of the interview, most of his clients trusted him enough to pay 50 percent of the cost up front with a ninety-day window to ship. But he admitted that with the capital he had been able to accumulate, he could almost always ship within a few weeks, and he could ship immediately if he had the items already in stock.

In 2005 Mango already had twenty-six handicapped adults working there, eight of whom were women and eighteen of whom were men. While the youngest was twenty, the rest were between twenty-five and forty-two years old. Most had been at the workshop for at least eight years. They worked mainly for food, which was provided for them daily, as well as a salary of 3,500–5,000 Kenya shillings per month (US$50–$75 in 2005—more than twice what Simon's salary had been to sell curios from the kiosk outside of Fort Jesus). Because the men and women who worked for Mango all lived permanently with their parents, this amount of money made a big difference for their families. Although one could argue that the workshop was exploiting these individuals by paying them US$3–$4 per day to make jewelry that would later be sold to wealthy Americans and Europeans, Mango was also providing an important service not being provided by the government—the care of the mentally handicapped—and making a positive difference in the lives of these people and their families.

Although many of the established cooperatives had lost their main international customers by not coming online more quickly, their business was clearly finding its way into the hands of those who understood how to market their workshops using NGO aesthetics to market marginality and produce a transparent connection with overseas buyers. More established cooperatives like Akamba Industry now all have websites, although they continue to struggle for a unique online presence amid the competition. Akamba Industry has also developed a much more diversified marketing strategy and now sells crafts and soapstone in addition to wood carvings. This diversification has kept them competitive, but it has also meant an increase in outsourcing to producers who are not cooperative members.

While many individual enterprises have thrived over the last decade, internal rivalries and interfamily competition continues in Mombasa's informal neighborhoods. In addition to witchcraft accusations, both the Kisii cooperative and Magongo Market have suffered destructive fires in the last ten years. It is unclear who started those fires, but there is no shortage of allegations or suspects with motives. Such market burnings and accusations are evidence of the competition accompanying the shift in the moral economy of development away from the cooperative model.

As with the broader concept of freedom, free market ideology heralds creativity as an undeniable good. But two questions remain: When are you being innovative and when are you being exploitative? Is exploitation intrinsic to a system that values innovation at the expense of a social safety net? The stories in this chapter cast light upon a moral economy of creativity and innovation and the ongoing debate over what ethical and moral development looks like in Kenya. Old structures like the cooperatives are losing business to accumulaters who outsource production to family, personal networks, and the marginalized. This ability has allowed many savvy Kenyan (as well as Western) businesspeople to live the Africa Rising experience and, for the first time, outcompete cooperatives and the European and South Asian businesspeople who long dominated the export business. However, such success hurts many of those long-established in the industry and hinges on the ability to survive on smaller profit margins and manipulate personal connections to lower costs and push production to the more marginalized in society—children, women, and the disabled.

SEVEN

From Ethnic Brands to Fair Trade Labels

DURING THE CHRISTMAS SEASON OF 2010, I was delighted to find so many of the Kenyan arts and handicrafts I had studied since 2001 readily available for purchase in a small boutique a few blocks from my New Jersey apartment. The store sold a variety of small crafts and handmade toys, as well as carvings from places as distant as Kenya, Bali, and Mexico. While nearly all the assorted toys, crafts, and carvings from Kenya carried a "Fair Trade Product of Kenya" sticker, small cards additionally described the raw material, the ethnic group, or the NGO that specialized in making and exporting a particular product line. Handicrafts labeled with ethnic identifiers were regular in the Kenyan curio or "tourist art" industry even before the onset of mass international tourism in the late 1960s. Although such carvings have long been termed "nontraditional" for their relatively recent economic origins (Crowley 1970:47), ethnic labels and brands such as Kamba Wood Carving and Kisii Soapstone presumably bring a competitive edge by making the art to which they are attached appear to be in its "natural'" setting, or "closer to the context of its creation or use and therefore less likely to be inauthentic or fake" (Steiner 1995:152).

But in preparation for the 2010 holiday season, the front of the small New Jersey shop was dominated by a display of white soapstone sculptures that seemed abstract at first glance and had little of the ethnic or "tribal" imagery that often characterizes African art produced for Europeans and North Americans. These top sellers instead were elongated human-like forms attached to one another and characterized by their lack of detail or colorful design. Some were symmetrical images of two torsos embracing, and others appeared to be hollowed-out domes formed by interlinked human bodies (see figures 13–17 later in this chapter). Although some were accompanied by cards reading "Kisii soapstone" (as much an ethnic as a regional and material marker), these carvings were different from the decorated bowls, candlesticks, and human and animal figurines more typical of soapstone carvings made in Kenya over the last several decades. These new carvings, designed largely for the global handicrafts market, depicted a type of abstract interpersonal connection through space—a motif also increasingly popular on the beaches and roadsides of Mombasa.

But such changing motifs of Kenyan art were precisely what you would expect from an East African industry founded on innovation and adaptation, as Kenyan traders increasingly accessed the international market through cell phones and the Internet beginning in the early 2000s. In my research for this book over the last fifteen years, I have repeatedly been told that the real challenge to Kenyans selling curios and crafts has become keeping up with a changing market. A crafts exporter explained to me in 2007 from his stall in Magongo Market: "You know, these tribal carvings that Kambas make. Those are not the hot commodity right now. What all my customers want right now is Fair Trade, handmade things, made of garbage or recycled goods. But not the tribal carvings" (author's interview, September 18, 2007, Mombasa). His observation suggests that among his clients (many of whom owned crafts stores in the United States or Great Britain), Africa or Kenya may no longer appear in the imagination as necessarily "tribal"—in the sense created by the image of the Maasai warrior, for example. However, through Fair Trade, ethical buying movements, and the NGO aesthetics that now saturate the symbolism and labeling of Kenyan crafts, Africa continues to be represented as in need of Western help and patronage. Even Western readers of *Time* and the *Economist* know that there are important economic and cultural changes taking place in Africa—after all, they now know that Africans have cell phones. But even though many are fascinated by the story of Africa Rising, the story is clearly not that Africa has risen. Kenya's crafts industry has found a way to not just sell a product but to actively participate in the Africa Rising experience.

I do not wish to suggest that American and European consumers and tourists visiting Kenya have stopped purchasing souvenirs and toys decorated with "tribal" images. Tribal and ethnic imagery is still highly valued within the global economy today (Comaroff and Comaroff 2009). Ethnic and tribal labels have long appealed to transnational elites' understandings of what is culturally "authentic," "traditional," or simply *real* about an "Africa" politically constructed as a binary opposite to the "rationality" and "modernity" of the West (Graburn 1976; Steiner 1994; Phillips and Steiner 1999a, 1999b). But the binary model of African tradition and Western modernity is increasingly impractical when applied to complex local situations, as much in New Jersey as in Mombasa. For tourists to the Kenyan coast I have interviewed, tribal and traditional motifs were unconvincingly "old" and "traditional" and not purchased for those qualities. Rather, such carvings—particularly those made at the Kamba cooperative in Changamwe—were more commonly referred to as "toys" or "souvenirs," unable to sufficiently "push back" and produce "the ultimate tourist commodity—experience" (Bruner and Kirschenblatt-Gimblett 1994:435, 449).

While everyone seems to love hating tourists, I find it limiting to view international tourists consuming invented traditions of Africa simply as "dupes." Tourists and their tastes are diverse and ever-changing. As a result, as Sally Price (2007) put it, "Art adjusts" (603). I am particularly interested in what Price has referred to as "shifting authenticities." This is not to suggest that such changes are new—African art has, of course, been changing since long before European contact (Bascom 1976:303; Biebuyck 1969). Yet, it is notable that as more Kenyan traders have shifted from the local roadside economy into the larger international business, there has been a corresponding increase in Fair Trade and explanatory labeling as well as motifs representing interpersonal connection across space like those described above. This shift is not just because of a changing market, but also because of the desires and political sensibilities of the Kenyan traders and exporters themselves.

The rest of this chapter highlights the recent diversification and changes in Kenya's tourist art to illustrate how the politics of social change are expressed symbolically through Kenya's tourism and curio industries. For example, Kenyan artisans and traders must adapt not only to a variety of international tourists and export markets but also to increasing environmental pressures and a recent rise in domestic tourism in Kenya. Amid this constellation of issues, I am particularly interested in the emergence and popularity of the motif of interconnected people described above, which I term the *art of connection*. The symbolism of egalitarian and transparent connection found by Kenyan traders, tourists, and Western buyers carries the same ideal prized by the transnational elite that focuses on equality while ignoring inequality. There is, for example, no obvious *art of disconnection*.[1] This same symbolism of transparent connection is also precisely the economic and sociocultural ideal branded through the Fair Trade sticker. Such changes demonstrate the importance of innovation and adaptation by Kenyan artisans and traders to keep pace within a competitive global market and adjust to a diverse and skeptical consumer base.

Over the course of many years, my research in Mombasa evolved from an investigation of roadside art traders in Mombasa's Old Town in 2001 to the much larger project exploring how art traders and particularly international exporters were using the Internet and cell phones in their daily business routines. My interest has, therefore, been largely on the economic foundation of East Africa's art industry and how those economics shape the aesthetics of the arts and crafts eventually sold. In this chapter, I focus on how that economic context has shaped the aesthetics of the art itself.

AFRICAN ART AS GLOBAL CULTURAL COMMODITY

Gesturing to an array of baskets, painted carvings, antique coins, wire jewelry, and wall hangings, a Kamba woman in her early thirties remarked to me in 2006: "It never used to be this diverse" (author's interview, March 28, 2006, Mombasa). Standing in the doorway of her shop, located on Ndia Kuu Road in Mombasa's Old Town, she was referring to the overall variety of goods being sold in Mombasa and originating from remote production locations throughout East Africa. Using examples from her own shop, she pointed out the decoration, beadwork, and painting that was applied to products such as Kamba wood carvings, which had for decades been plain, undecorated wood. Although she did not specifically market products in her shop as originating in different countries, she sold wood carvings from Tanzania, "ebony" bowls and candlesticks from Malawi, malachite bowls and jewelry from the Democratic Republic of the Congo, baskets from Uganda, and batiks from Zimbabwe. She argued to me that this increased diversity of product types and origins, as well as the increased decoration on items, was a result of both increased competition and cell phones. It was a cell phone that allowed her to remain seated in the shaded doorway of her shop while calling her Congolese malachite dealer, her Malawian bowl suppliers, and the wholesalers in fabrics and pillowcases from Zimbabwe. Most importantly, she did not have to go to these places in person.

As I looked at the array of items in her shop, only some of which were made in Kenya, I began to understand her point. New technologies for facilitating communication between producers and consumers, when in the hands of clever and connected intermediaries like her, left a visible mark not just on the economic organization of the crafts industry but also on the products being sold. Her job was to make the connection between the customer and the producer appear to be intimate and personal, even if the actual links in the multiple commodity chains were extremely complex.

Despite this complexity and the diversity of items being sold through Kenya's crafts industry, the words *curios, crafts, handicrafts,* and *tourist art* are all used synonymously as translations for the single word *sanamu* (Swahili for "art"), which is the primary term used in Mombasa for the variety of soapstone and wooden carvings, baskets, batiks, and jewelry sold around the tourism industry and exported from Kenya. Although the term *vinyago* is often used to refer to larger carvings (which comprise a major component of Kenya's curio and handicrafts industry), even these are included in the broader term *sanamu,* which refers to almost any type of art made by an *msanii,* or artist. In other words, what in English are Kenya's curios are in Swahili simply Kenya's art. So while the curio cabinets of North America and Europe are generally reserved for artifacts from a long-lost African past, the "curios" *(sanamu)* sold in Kenya can also reflect cultural hybridity, change, and an Afropolitan understanding of difference, tradition, and modernity.

While of a much lower class than typical Afropolitan consumers (and unaware of the term), the Kenyan traders and exporters I have known for over a decade are still actively engaged in constructing proud, modern, and mobile African identities unified through an aesthetic of cultural and symbolic blending and hybridity—Afropolitanism's core idea (Dabiri 2014; Mbembe 2007). Sidney Kasfir (1999a:65) has provided extensive evidence of how the new African art that emerged in the 1950s and 1960s involved a great deal of cultural brokerage by a rather small number of African traders and Western supporters—early Afropolitans, I would suggest. Such cultural brokerage leads to change and innovation, which have never been new to Kenya's curio industry.

As early as the 1950s, the "tribal" and "traditional" nature of African carvings was already being questioned. Walter Elkan, for example, wrote that the Kamba carvings "have an exotic but suspiciously uniform look about them and at the back of everyone's mind there lurks the suspicion that really they are all mass-produced by machines" (1958:314). Kenyan carvers and traders have long been aware of such skepticism as well as the diversity of their customers and their changing expectations. During the 1980s, Changamwe's Akamba Handicraft Industry Co-operative Society first began making an official marketing distinction between "ethnic" lines, with tribal imagery intended for the local market, and the quite different export lines, which included nonethnic decorative animal carvings and functional items (Jules-Rosette 1984:210). This distinction rested on the assumption that tourists to Kenya wanted items with more "local color" (Jules-Rosette 1984:210), such as Maasai figurines, whereas export products did not need to explicitly market the carvings' origin. This is largely because, as Andy Redfern and Paul Snedker (2002) have discussed, by the 1980s, many of the crafts sold on the global market of the 1960s "began to look tired and old-fashioned in the market place" (6). They postulated that this was largely because the novelty of such products throughout the 1970s and the initial boom in international tourism had attracted buyers. This would also help explain why so many European and North American crafts stores began to take huge losses in the 1990s, just as the Fair Trade coffee and foods movement was gaining popularity and helping to revive the industry (Redfern and Snedker 2002:9).

The Kenyan crafts industry has adapted and survived, albeit with mixed stories of success and failure. I suggest that the survival of Kenyan exporters, artists, and cooperatives is largely because Kenyans and other Africans have been regularly producing a variety of images other than "ethnic and tribal arts" during the decades since independence in the 1960s. Such products include carvings of animals, baskets and bags, paintings, and crafts emblazoned with abstract geometric designs (see Jules-Rosette 1984:210). Kristina Dziedzic Wright (2008), for example, has described the emergence of coconut crafts made on the island of Lamu on the northern Kenyan coast, again signaling the importance of creativity in materials and designs in response to an evolving tourism industry and consumer base.

Because much of the value of ethnic and tourist art rests in consumers' expectations and understandings of "authentic Africa," as the circulation of images representing Africa change, so too do tourists' and art buyers' understandings of what Africa, Kenya, or Mombasa *really* looks like, or how they are *really* experienced. In his classic 1976 work on tourism, Dean MacCannell (1976) argued that tourists were doomed to failure in their quest for authentic cultural experiences since tourism industries were created for them and thus by definition lacked the natural or pristine elements that tourists desire.[2] His argument, however, is focused almost solely on white Euro-American tourists and on tourists more generally as a homogeneous population with static assumptions about what an authentic culture might look like.

My data and findings resonate more with Edward Bruner (1991), who argued that "most tourists are quite satisfied with their own society, most are not alienated, and they are not necessarily seeking an authentic experience elsewhere" (240). Bruner continued: "Tourists are not dupes, and they realize that the native performances on their tour itinerary are constructions for a foreign audience. Tourists are willing to accept a reproduction, as long as it is a good one" (240). This suggests that, while tourists may not view ethnic labels, images, and commodities as completely authentic, precolonial cultural artifacts, they are satisfied when items are produced well and in a way that feels comfortable to the Western consumer. This reality is precisely what has opened up a new space for innovative African traders and artists to push the symbolism sold through Kenya's crafts industry in new directions.

The Kenyan case, therefore, challenges the simple model of the "art-culture system" (Clifford 1988), which holds that works of art and cultural "artifacts" are subject to appraisal as authentic or not within the greater Western quest for modernity (Clifford 1988:224). As the model goes, age and exotic qualities create distance between consumer and producer, and for Western consumers, the experience of evolutionary distance and their own modernity. I agree with Elizabeth Davis (1999) that James Clifford's (1988) model, like Dean MacCannell's (1976), no longer captures the complexity of change within art markets.

Some of what is lacking in Clifford's (1988) model is that much of what is being commodified through Kenyan curio art (and African art more generally) is not simply an object but an interaction or an experience. Indeed, face-to-face encounters between artisan and art buyer privilege the immediate context of production over an exotic or traditional "authentic context" (Davis 1999:486). It is to this immediate, modern context that much of the art market is turning.

Elizabeth Davis (1999) found in Niger that the Western neocolonial habit of collecting objects considered authentic for being "exotic" is indeed giving way to more hybrid "modern" objects and complex cross-identification between Tuareg artisans and their customers. Resonating with my own findings from Kenya, she discusses how "creativity and novelty have become crucial in the competitive and faddish Western market" (489). In the Kenyan case, this market includes not only long-term expatriates but also retirees and "pensioners," students, return tourists, and domestic Afropolitan tourists. Davis calls such changes evidence of a new process, "entirely distinct from that which imbues exotic objects with appeal in the West." The "modern" artisanal objects, Davis found, represent "a striking transformation in the relations between Westerners and non-Westerners." She explains: "A material world assembled with Tuareg-style Western objects offers Westerners the comfort of familiarity, while it promotes an ethically comfortable affiliation with local people" (499).

Inspired by such findings, I turn now to the hybrid and modern appeal of contemporary tourist art and handicrafts in Kenya. It is precisely this hybrid nature of "global crafts" that generates heated debates about their artistic merit and authenticity (also see Chibnik 2003:2).

ETHNIC AND MODERN SUBJECTIVITIES

Both Sidney Kasfir (2004) and Kristina Dziedzic Wright (2008) have discussed the emergence (or reemergence) of new craft forms, including "Swahili" wood carving, made in the town of Lamu on the northern Kenyan coast. Both found that ethnic identity played an important role in the positioning of artists and art vendors. I found a similar language and awareness of ethnic difference in Mombasa, particularly when traders discussed innovation and new motifs. Intellectual property was often spoken of in the collective, or ethnic, sense (such as Kamba, Kisii, Maasai, or Swahili), despite the constructed nature of the ethnic groups in question and the ostensibly ethnic traditions of African art. For example, young Kamba-speaking men who migrated to Mombasa often tried to use ethnic connections and affiliations to find employment around Changamwe's Kamba wood-carving cooperative, even if they had no direct connection to Wamunyu or the families that had originated the tradition in the early twentieth century. Almost inescapably, national and local ethnic politics often seeped into the relationships among curio vendors working along Mombasa's roadsides or in carving cooperatives.[3] The vast majority of traders were Kamba, Kisii, or Kikuyu in background—all broadly constructed ethnolinguistic groups not generally considered "indigenous" to Kenya's Coast Province. Ethnic tensions in Mombasa primarily involved issues of migration, land ownership, and the licensing of businesses—all issues central to the livelihoods of my research participants. It is perhaps then not surprising that I have found nonethnic products competing for shelf and suitcase space not only because of shifting tourist desires but also because of a distance created by traders between their tourism-related businesses and the violent realities of ethnic politics in urban Kenya. So it was not simply a changing consumer base but also the politics and context of the interaction between vendor and buyer that applied pressure to the symbolics and meanings of the art.

Many art dealers who identified as modern, urban Kenyans were wary of presenting themselves as tribal or ethnic, particularly during the 1990s and 2000s, when a return of multiparty politics to Kenya contributed to cyclical spikes in ethnic tension around election years (see chapters 2 and 3). While ethnic identity and knowledge of indigenous languages was often useful to savvy entrepreneurs, traders and migrants who had experienced discrimination and political targeting by other Kenyans because of their ethnic backgrounds often welcomed a shift in how they were portraying Kenya to cautious tourists from overseas. This was particularly the case for individuals who were striving daily to downplay their ethnic identity and finding more security in representing themselves as modern Kenyans rather than ethnic migrants. Further, many traders I interviewed were multiethnic and feared being cornered into a particular political identity category. Although politicians drew on ethnic differences and images to divide and rule Kenyans or foment political violence, "tribalism" was the opposite of what many Kenyans who depended on the tourism industry hoped for the future of the country.[4]

As ethnic identities were politicized by Kenya's political elites in feuds over election votes (especially in 1997 and 2007–2008), traders I knew who depended upon tourism and economic stability became perturbed by ethnic or "tribal" rivalries and performances. Kenyan art that showed the nation to be modern, changing, and new represented Kenya as welcoming to tourists without playing on labels, brands, and symbols that were often politically sensitive. The traders appealed to tourists on their own terms, as modern or worldly with a global identity and not "tribal" or "traditional" in either a cultural or economic sense.

Nevertheless, traders were aware that they could lose their symbolic capital and attraction by appearing *too* modern, entrepreneurial, or capitalistic. There was a threshold, and savvy traders and exporters were always walking a fine line. As an exporter told me in 2005: "When [tourists] find that there is Internet everywhere, and people are getting cell phones, they get disappointed, and they say, 'I never thought it would be this way.' So I think we bring a very different reality" (author's interview, September 23, 2005, Mombasa). His job—the production of this "very different reality"—involved finding overlap and points of collusion between tourists' expectations and his own pursuits within the political and economic realities that directed his lifestyle.

Throughout these changes, the symbolic value of the "tribal" Maasai did not vanish. If anything, the desire for photographs and sex with "tribal"

Africans has replaced the need for a wooden caricature (see Kasfir 2004; Meiu 2011). The masculine image of the patriarchal Maasai warrior is still prominent in the Western imagination and epitomizes the most picturesque, unchanging, and potentially "authentic" representation of "tribal Africa" (Hodgson 2001; Kasfir 2007; Spear and Waller 1993). Such Western stereotypes, while social constructions, were not lost on Kenya's art traders. One male exporter in his thirties commented in 2005 of the symbol of the Maasai warrior as "authentically African": "Usually women from outside [of Kenya], they come and marry Maasais [sic] because they have this whole symbolical . . . 'This is like a *real* Kenyan. A real African.' But the Maasai, it's not like they like being that way. They want to be modern, but in order to be modern, by being these Maasai they can get the money to be modern" (author's interview, September 10, 2005, Mombasa).

Similar to the Maasai described in this quote, Kenyan art traders with dreams of becoming wealthy entrepreneurs and experiencing the lifestyles they saw portrayed in international media were trying to open new spaces for representation that better fit their own desires. Many exporters and intermediaries, especially those with close connections to producers (through family, for example), blended the desires of international buyers with their own notions of modernity to develop new, Afropolitan motifs and ways of marketing the art that they felt expressed their place in modern Kenya as well as the transnational, creative, and innovative nature of their businesses. For example, as the exporter quoted above told me quite directly, "I would take authentic and modern just in one category." For him, what was most *authentic* on the curio market was what was *new* and had been least copied. He explained: "I would just take authentic and modern together with [Kenyan] artwork [arts, curios, and handicrafts]. Most people from my experience, they are really looking for something that is very unique. It's really Kenyan. It's not something fake. You talk to some of those people from U.S. and they tell me that point: 'We don't want stuff that has been in the market for more than ten years.'"

This very Afropolitan aesthetic of the hybrid and the new as most valuable could also be seen in the marketing of products. A product line called Swahili says that its products "are designed with the needs of modern living in mind, blending beauty and functionality. We collaborate with a talented pool of African artisans to extract contemporary products from indigenous textiles, symbols and traditional crafts. New color palettes, materials and designs make the handmade treasures we offer truly exclusive."

In this description, we see not just an emphasis on the "modern" being a blending of the indigenous and traditional with the new, but we also see the production of a value for Kenyan crafts that moves beyond the visibly traditional to that which is modernly functional, particular to middle-class individuals. These products are meant to appeal both to white international tourists as well as to middle-class Africans, or Afropolitans.

INNOVATION AND THE ART OF CONNECTION

Since Mutisya Munge carved his first wooden animals and figurines, Kenya's curio and handicrafts industry has survived and thrived because of carvers' innovation and transethnic sharing. Sally Price (2007) noted, that when artists once dubbed "primitive" find themselves operating in an expanded, international economic environment, the result can be innovation in artistic forms, alternative materials, and new interpretations of the art itself. For example, several innovations emerged in soapstone and wood carvings out of collaboration between Kamba and Kisii carvers who were hired during the 1960s and early 1970s to copy West or Central African art for export or sale locally in Kenya (Miller 1975:29). Even though curio art today is often sold or marketed with very specific ethnic brands to increase value, these monoethnic labels have long been deceptive since artisans have for decades learned from one another across ethnic boundaries. This transethnic reality of African art is, indeed, one of the most important sources of innovation.

By the mid-1970s, artists from around the town of Kisii in southwestern Kenya were regularly carving small soapstone animal figurines, inspired by similar Kamba wood carvings but with their own unique innovations. For example, unlike the detailed and precise realism of Kamba animal carvings, the emerging Kisii animals have been described as "simple" and "nearly abstract" (Miller 1975:30), with "geometric balance, and smooth, usually undetailed, surfaces" (31). Indeed, any experienced soapstone trader can easily differentiate between a Kamba-style and a Kisii-style soapstone elephant, even if it is all marketed eventually as "Kisii soapstone," referring to a town and region as much as an ethnic group. The Kamba and Kisii styles were entirely different, which was a major reason why so many Kamba carvers (or at least carvers trained in the Kamba animal-carving tradition) found employment carving soapstone animals for Kisii exporters and wholesalers to diversify the types of animal motifs they sold.

Because it is cheaper than wood, soapstone has also long been a practical medium for stylistic experimentation. Carvings of human pipe smokers and water bearers made from soapstone began appearing on the Kenyan market by the early 1970s (Miller 1975:31). Other forms emerged with time, such as "thinking men or women with bare breasts. Even ten years ago you could not find those," I was told in 2001 by Dennis, a Kisii vendor with a roadside kiosk (author's interview, April 20, 2001, Mombasa). Dennis, born and raised in Tabaka, near the soapstone quarries, finished his secondary school education before going to work for his uncle Nyambuto selling soapstone carvings in Mombasa. He had grown up carving, but he told me that most young men like him wanted to work in the formal sector rather than in the soapstone business. However, after finishing school, the offer from his uncle to manage several of his kiosks outside of Mombasa's Fort Jesus was too promising to pass up. Having literally grown up next to the soapstone quarries, he and many other such young men brought fresh energy to the industry and new ideas for how to develop the newest and most innovative carvings.

One form of soapstone sculpture that came to prominence beginning in the early 1990s represented social connectivity in the form of abstract, interconnected people. These carvings were also a practical way to lighten the heavy soapstone by hollowing out most of the material. It was common, for example, to find simplified carvings of a "mother and child," a tall figure stretching down to embrace a shorter one, who was looking and reaching up (see figure 13). There was also a "family" motif, depicting combinations of parents and children, abstractly organized around a single soapstone base, and there was "the lovers," depicting two individuals embracing. During my time in Kenya, I frequently found myself helping visiting friends or relatives seek out sculptures matching the number of children in their own families. This was, undoubtedly, a reflection of Western consumers' emphasis on the nuclear family as central to social organization. Sexualized sculptures of abstractly carved naked women or of interconnected lovers (often with enlarged and pronounced sexual organs) were also a popular item among tourists, reflecting the larger sexualization of Kenya through the tourism industry. These items were all produced by hand on a massive scale by very talented artisans who had, in most cases, been carving from the time they were children.

Maybe not ironically, I have heard both tourists and Kenyan vendors refer to these plain, smooth stone sculptures as a type of "modern art." Many tourists with whom I spoke derived the "modern" interpretation from the

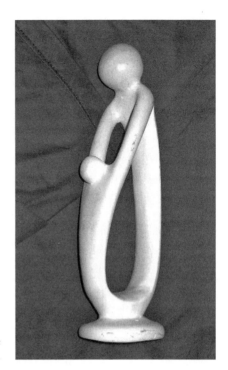

FIGURE 13. A family-motif soapstone
carving of mother and child.

features having been smoothed away, leaving simplified, abstract representations of interlocking human bodies that lacked specific ethnic, racial, and
often even gender identifiers, the exception of the explicitly sexualized carvings. But even in the sexualized carvings, the individuals could not necessarily be identified as African or European—the particular combination desired
was left in the mind of the interpreter. Nelson Graburn (1976) has noted the
importance of simplification in ethnic and tourist arts: "Simplification is
aided by the fact that the buyer does not know the meaning of the omitted
detail" (16). This simplification is central to both the art of connection as
strategy and artistic motif by creating a space of ambiguity or uncertainty
from which meaning can be produced. This openness to interpretation allows
both buyers and sellers to go beyond being passive consumers of meaning. All
parties are invited to use their imaginations to creatively interpret the connections being depicted in the art and to experience the art by producing
their own meanings from it.

In another common style, the figures are interlocked within a dome or
column of human torsos, heads, and appendages, with some upright, some

FIGURE 14. The art-of-connection motif in a Makonde-style
soapstone carving, demonstrating interpersonal connectivity.

upside-down, and others elongated until one figure's legs became another's
arms (see figure 14). From this basic concept have come a variety of other
motifs of varying sizes and styles—some of wood but most of soapstone—all
of which represented egalitarian connection (see figures 15–18). I interpret
these as a literal representation of human interconnectedness desired by both
tourists and international art dealers. Rather than play on dubious tribal
imagery, these sculptures literally represent the very contact that makes contemporary tourism experiences "real." "This is the future here," an American
tourist in her twenties told me in 2006, referring to a small carving she had

FIGURE 15. A rosewood carving of a motif depicting social connection.

purchased of interconnected people holding up a globe, "since tourism has become a global experience, or [an experience] of togetherness." In this case, this sense of global connection was sold to her through Kenya's tourism and curio industries, marketed to satisfy her desire for an egalitarian world order made possible through NGOs and transparency rather than a stereotypical assumption about an Africa of "primitive" or "tribal" art.

Meanwhile, although I did hear traders refer to these sculptures as "modern," most dealers called the complex carvings of interlocking people as "Makonde," referring to one major source of inspiration—complex Makonde wood carvings made by peoples of Mozambique and Tanzania (Kasfir 1999a; Kingdon 2005).[5] By the early 1980s, the Kamba carvers of the Makindu

FIGURE 16. An example of the symmetry often found in "modern" soapstone carvings.

cooperative in Kenya specialized in copying Makonde carvings (which they called *kisanza*; see Jules-Rosette 1984:126). The Kenyan government's Handicraft Unit also observed innovation and adaptation, reporting of the Makindu carvers: "Unlike other wood-carving Societies in Kenya, the group not only specializes in sculpture carving (Makonde Carvings) but also use variety of wood species such as Olive Wood, Ebony, Mahogany 'Itula' and White Ebony."[6] In Tabaka in Kisii District, at the site of the quarries and most soapstone carving, I was told by carvers and a workshop manager that motifs of interconnected people had been regularly produced since the early 1990s and had developed out of the sharing of knowledge between the Kisii, the Makonde, and Shona carvers from Zimbabwe.

But unlike many of the intricate Makonde carvings, which had a firm ethnic label and played on notions of Africa as "exotic" or "grotesque" (Graburn 1976:18), Kenyan soapstone carvings were highly simplified,

FIGURE 17. An abstract and simplified figure carved of soapstone.

smoothed, and polished so as to reveal no race or gender. Indeed, Kenya's soapstone carvings were most similar to the modern-looking sculptures that have been produced by Zimbabwean carvers for decades (see Larkin 2011; Zilberg 1995). Representing a blank slate for interpretation, these sculptures elicit a creative interpretation from both the buyer and the vendor, who could have numerous understandings of each object's meaning. The intriguing sculptures had the potential to represent the new, modern connections developing in Africa and Kenya, which traders and travelers together celebrated as part of their greater transnational mobility made possible through international tourism and the use of new technologies. These new art motifs were

FIGURE 18. A soapstone wholesale shop in Changamwe, filled with various types of family motifs and interconnected figures. Photo by author, 2006.

not ethnic but rather were the product of interethnic cooperation and sustained connection. By hiding inequality and stressing connection over disconnection, such sculptures appear to represent the free mobility dreamt of by traders and romanticized by the transnational elite. Indeed, there was no *art of disconnection*. There was, however, very clearly an *art of connection*. The friction and awkwardness of global connectivity was not being portrayed. Rather, the ideal freedom of movement inherent in globalization rhetoric was being produced, consumed, and experienced through the art.

The case of sculptures that appear abstract and that are labeled "modern," carved by "Kambas," and marketed as "Kisii" while often called "Makonde" by traders demonstrates the pervasive ambiguity central to the politics of labeling ethnic or "tribal" identity in Kenya's curio art. Such contradictory identity politics is typical of colonial identity constructions and the global handicrafts business more generally.[7] Such origin-ambiguity is more the rule than the exception, which provides an essential flexibility to marketers and intermediaries who are responsible for producing a certain sense of transparent connection within an international commodity chain characterized by inequalities at all scales. Just as the careful balancing of perception and reality—revelation and obfuscation—becomes central to crafts traders' strategies (or art) of making and maintaining connections, the art-of-connection motif has emerged, representing the transparency central to the ethical connections that render invisible the central businesspeople and the complex insecurities and inequalities that shape their lived experiences and strategies. The art of connection not only depicts trust but also works to simplify complex realities, pushing the production of meaning onto consumers and thereby further distancing the meaning produced through the art from the realities and insecurities of Kenya's crafts industry.

THE WOOD CRISIS AND THE
ENVIRONMENTAL IMPACT

Environmental pressures on innovation and changing aesthetics in Kenyan tourist art and in global crafts more generally have been a source of risk and uncertainty for traders and carvers alike. But as I will discuss in this section, "Good Woods" labeling and clever new artistic motifs have been successful within the context of these environmental pressures by appealing to ideals of ethics and environmentalism.

While wood carvings are light, inexpensive, and attractive to souvenir-seeking travelers, the trees most prized by buyers and carvers alike have been in a state of depletion for decades (Belcher, Cunningham, and Campbell 2005:1). Most of the wood preferred for Kenyan carving comes from slow-growing and endangered species such as rosewood and African blackwood, which are valued for their fine grain and the fact that they rarely crack, even in the cold climates of the northern hemisphere (Cunningham 2005:13).

Since the earliest days of Kamba wood carving, traders traveled long distances to obtain the best wood. During the 1960s and '70s, Mombasa's Akamba Industry was repeatedly involved in negotiations with Kenya's forestry department over access to cheaper wood.[8] As early as 1974, a United Nations study found that it would take only five years for the type of wood most commonly carved by the Kamba, *muhugu (Brachylaena huillensis),* to become exhausted in the readily accessible areas of the country.[9]

Despite these constraints, wood-carvers I interviewed at the wood-carving cooperative in Mombasa still preferred muhugu, teak, rosewood, and African blackwood, all of which could be found in the Central Province forests around Nyeri and Mount Kenya. Nairobi, in fact, had seen an earlier boom in urban wood carving than Mombasa, particularly during the Second World War, largely because of the proximity of wood and the soldiers stationed in the city. But by the early 1980s, although muhugu and African blackwood could still be cut in Kenya, government regulations limited carvers to purchasing only three logs per month from the Karura and Ngong Forests just outside of Nairobi (Jules-Rosette 1984:120). The result was that many traders either moved to Mombasa to access coastal forests or imported wood from Tanzania and Malawi. Then in the mid-1990s, the government applied strong restrictions and regulations to the cutting and use of muhugu from the central Kenyan forests (Schmitt and Cunningham 2002). The resulting spike in the price of raw material for carving increased competition just as Kenya's tourism industry, the national economy, and the international crafts industry fell into several years of recession.

Other than shifting to soapstone (a common strategy for many Kamba carvers), one way to deal with this environmental pressure was to carve wood newly certified as environmentally friendly, or simply "good." Since the mid-1990s, NGOs have emerged on the Kenyan coast to help convince woodcarvers to carve neem, mango, or jacaranda rather than the rare muhugu, African blackwood, rosewood, and teak (Choge, Cunningham, and Ellery 2005; Schmitt and Cunningham 2002; Schmitt and Maingi 2005). The major efforts came from the World Wildlife Fund and the Kenya-based Good Woods Project, which pushed certification as a means of limiting the destruction of East Africa's remaining coastal forests (Schmitt and Cunningham 2002:260–61). The Good Woods movement was helped by "ethical sourcing" by groups such as the U.S.-based Mennonite Central Committee, which was buying an estimated US$250,000 worth of carvings from Kenya each year, largely from Kamba cooperatives (Schmitt and Cunningham 2002:261).

In a related trend, as the rare hardwoods became more expensive and harder to find, traders adapted styles that would portray the authenticity of the wood to maintain a higher price for the carvings. As neem became the most common type of wood in the Kenyan market—80 percent of the wood carved in Mombasa's Kamba wood-carving cooperative in 2005[10]—many of the very soft and light-colored neem carvings were painted black and marketed as "ebony." While increasing the value of genuine African blackwood, the practice of painting neem black brought an additional challenge to the vendor: to visually demonstrate that the wood was authentic. By leaving the outer bark on the wood to reveal the separation between the darker core and

FIGURE 19. A curio vendor polishes a large African blackwood sculpture. The dark inner wood portrays interconnected human forms, and some of the bark and light outer wood is left in place to demonstrate the authenticity of the wood. Photo by author, 2001.

the lighter periphery, artisans and vendors made the identity of the wood explicit. This was usually practiced with the darker and more valued hardwoods—usually rosewood, muhugu, or African blackwood (see figures 19 and 20). As a result, all types of carvings made that revealed the authenticity of the wood in this way were soon found throughout East African curio shops and markets, appealing to an environmental rather than a tribal or traditional notion of authenticity. An adaptation of this idea—cross sections of rare rosewood, blackwood, or muhugu logs sold as coasters—would become the epitome of transparent woodcraft. These coasters were both functional and ethical, using only a minimal amount of material while also demonstrating the wood's authenticity and rarity.

FAIR TRADE AND MARKETING ETHICS

As the case of "Good Woods" certification shows, innovation in marketing Kenyan carvings and handicrafts did not come only in the materials used and the forms produced but also in the explanatory labels and explicit markers

FIGURE 20. An African blackwood carving that reveals the dark heartwood and the light outer wood and bark.

applied to the products at the points of sale, export, and import. The first independent Fair Trade crafts store opened in Europe in 1969, and by the 1990s the movement took a more bureaucratic form and shifted from "alternative" trade (alternative to a free market price) toward labeling and certification of products as having been produced under "fair" conditions (Redfern and Snedker 2002:9–12; Low and Davenport 2005:144). The 1990s rise in international Fair Trade labeling and certification was, therefore, timely for Kenyan intermediaries and exporters, who were able to use the Fair Trade label to maintain a high price for their products—authentic or valuable not because of "primitive, tribal" symbolism but for the assumptions that the production process was fair and ethical (Reichman 2008:103).

The product certification aspect of Fair Trade came out of a late 1980s strand of the larger movement, and European Fair Trade labeling groups began organizing under an umbrella group, the Fair Trade Labeling Organization (FLO), in 1997 (Raynolds and Long 2007:17). As Laura

Raynolds and Michael Long (2007:19) pointed out, partially because of such organizations, the Fair Trade certification system has since the late 1990s become much more industrial and bureaucratic. It was common at Mombasa's Akamba Industry and other workshops and cooperatives for international buyers to send their own stickers, often printed with "Fair Trade," to be applied to all products before they shipped. One U.S.-based company even had a Mombasa cooperative place price tags with bar codes as well as "Fair Trade" labels on items before shipping rather than pay their employees in the United States to do the job. "Apparently the Fair Trade stickers keep them from paying someone on their end," the head of exports at the cooperative told me, admitting he did not actually understand the labels' significance.

But many intermediaries like Davis did understand. When he was still working as a full-time exporter, his job included daily visits to one of Mombasa's chronically packed and slow Internet cafés to check his e-mail for new orders, updates, and inquiries. He was always worried about what would happen if he could not satisfy his buyers with *new* products that would sell on the European and American crafts markets. His job entailed communicating with production cooperatives and workshops located from Nairobi to Kisumu in Western Kenya to Dar es Salaam, Tanzania. It was, however, essential that none of these producers became directly connected to his buyers, lest his own intermediary position become needless. As a final step before shipping his orders, all of the products, regardless of their origin, were labeled with the ordering company's website and "Fair Trade product of Kenya" stickers, which his employers had sent ahead of time (see figure 21).

It was obvious to many exporters that Fair Trade and other labels such as "Handmade in Kenya" functioned primarily to attract customers. "Besides," as Davis would tell me one day while, pointing to some handmade items he was repacking and labeling with Fair Trade stickers, "I know these were made by *chokoras* [street kids]." His tone implied that their production was anything but fair. He knew from experience about the potential for young Kenyans to be exploited by businesses that paid small amounts of money or food for days of work. But that was also the economic foundation of his business. Walking through the musty and humid rooms of his two-bedroom apartment, which were literally overflowing with boxes of handicrafts sent to him from all over East Africa, he pointed out explanatory labels with phrases like "Teenage mothers and girls," "Empowering Women, Children, and Orphans," and just "Women and Children," all of which promoted the same NGO aesthetics of Africa as vulnerable, immature, and in need of outside

FIGURE 21. Men applying Fair Trade stickers to products before repacking them in their boxes and shipping them to the United States. Photo by author, 2006.

help. On that day, I could not find a single production group with an ethnic or "tribal" brand.

Since Fair Trade has a specific mandate to help "disadvantaged producers" (Raynolds and Long 2007:28), it has dramatically increased the opportunities and potentials for performing marginality though these same NGO aesthetics. While transparency markers like Fair Trade stickers add value when placed on handmade Kenyan carvings, art, and souvenirs, the same is true of an array of products and explanatory labels that describe an interaction between a deserving producer and a charitable consumer. For example, Global Village, a major dealer in Kenyan Fair Trade handicrafts based in the United States, markets Kenyan wood carvings in its U.S. shops with small cards that read "Muhugu Wood from Kenya." These cards, of course, do not note the environmental effects of the overcutting of muhugu. On the back of these cards "Your purchase makes a difference" is printed in bold. But do American consumers realize that difference is deforestation?

Fair Trade and "trade not aid" movements do not generally exploit tribal or primitive constructions of Africa but instead take advantage of a Western call for a global community without boundaries—an idea that is manifested

and engaged with in numerous ways through popular culture and the advertisements of companies like the Body Shop and American Express (Kaplan
1995:46). Fair Trade marketing has become similar to volunteer-tourism
programs, which combine, as Kate Simpson (2004) put it so aptly, "the
hedonism of tourism with the altruism of development work" (681). Such
programs, as well as unscripted gap-year traveling to Africa by Western students,[11] make development doable, knowable, and understandable, particularly for young travelers who encounter their African "Other" for the first
time (Simpson 2004). The problem with such programs and travel trends,
Simpson (2004:683) argues, is that they (like Fair Trade marketing) offer a
highly simplistic understanding of development, where enthusiasm and good
intentions become more important than understanding the historical and
political roots of poverty, underdevelopment, and social inequality. The
changes in the marketing of both tourism and tourist art represented by the
Fair Trade label point to a larger change in the way that Africa and the countries of the Global South are being viewed, marketed, and consumed in the
twenty-first century. The message from Fair Trade and volunteer tourism
alike is that while Africa may not be tribal or primitive, it is definitely poor
and greatly in need of consumers' help.

THE AESTHETICS OF DOMESTIC TOURISM

The changes in Kenya's curio and handicrafts industry are due not only to
movements originating outside of Kenya, such as Fair Trade, but also to the
growth in Kenya's domestic tourism industry and Afropolitan aesthetics
more generally. The Kenyan government, recognizing the importance of
domestic tourism, created the Domestic Tourism Council (DTC) in 1984,
which was responsible for promoting tourism in Kenya. Isaac Sindiga (1996)
has argued that the DTC had little impact, largely due to an "outward tourism orientation" and the lack of concessionary rates for Kenyans with low
incomes. Through the mid-1990s, companies that promoted tourism among
Kenyans were almost nonexistent, and the government provided little infra-
structural support beyond the school groups of young Kenyans that
accounted for most of Kenya's domestic tourists (Sindiga 1996:24).

The domestic tourism boom experienced in Kenya since the late 1990s has
largely been a product of a revived national economy and the active promotions from the Kenya Tourism Board (KTB), with the goals of developing "a

culture of holiday travel for Kenyans" and creating "curiosity and [beginning] to change attitudes."[12] The KTB initially undertook research in 2002 to understand the market conditions and potential of domestic tourism and in 2004 began its "discover, explore, experience" campaign, "launched to create awareness and desire" among Kenyans. As a result, much of the steady rebound in tourism in Kenya since 2003 (with a few dips in 2008 and 2014 following travel advisories) has been due not only to international tourists but also to Kenyans learning to be tourists in their own country (Mugambi 2007).

Kenyans' understandings of being modern are part of a cultural imaginary that is apparent in the Kenyan popular culture industry targeted at residents of Mombasa and Nairobi. Tourism is a major part of this, as Kenyans increasingly see the consumption of leisure as a way of being modern. But domestic struggles over cultural authenticity are only beginning to be reflected through Kenya's mass-produced arts and crafts. At the same time, Kenyan voices are being heard through the music and entertainment industry, which is increasingly dominating YouTube channels and tourist spaces such as Mombasa's renowned nightclubs and beach parties. And despite contrary assumptions by many curio vendors, up-country Kenyan tourists visiting Mombasa during the Christmas and Easter holiday seasons *do* buy curios.

One trader from just north of Mombasa set up a table at the public beach on Mombasa's North Coast to sell curios just before Christmas in early December 2005 (author's interview, January 8, 2006, Mombasa). Each day, his location at the public beach was packed with thousands of Kenyans to whom he actively marketed his small, functional soapstone items. Within a few weeks he had sold all of his stock, consisting mainly of practical items such as drink coasters, boxes, and small dishes. When I asked him in January 2006 what had happened to his stock, he proudly said that he had made very good money selling it all. "But it was up-country tourists," he said. "They were the ones doing business. But none of *them*," he said, pointing out some of the white tourists walking past, "not even *one* of them bought from me. Even all of my beadwork," he said, pointing to a yellow plastic bag under the table on which he was selling some cassava chips. "That's full of beads and materials for making necklaces. But I'm taking a break right now. Business is good."

During the years I spent conducting research with curio traders in Mombasa, it remained a common myth that Kenyan tourists did not buy curios. However, one trader told me in the hotel shop that he managed for its Indian owner: "You know, those Kenyans who just come for a short time, like

Christmas, those are spenders. They spend a lot" (author's interview, October 7, 2005, Nyali Beach). Success for such a businessperson came from adapting to the Kenyan tourists, since Kenyans' aesthetics, in his opinion, overlapped with those of Afropolitans and other foreign tourists. He told me why he thought Kenyans had started buying from his hotel shop:

> You know, there are many changes. You know, the mentality of people in the past, they were thinking "OK, a hotel like Nyali is a hotel for whites." You see? They had the mentality "if I go to, um, Mombasa Beach, it is high-class people." But because of how we have developed—a little bit I think it is because we have been to school. Children who have been to school they already know "OK, I have no difference from a white person." So it was not economical, it was just a mentality, yes. Because those people who afford to come to Nyali now, it is not that they did not have money. But they thought this was just for whites. But now those matters have stopped. We get every kind of person [coming to the shop].

He also explained that, from what he had seen in his hotel shop, international tourists tended to buy all the same products that Kenyan tourists bought, such as beaded sandals, simple jewelry, and lightweight shirts. For him, marketing mainly to Kenyan tourists attracted foreigners looking for items that were not only new and different but also *authentic* in that they were used and consumed by modern Kenyans. He gave the examples of beaded sandals and embroidered African shirts. He said if an international tourist saw a Kenyan tourist wearing such clothing, she or he would want to wear it in order to get the real Kenyan experience.

Afropolitan-themed bags, fabrics, and jewelry now commonly accompany carvings, depicting transparent connection on the shelves of Mombasa's craft shops. New hybrid styles that portrayed a positive and modern African identity grew in popularity, not only because the tourists were changing but also because the producers and vendors were becoming tourists. One brand of Kenyan handmade products described its designs as having "the needs of modern living in mind, blending beauty and functionality." This branding of functionality and modern living reflects a pivot in much of the crafts industry to meet the demands of not just international tourists but also domestic, Kenyan, African, or Afropolitan tourists.

While Afropolitanism has been critiqued for the elite consumption patterns that help define it (Dabiri 2014), those consumption patterns can help to promote Kenyan crafts businesses. Further, Kenya's domestic tourists represent a much broader demographic. In Mombasa, even working-class and poor Kenyans would struggle to make their way to the beach (especially on Sundays) if just to walk, drink a soda, and maybe buy a small bracelet. Those Kenyans, while not the elite, did buy crafts. As a result, their tastes did influence things like the beadwork sold from tables around the North Coast tourist hotels. There is also a type of "poor man's Afropolitanism," or possibly "Afropolitanism from below," in Kenyan traders' preference for the modern global crafts and accompanying resistance to ethnic labels and motifs. This is not to withdraw from the critique of the ways that Afropolitanism mirrors Western consumerism. Indeed, the marketing of marginality continues the production of images of Africa as poor and needy. However, when deployed through ethical branding, these images are not simply pessimistic. There must be a possibility for eventual advancement and development if the purchase is to actually help to make a difference. The art of connection and NGO aesthetics are rooted not in images of a tribal or primitive Africa but of an Africa Rising although not having risen yet. This is a reality that resonates with crafts traders, international tourists, and Afropolitans alike, thus reassuring a new generation of tourists to Kenya as the images and meanings produced through their consumption patterns and imaginations continue to reciprocally serve as the "handmaiden of the Africa Rising narrative" (Dabiri 2014).

Kenya's curio industry has been in a state of adaptation and innovation since its inception in the early twentieth century. As I have discussed, an exploration of how artisans and traders of tourist arts and handicrafts adapt to a changing market moves beyond theories of a homogenized population of authenticity-seeking tourists (MacCannell 1976) or a global "art-culture system" (Clifford 1988). While it is easy to make assumptions about tourists' desires, the examples of Fair Trade and environmental certification, carving figures to reveal the type of wood, and producing abstract sculptures showing human interconnectedness all demonstrate the diversity of genres and motifs as well as the importance of nuance and innovation in the global crafts business.

The continued importance of the Fair Trade label in connection with African crafts reveals a continuation of the West's paternal obligation to market solutions to Africa's problems, but the ways such labels and other innovative symbolic markers have been adapted to the global market by Kenyan traders reveal that the power dynamic within the industry is complex. This innovation pushes the envelope of what is possible in the future for the production of arts and crafts in Kenya and for the larger representation of "Kenya" and "Africa" to a global audience. Indeed, much of the shift from ethnic brands to Fair Trade labels I have described is about a shift from a local market that long relied on "tribal" images to give Kenya that so-called authentic Africa feel to a global export market that is largely controlled by technologically savvy businesspeople from around the world with new ideals of enacting and representing global citizenship through their businesses and the images they broker and sell.

Conclusion

THE STORIES PRESENTED IN THIS book capture the lived realities of struggling Kenyans' fleeting connections to the global economy, with all the risks and insecurities associated with these new connections and the new mobilities and imaginations made possible by digital technologies. People strategically approach new connections in terms of their risks. The art of connection in modern Kenya involves the production and maintenance of transparent connections: economically between producer and consumer and politically between citizen and state. Despite being rooted in illusion, the art of connection illustrated by Fair Trade branding emphasizes intelligibility and simplicity over complexity to create an "ethical scene" (Ballastero 2012). But transparency also implies a simplification or obfuscation of underlying complexities. By applying a Fair Trade sticker, Kenyan exporters operating over long distances are able to give their clients the experience of connecting directly and transparently to artisans while simultaneously erasing their own presence and avoiding any questions about their actual business ethics.

The new art of connection, along with much of the new branding and marketing of Kenyan crafts, involves the obfuscation of economic complexities—Kenya's technological modernity and the country's politically sensitive issues such as ethnic conflict. The stories presented in this book speak to the persistent reification of ethnicity and ethnoterritorialism in Kenya and on the coast (McIntosh 2009). I found that, in addition to being central in framing the lived realities of political and economic change in Kenya today, ethnicity is something that can be resisted, particularly when ethnic tropes emerge through divisive politics. Though ethnicity is central to their lives, Kenyan traders label ethnic tensions "political" and have even moved to de-ethnicize their products. But while ethnicity can be the source of insecurity, it can also be just the opposite—a source of security. Ethnic and kin networks provide an essential social safety net and are only becoming more important for making and maintaining economic connections. When not politicized around elections and economic transition, ethnicity can be a source of pride and security. Indeed, "Africa works" because of such patronage networks, which may appear "informal" or dysfunctional but are in fact central to social and economic life (Chabal and Daloz 1999). Further, the move from ethnic brands to Fair Trade labels was not inevitable but the product of the insecurities that shaped people's business strategies.

While the principle of having an alternative, "fair" option to the free market, is admirable, we must be aware of the trap of marketing marginality and Africa Rising through Fair Trade and NGO aesthetics. But the problems of oversight illuminated in this book can be fixed. They must first, however, be discussed. Before any ethical system can be successfully established, there must be an awareness of discussions of moral economy and business ethics already taking place on the ground. Steps have already been taken in recent years to establish special Fair Trade units in Kenya to help with licensing, regulation, and oversight.[1] But being intrinsically rooted in a market system, Fair Trade companies must continue to promote their brand and "race to the bottom" in order to compete. We must be realistic when evaluating Fair Trade and ethical branding as symptoms of rather than solutions to the larger problems of inequality, exploitation, and insecurity within the global economy today.

Connecting to the global economy comes with all types of new risks and can be dangerous. As demonstrated with the examples of Maria and Davis, many aspiring young Kenyans are struggling within an economic environment that is more informal and intertwined with one's person and social life than ever before. Enabled by new policies of economic informalization and telecom liberalization, this new modern Kenyan "workstyle"—or blending of work and lifestyle (Beck 2000; Deuze 2007)—while allowing independent traders and agents to "work it alone" and feel free of government regulations and the pressures of personal social networks, is characterized by the new risks and insecurities that accompany their new connections and mobilities.

Although I agree with the *Economist*'s argument that the "real" digital divide is located within rather than between countries ("The Real Digital Divide" 2005), speaking of a strictly *digital* divide within an economic envi-

ronment defined by insecurity distracts attention from the historical formation of social inequality that has already shaped the economic culture. In
Mombasa, the digital-power divide has emerged out of the social context in
which the usage of new technologies has been shaped by concrete, deliberate
policy decisions that have complex, reverberating social, cultural, and
economic effects. As is true elsewhere in the world, blending a life of work
and leisure through the use of digital technologies does not set the individual
free but places the individual in the hands of the fickle and unpredictable
global economy (Beck 2000). Because the responsibility to manage risk has
been abandoned by the Kenyan state and left to individual citizens and informal social and ethnic networks, the story of the digital divide among my
research participants became one of ups and downs, precariousness, and
intense competition. These findings are important for future studies of
Africa's urban informal economy and create a multitude of new questions
and opportunities for further research.

The need for risk management is one main theme that emerges from this
book's stories. M-PESA has become central to mitigating the risks involved
in everyday monetary transactions in Kenya. But just as we must think critically about their use of notions of transparency to rationalize their actions
and generate trust in citizens, we also must be wary of the value that government, corporations, and development institutions place on the financial
inclusion of poor people living on the margins who have limited means for
managing risk. Safaricom's success has been largely rooted in its ability to
gain the trust of Kenyans, who turn to mobile money systems like M-PESA
to manage the risks of their new business models. But, as one Mombasa businessman told me, Safaricom simply places the liability back onto the customer. There is no denying that rural and urban Kenyans can now perform
more financial functions with their phones than wealthy urbanites in the
United States can: they can withdraw money from ATM machines, buy gas
and other goods, and send money internationally. Indeed, the success of
M-PESA in Kenya has made it a model for banking in many other parts of
the world. But Safaricom is making enormous profits, and M-PESA has
extended the realm of global finance into the lives of even the world's poorest
and most marginalized. Development institutions should understand that
poor Kenyans struggling in the shadows of the global economy have not only
much to gain but also much to lose from financial and technological inclusion, especially when they lack formal means of managing the risks that
corporate marketing is inviting them to take.

This book is not an attempt to demonize or to place blame upon African governments. The cases I present demonstrate that insecurity has been perpetuated by inconsistent regulations and a continuation of laissez-faire policies of microinformality. But this book was made possible only with the permission of and through collaboration with the Kenyan government, Kenyan academics, and Kenyan universities and state institutions. After decades of pressure from international institutions like the World Bank and the IMF to privatize (and thereby informalize) its economy, Kenyan policy makers have understandably struggled to regulate the economy. East African leaders have for centuries had to decide how to negotiate and handle the region's connections to the rest of the world and the global economy. In 1728, a joint delegation of representatives from Mombasa Island and the hinterland communities traveled together to Muscat to invite the Sultan of Oman to oust the Portuguese from East Africa (Willis 1993:27). In the newly independent Kenya of the 1960s, President Jomo Kenyatta's government strategically invested in tourism and crafts industries that would drive the economy as well as reassure the international community that Kenya was still safe for Western visitors and investors alike (Cooper 2002:174). Today President Uhuru Kenyatta, like so many other African leaders, is increasingly challenged to evaluate the risks and benefits of doing business with Chinese companies (Ellis 2011a, 2011b).

What this book has demonstrated is that Kenya's small-business economy is a valuable national asset and essential to connecting the country—economically and symbolically—to the rest of the world. Despite the importance of relations with China, Britain, and the rest of the international community, Kenya's connection to the global economy is taking place in the workshops and cybercafés, along beaches and urban roadsides. Those important interlocutors and culture brokers should be nurtured and enabled for the benefit of the wider Kenyan nation.

The stories in this book demonstrate that when leaders can gain the trust of citizens, the government can play a central role in addressing the needs of Kenya's businesspeople at all scales. As I discussed in chapter 4, formalization and economic regulation can be both nurturing to businesses and increase the legitimacy of the state if they are done in a way that benefits the people.[2] Beyond simply opening the doors to international capital, governments today have a central role to play in helping small businesses access secure economic environments and manage risk. But if ethnic groups and impoverished traders continue to be targeted and treated as election fodder, the government will just continue to push some of Kenya's brightest and hardest-working men and women to pursue potentially dangerous opportunities in a fickle global economy where all risk continues to be placed on their shoulders. By exposing the complexities of the global economy, I hope to increase understanding of it and implementation of policy that will work best for governments, people, and businesses alike.

NOTES

CHAPTER 1. THE ART OF CONNECTION

1. For more on the ethnographic study of handicrafts industries of the Global South, see Chibnik 2003; Graburn 1976; Phillips and Steiner 1999a, 1999b; and Steiner 1994, among others.

2. Kisii speakers of Nyanza Province in southwestern Kenya can also be called the Gusii or Wagusii in Swahili. My point is not to essentialize ethnic groups or communities, but because most of the cooperatives and marketing of soapstone was done with the Kisii spelling, I have also chosen to use this spelling to refer to members of the ethnic group, a language, and a region of Kenya. There is also a Kisii Town and a Kisii District (now Kisii County). Similarly, the term for "Kamba people" in the Kamba language is *Akamba,* using a prefix of *a-,* whereas in Swahili the prefix would be *wa-.* I have tried as frequently as possible to use the English *Kamba* for consistency. However, because the name of the Kamba woodcarving cooperative in Mombasa was the Akamba Handicraft Industry Co-operative Society Limited and was commonly referred to as "Akamba Industry," both *Kamba* and *Akamba* appear regularly in the text.

3. Similarly, Clark (1988) called for focused attention on street traders and other "informal" economic actors who have been increasingly emerging as significant political and economic actors. Also, Behrend (2000) identified "globalization from below" among Mombasa's roadside photographers, and Simone (2001, 16) was concerned with how urban Africans act through a process he termed "worlding from below."

4. A great deal has been written that both perpetuates (see Mahajan 2008; Bright and Hruby 2015) and critiques (see Bond 2014; Taylor 2014) the Africa Rising narrative.

5. See *Economist,* December 3, 2011; *Time,* December 2, 2012.

6. See *Economist,* May 13, 2000.

7. See *Time,* January 16, 1984; March 30, 1988.

8. Also see Bond (2014) and Taylor (2014) for critiques of the Africa Rising narrative.

9. While there is far too much written on the topic of Afropolitanism to review here, see Eze 2014; Lemma 2013; Mbembe 2007; and Wawrzinek and Makokha 2010.

10. All names of research participants are pseudonyms.

11. By 2015 he was using a smartphone, which I had bought him, to work as an informal photographer in his migrant neighborhood in Mombasa. For a few shillings, he would take pictures for his neighbors and friends in the community and then e-mail them to them using his smartphone's capabilities.

12. In 2002, demand for mobile phones increased by 69.6 percent, with 630,000 mobile phone subscribers in 2001 and just over 1 million in 2002 (Kenya 2003:28). By 2013, 75 percent of Kenya's more than 40 million people had mobile phones (Kenya 2014:7).

13. See Adey et al. 2014; Glick Schiller and Salazar 2013; Hannam, Sheller, and Urry 2006; Porter et al. 2010; Sheller and Urry 2006; and Urry 2007.

14. See Chibnik 2003; Graburn 1976; Kasfir 1999a, 2007; Phillips and Steiner 1999a, 1999b; Steiner 1994, 1995, 1996; and Stoller 2003.

15. There have been several reviews of the early development of tourism in Kenya. See especially Akama 1999, 2002; Ndege 1992; Ondicho 1999; and Sindiga 1999.

16. Other notable government acts included the 1945 National Parks Ordinance, which protected national parks as a valuable resource and asset for attracting tourists, and the creation of the Ministry of Tourism and Wildlife in 1958, which Ondicho termed a "hallmark event pointing to the prime-moving role the government was going to play in promoting the growth of tourism" (1999:51).

17. See the report "Development of Tourism in Kenya," dated March 4, 1970, from the Ministry of Tourism and Wildlife, document 108, in the file "Coast Provincial Administration, Tourism 1965–1971," Coast Provincial Files, Kenya National Archives, Nairobi, serial number CA/21/53, box 105, shelf 4659, room 6.

18. For more on the interest and investment of the Kenyan state in the development of basic infrastructure for the tourism industry, see the memo, "Coast Tourist Development," by J. Knightly, Coast Provincial Town Planning Officer, to the Coast Provincial Commissioner, dated May 24, 1971.

19. From an academic standpoint, the art has value because it tells a very real story about the cultural politics of neoliberal capitalism and the risks and inequalities that shape diverse experiences of globalization. Kenyan crafts tell a deeper story about colonialism, African ingenuity, and the innovation needed to compete in the global economy.

20. For more on ethical consumerism, see Barnett et al. 2010; Lewis and Potter 2010; and Carrier and Luetchford 2015.

21. One of the few downtown hotels that did not close or change name during my extended research period (2001–08), the name was locally pronounced "hermz."

22. See box 1.1 in Belcher, Cunningham, and Campbell (2005, 8).

1. The name Mvita does not necessarily derive from the Swahili word *vita* (war). De Blij (1968:5) wrote, "the Swahili name for Mombasa is Mvita, which, according to the most generally accepted interpretation, means 'place of war.'" However, he added, "The derivation of the word *Mvita* is still a matter of debate" (5n4). He noted that the name could have come, for example, from the word *kufita* ("to hide" in the Kimvita dialect of Swahili; *kuficha* in standard Swahili). Another explanation is that the original settlement was simply named after the Shirazi leader Shehe Mvita, who according to certain oral traditions established Mvita town after acquiring land from an earlier, non-Islamic ruler, a queen named Mwana Mkisi (Nurse and Spear 1985:73). Loaded with symbolism, such stories, which are found along the East African coast, have questionable historical accuracy.

2. See Barkan 1998; Barkan and Ng'ethe 1998; Ndegwa 1998b; Wolf 2000.

3. See Ndegwa 1998b; Oded 2000; UNDP 2002:7; Wolf 2000.

4. As John Middleton (1992:1n1) pointed out, the Arabic word also means "edge" or "border." The Swahili as originally termed were therefore not only the people of the coast, but the people at the edge or border of Arab or Islamic civilization. In this sense, the Swahili were the *ethnics* of the Arab world—the "Others" at the border of empire.

5. See Arens 1975, 1976; Caplan 2004; Eastman 1971; Mazrui and Shariff 1994; Salim 1973; and Parkin 1989, among others. I do not wish to dwell on the question of who is and who is not a "Swahili," as the term can be an empowering category in certain instances and derogatory in others. Like other Westerners who learn Swahili, I was often called *mswahili* (a Swahili) by other Kenyans, demonstrating the term's multiplicity of meanings and usages.

6. The formation of the Theneshara Taifa during the sixteenth century resulted primarily from the expansion of Galla (a generalized and somewhat derogatory term for the ancestors of Kenya's Oromo, or Orma) pastoralists to the interior of Malindi along the Sabaki River. This violent expansion pushed both the coastal Muslim and the hinterland populations, upon whom the coastal merchants relied for trade goods, to the protection of Mombasa Island and its fortified kaya ridge in the immediate interior (Berg 1968:40, 46; Willis 1993).

7. For more on the Mijikenda, see Brantley 1981; McIntosh 2005, 2009, 2010; Morton 1972, 1977; Parkin 1989; Spear 1978, 1981; Waaijenberg 1993; and Willis 1993, among others.

8. *Miji-Kenda* is Swahili; the very similar *Midzi-Chenda* is the term in the various Mijikenda languages, demonstrating the closeness and at times interchangeability of the Swahili and Mijikenda languages. For more on the similarity and history of the Mijikenda and Swahili languages and dialects, see Nurse and Hinnebusch 1993; and Nurse and Spear 1985.

9. For example, the people of Kaya Giriama were simply called the *Wagiriama* in Swahili (*Agiriama* in the Giriama language), or "people of Giriama." Likewise,

the people of Kaya Chonyi were called the *Wachonyi* in Swahili (*Achonyi* in the Chonyi language), or the "people of Chonyi." There was tremendous cultural and linguistic similarity among the various hinterland populations, as well as the Swahili, to whom they are intimately linked socially, historically, and economically. See Spear (1978, 1981) for the most comprehensive analysis of the history and primary institutions of the communities of Mombasa's immediate interior.

10. Making any natural or ancient differentiation among the various communities of the East African coast is difficult because the region has a long history of linguistic, genetic, and cultural exchange. There is now very good linguistic and archaeological evidence of continuous occupation of the coastal hinterland from the early Stone Age through the modern period, with considerable mutual influence among Bantu-, Cushitic-, and Nilotic-speaking groups occupying the area during that time (Spear 2000:269). Summarizing largely linguistic and archaeological interpretations of historical migrations of the Northeast Bantu, Spear (2000) concluded that the descendants of the communities that would become the Mijikenda, Pokomo, and Swahili were present on the Kenyan coast by the first century A.D. The differentiation into separate dialects took place throughout the first millennium, with Swahili emerging as a distinct language by the ninth century (Spear 2000:258–59, citing Nurse and Spear 1985 and others).

11. The Mijikenda kaya originally functioned primarily as ritual centers and defensive settlements to which farmers would return at night after spending days working in the fields on the interior ridge (Spear 1978).

12. By combining a number of sources, such as the writings of the missionary Krapf, Spear (1978:136) estimated that the Mijikenda still controlled the interior trade with the Chagga and Kamba through the 1830s. It was during the 1840s, after Mombasa had fallen to the Busaidi Sultan in Oman (in 1837), that the Kamba came to dominate the trade route to Mombasa (Spear 1978:136). The missionary Krapf wrote of the Kamba in the 1840s that they "go in caravans of from 200 to 300 persons into the interior to fetch ivory, and form in a general way the commercial medium between the coast and the interior, into which they journey a distance of from 200 to 250 leagues" (1860:144). Beginning in the 1850s, Mombasa and other "Swahili" of the coast became the most common on the Chagga route and made inroads in the trade with Kamba ivory traders operating through Kitui (Spear 1978:136; Steinhart 2000).

13. In 1885 the affairs of the British East African Association were headquartered in Mombasa. In 1888 the British presence increased with the commissioning of the Imperial British East African Company, which would form the backbone of the British East African Protectorate declared in 1895. Kenya would not officially become a colony until 1921. For a comprehensive look at the role of the coast in East Africa's and Kenya's history, see Brantley 1981; Cooper 1977, 1980, 1987, 2002; Kanyinga 2000; Kirkman 1983; Morton 1990; Nurse and Spear 1985; Oded 2000; Ogot and Kieran 1968; Pouwels 2001; Presthold 2004, 2008; Salim 1973; Spear 1978, 1981, 2000; Sheriff 1987; and Willis 1993.

14. At the onset of British involvement in East Africa, Muslims (as opposed to non-Muslim Africans) had a significant advantage in acquiring land, partly because the process was dominated by Arab administrators and partly because the announcements for registration were made inside mosques (Kanyinga 2000:59). The result was, as Kanyinga has suggested, a massive dispossession of land farmed by Mijikenda peoples by the coastal Muslim elite, many of whom had close ties to the Busaidi sultanate in Zanzibar. In the early days of British rule, huge tracts of land were given to a very few Muslim Swahili and Arab families, including the Mazrui (although they had also opposed the Busaidi), opening up this land for sale to other Arabs as well as Indian and European investors (Cooper 1980:198–201; Kanyinga 2000:59).

15. As suggested by Willis (1993), it was this development that led many Giriama, particularly in Malindi, to begin converting to Islam in order to gain access to the private ownership rights of the Muslim Swahili.

16. Post–World War II colonial favoritism toward the Arab, Indian, and Swahili merchants and urban gentry was at least partially a result of a British attempt to keep Mombasa from being drawn into the Mau Mau resistance of the 1950s. When the Emergency began in 1952, the effects of Mau Mau could barely be felt on the coast. Salim (1970) suggested this was largely because the Swahili and Arabs of the urban coast, primarily Mombasa, were enjoying late-colonial prosperity. Salim gave the examples of the Arab Secondary School and the Mombasa Institute of Muslim Education (MIOME), completed in 1950 and 1951 respectively, as examples of the "educational, economic, and cultural revival" of the period (216). This was combined with the expansion of the radio program "Sauti ya Mvita," (the voice of Mvita), which according to Salim "became the found and focus of a coastal Muslim cultural revival" (216).

17. For more on the particulars of Mombasa Island politics from the 1950s through the turn of the twenty-first century, see Ombongi (2005:300–305).

18. For more on the contrasting politics of national development in Kenya and Tanzania from independence through the 1970s, see Barkan 1984.

19. See "Mombasa District Monthly Report, August 1965," by C. K. Githinji for District Commissioner, Mombasa, signed September 10, 1965, document 24 in "Mombasa District Monthly Reports, 1963–1972," Coast Provincial Administration Files, Kenya National Archive, Nairobi, serial number CA/16/149, box 81, shelf 4651, room 6.

20. See "Mombasa District Monthly Report, February 1968," by G. H. Omondi for District Commissioner, Mombasa, dated March 27, 1968, document 50 in "Mombasa District Monthly Reports, 1963–1972," Coast Provincial Administration Files, Kenya National Archive, Nairobi, serial number CA/16/149, box 81, shelf 4651, room 6.

21. I say "perceived shortage" because the problem is not a net lack of land but a highly politicized, uneven allocation of land that left very large parcels in the hands of very few landlords and the vast numerical majority without legal title.

22. The multiparty 1992 and 1997 elections were the first since independence and were followed with much expectation and scrutiny. See Barkan (1993) and Throup

and Hornsby (1998) for evaluations of the 1992 election. For more on the 1997 election and a discussion of political change since the 1992 election, see Barkan 1998; Barkan and Ng'ethe 1998; Harbeson 1998; Holmquist and Ford 1998; Kiai 1998; and Ndegwa 1998a, 1998b. For more on violence in Mombasa surrounding the two elections, see the Human Rights Watch report (HRW 2002) that focuses on the 1997 "Kaya Bombo" violence and also makes multiple connections with events related to the 1992 elections. See Oded (2000) for a discussion of the politicization of Islam in Kenya and for an in-depth discussion of the impact of the 1992 and 1997 elections on Kenyan Muslims.

23. *Kangas* and *kikois* are anglicized plurals commonly used with tourists. In standard Swahili the plural of *kanga* is *kanga,* and the plural of *kikoi* is *vikoi.*

24. Although I first met Mama Wanjiru in 2001 and saw her and her family on a regular basis throughout my research, unless otherwise noted, all quotes from Mama Wanjiru come from my interview, October 27, 2005, in Mama Wanjiru's house in Mombasa.

25. There was a conceptual linkage between the cutting and planting of trees and land ownership in much of Kenya and on the coast (Parkin 1972:ch. 4; Waaijenberg 1993; Willis 1993:120). In much of Kenya, land rights were obtained through "first settlement," as land became the property of the first inhabitant to cultivate and make productive use of the land (Kanyinga 2000:32).

26. I first heard such stories and discourses during fieldwork in 2001. They were repeated again during interviews and discussions with roadside vendors when I was working outside of Fort Jesus in October 2005.

27. Author's interviews: October 17 and 18, 2005, with former employees of Mama Wanjiru; October 19, 2005, with Njoroge; October 27, 2005, with Mama Wanjiru. Because Njoroge's grandmother passed away before I was able to speak with her, I was unfortunately not able to interview her personally to learn more about her past.

28. Author's interviews: October 17, 2005, with former employee of Mama Wanjiru; October 19, 2005, with Njoroge; October 27, 2005, with Mama Wanjiru.

29. This is all from author's interview, October 19, 2005, with Njoroge, Mombasa.

30. See Bravman 1998; Lynch 2011; McIntosh 2009; and Osborne 2014, among others.

31. *Miraa,* better known as khat, is a mild stimulant legally grown and consumed in Kenya. It is also a major export, primarily to Somalia, the Middle East, England, Italy, and Germany, although it has recently been banned in the United Kingdom and is illegal in the United States.

CHAPTER 3. CRAFTS TRADERS VERSUS THE STATE

1. For more specifics on this issue, see exemplary files in the Kenyan National Archives, Nairobi, including "Tourism 1965–1971," Coast Provincial Administra-

tion, serial number CA/21/53, box 105, shelf 4659, room 6; and "Hotel Trade–Beach Security 1959–1983," Coast Provincial Administration, serial number CQ/18/1, box 14, shelf 353, room 1.

2. Although academic sources (Elkan 1958; Kasfir 1999a; Jules-Rosette 1984) have Mutisya Munge first learning to carve while in Tanzania, many carvers I have interviewed who were born in the 1930s and '40s believed that he also witnessed carving traditions in the Congo and Malawi before returning to Wamunyu to develop his own techniques (see particularly author's interview, November 2, 2005, with three Kamba members of Mombasa's wood-carving cooperative). Whether these stories are factual or not, they emphasize the main message: that Munge incorporated a variety of Central and East African artistic elements into what would eventually emerge as a unique "Kamba" form of art.

3. Jules-Rosette (1984:107) noted that the exact year when Mutisya Munge returned to Wamunyu was unclear. Some of her sources set the date as early as 1918 and others as late as 1935 (107n4). From her evidence, she concluded that he returned sometime between 1918 and 1929, although the exact date will probably always remain uncertain (107).

4. Mount (1973:40) noted that the majority of African souvenir art dealers came from only a few ethnic groups, such as Hausa and Wolof speakers of West Africa and Kamba speakers of East Africa.

5. Also see the file "Akamba Industries Co-operative Society, Ltd. 1950–1958," which was compiled largely by the Ministry of Co-operatives and Social Services. It can be found in the Kenya National Archives, Nairobi, serial number TR/8/103, box 108, shelf 6615.

6. See By-Laws of the Akamba Industries Co-operative Society, Ltd., document 3, and the "certificate of registration official," document 4 in the file "Akamba Industries Co-operative Society, Ltd. 1950–1958," Ministry of Co-operative Development, Kenya National Archive, Nairobi, serial number TR/8/103, box 108, shelf 6615.

7. Letter from Mr. Hayes, District Officer, Co-operative Department, Machakos District, to Registrar of Co-operatives, August 2, 1950, document 2 in the file "Akamba Industries Co-operative Society, Ltd. 1950–1958," Ministry of Co-operative Development, Kenya National Archive, Nairobi, serial number TR/8/103, box 108, shelf 6615.

8. See letter from Andrew Ndeti, Co-operative Inspector, to Registrar of Co-operative Societies, October 11, 1951, document 30 in the file "Akamba Industries Co-operative Society, Ltd. 1950–1958," Ministry of Co-operative Development, Kenya National Archive, Nairobi, serial number TR/8/103, box 108, shelf 6615.

9. See letter from Rural Industries Officer, Machakos, to Registrar of Co-operative Societies, February 7, 1952, document 35 in the file "Akamba Industries Co-operative Society, Ltd. 1950–1958," Ministry of Co-operative Development, Kenya National Archive, Nairobi, serial number TR/8/103, box 108, shelf 6615.

10. These apprentice-based workshops, Elkan (1958:319) noted, served as warehouses for stockpiling carvings, making it possible to assure quick turnover on large orders.

11. See letter from the Acting Registrar of Co-operative Societies to the Machakos District Commissioner, dated Feb. 28, 1953, document 41 in the file "Akamba Industries Co-operative Society, Ltd. 1950–1958," Ministry of Co-operative Development, Kenya National Archive, Nairobi, serial number TR/8/103, box 108, shelf 6615.

12. Only the third attempt to register the Mombasa cooperative, officially titled the "Akamba Handicraft Industry Co-operative Society Ltd," was successful. The first two attempts, made in 1960 and 1961, were not accepted. It was only with the help of J. L. P. Pinto, Co-operative Officer, Mombasa, in late 1963 that the cooperative was finally registered by the Commissioner for Co-operative Development. It officially became a "body corporate" on December 23, 1963, when it was issued Certificate of Registration no. 1030. For more, see the file "Akamba Handicraft Industry Co-operative Society, Ltd. 1963–1978," Ministry of Co-operative Development, serial number TR/8/816, box 236, shelf 6658, room 2.

13. This early history comes from author's group interview with several founding members of Akamba Industry, November 2, 2005, Chaani, Mombasa.

14. See letter from O. K. O. Oulo, Co-operative Officer, Mombasa, to the Commissioner for Co-operative Development, July 5, 1965, document 144 in the file "Monthly Reports Mombasa—Department of Co-operative Development 1957–1967," Kenya National Archive, Nairobi, serial number TR/19/292, box 489, shelf 6743.

15. See Mombasa District Monthly Report, December 1963, from Regional Government Agent, Mombasa, to The Civil Secretary, Coast Region, January 10, 1964, document 2 in the file "Mombasa District Monthly Reports, 1963–1972," Coast Provincial Administration, Kenya National Archive, Nairobi, serial number CA/16/149, box 81, shelf 4651, room 6.

16. This letter was from B. E. Oyaro, Co-operative Officer, Coast Province to Town Clerk, Municipal Council of Mombasa, April 6, 1967. See document 6 in the file "Akamba Handicraft Industry Co-operative Society, Ltd. 1963–1978," Ministry of Co-operative Development, Kenya National Archive, Nairobi, serial number TR/8/816, box 236, shelf 6658, room 2.

17. It was written in a letter from Daniel A. Oyoo, Examiner of Accounts, Coast Province, to the Chairman of Akamba Industry, Mombasa, January 8, 1971, that the 8.6 acres of land were purchased in early 1970 "at an unbelievable throw away price of Shs. 43,765/- only," with a resale value estimated around 100,000 shillings. This was because the European owner of the farm sold to the cooperative was looking to leave Kenya and apparently was not willing to wait for a better offer. See unnumbered document in the file "Akamba Handicraft Industry Co-operative Society, Ltd 1963–1978," Ministry of Co-operative Development, Kenya National Archive, Nairobi, serial number TR/8/816, box 236, shelf 6658, room 2.

18. Ministry of Co-operatives and Social Services, Department of Co-operative Development, *Annual Report for 1971, Mombasa District,* January 21, 1972, section 2.6, page 4, Kenya National Archives, Mombasa.

19. See letter from E. M. Muhihu, Coast Provincial Commissioner, to Town Clerk, Mombasa, June 6, 1972, document 149 in the file "Hawkers Trade 1956–1974,

Mombasa District," Kenya National Archives, Nairobi, serial number CQ/18/4, box 14, shelf 353, room 1.

20. This particular comment comes from page 5 of the Minutes of the Third Meeting of the Handicraft Committee Held on Tuesday, November 8, 1977, document number 15 in the file "Handicrafts Development Plan—Ministry of Co-operatives 1972–1984," Kenya National Archives, Nairobi, serial number TR/10/24, box 413, shelf 6717.

21. This estimate is on page 2 of "Handcraft Co-operatives: A Survey on Potentials for Expansion and Development," Development Planning Division, Ministry of Co-operative Development, January 1978, Kenya National Archives, Nairobi, serial number TR/20/29, box 509, shelf 6749.

22. The total market value of production at the same time was estimated at 60–70 million shillings per year. These numbers come from page 2 of "Handcraft Co-operatives."

23. "Handcraft Co-operatives," page 5.

24. Records from the Municipal Council from the late 1980s and 1990s attest to the repeated harassment of curio and other vendors operating from downtown kiosks, particularly when formal business owners complained to the council and vendors who had been in place since independence were told to move without being given alternative locations. Minutes from meetings of the council reveal that kiosk-based traders brought several cases before it, most of which were thrown out before being heard.

25. For more on the specifics of structural adjustment in Kenya, see Kibua and Nzioka 2004; Manda and Sen 2004.

26. The 1998 bombings of the East African embassies killed more than 250 people, twelve of whom were American (Oded 2000:82). Also see the special issue of the *Daily Nation* with the front-page headline "Lest We Forget," August 3, 2008.

27. Between 2003 and 2004, tourism earnings increased nationwide by 51.9 percent (Kenya 2005a:194), with the number of fourth-quarter (high season) visitor arrivals for holiday increasing from 180,900 in 2003 to 258,400 in 2004 (195).

28. See Hotel Survey in *Kenya Coast Line Development,* prepared for the Ministry of Lands and Settlement by Mr. S.C. Lock, the ministry's Town Planning Advisor, August 1, 1967, documents 49 and 49a in the file "Tourism 1965–1971," Coast Provincial Administration, Kenya National Archive, Nairobi, serial number CA/21/53, box 105, shelf 4659, room 6.

29. Fifteen were in Malindi, three in Kilifi, and three in Lamu. See the list, generated by P.M. Otsianda for Provincial Commissioner, Coast, July 13, 1977, document 102 in the file "Hotel Trade—Beach Security 1959–1983," Coast Provincial Administration, Kenya National Archive, Nairobi, serial number CQ/18/1, box 14, shelf 353, room 1.

30. Many in Mombasa's more conservative Muslim and Christian communities took offense to tourists' proclivity to walk around the city in bathing suits, drink heavily in downtown bars and restaurants, and at times pick up young Kenyan men and women to accompany them on both sexual and nonsexual forays.

31. See Rakodi, Gatabaki-Kamau, and Devas 2000; and AMREF 1999 for the complete *Mombasa District Participatory Poverty Assessment* (1999).

32. Nassir solidified his political prominence by being one of the first to vigorously support Moi's candidacy as president immediately following Kenyatta's death in 1978 (Oded 2000:30). His friendship with Moi would continue for more than two decades, as Nassir was a devout supporter of Moi's Nyayo ideology and worked hard to garner support for Moi and KANU at the coast (Oded 2000:30).

33. Chang'aa is a locally brewed alcohol in Kenya, similar to moonshine.

34. See "Kiosk Demolitions Well-Calculated" 2001.

CHAPTER 4. NEGOTIATING INFORMALITY IN MOMBASA

1. See Weis (2008) for an analysis and discussion of the results from the 2007 election.

2. See Barkan (2004) for an overview of the 2002 general election.

3. For more on the history of the term *jua kali* and the sector in Kenya, see Bowen 1999; Daniels 1999; Ferrand 1996; Kabecha 1999; Kenya 2005b; King 1996; Macharia 1993, 1997; and McCormick 1987, 1993.

4. The Kenyan government and development agencies have more recently begun referring to the majority of such businesses as micro and small enterprises, or MSEs. Although the Sessional Paper No. 2 of 2005 defined MSEs as employing up to fifty workers (Kenya 2005b:5), its authors admitted that over 70 percent of MSEs employ only one person (2005b:6).

5. See Thomas H. Tudor, United Nations (ILO) Senior Advisor, "Recommendations on Policy and Organization for Handicrafts and Cottage Industries," to the Honourable Masinde Muliro, Minister of Co-operative Development and Social Services, December 15, 1971, document 1 in the file "Handicrafts Development Plan—Ministry of Co-operatives 1972–1984," Kenya National Archives, Nairobi, serial number TR/10/24, box 413, shelf 6717. On page 3, Tudor remarked, "as early as 1963 the International Labour Office (ILO) detailed an advisor at the request of the Ministry of Commerce and Industry, to undertake a survey and prepare recommendations [on handicraft development]." The result of that 1963 study was the 1965 release of the ILO report *East African Regional Survey of Handicrafts and Small-Scale Industries, Part III, Kenya.*

6. "Handcraft Co-operatives: A Survey on Potentials for Expansion and Development," January 1978, Development Planning Division, Ministry of Co-operative Development, in Kenya National Archive, Nairobi, serial number TR/20/29, box 509, shelf 6749.

7. "Handcraft Co-operatives."

8. The Sessional Paper No. 2 of 2005 on "Development of Micro and Small Enterprises for Wealth and Employment Creation for Poverty Reduction" (Kenya 2005b) reviewed policies and strategies outlined in the Sessional Paper No. 2 of 1992 on "Small Enterprises and Jua Kali Development in Kenya" (Kenya 1992).

9. When Moi became president in 1978, he had to negotiate a difficult political playing field. He was, however, successful very early at addressing citizens around the country and acquiring a populist image for appealing directly to Kenyans (Haugerud 1995:81). Early in Moi's career, diverse political factions within Kenya joined his side as his regime solidified and he vowed to end political factionalism and corruption (Miller and Yeager 1994:99–100).

10. This information comes from viewing the licenses themselves during research in 2001–2007.

11. In addition to the business permit, there were other taxes and fees for hanging goods outside of a shop or for employing someone to work in the street attracting customers into the shop. In one case, the 4,250 shillings (US$65) for the Single Business Permit became 7,480 shillings (US$110) with the additional fees (these licenses were viewed during author's interview, August 12, 2006, Mombasa).

12. Also see "Policy Makers Must Close Poor-Rich Gap" (2006). This article and Munene (2006) cited a study by Action Aid Kenya that made a big splash in May 2006 when released to the public, stressing the wealth inequalities in the country at a time when the economy was supposedly booming. The latter article called the "much-hyped economic growth" simply "ridiculous."

13. This was according to Dr. Ongong'a Achieng, the KTB's managing director, speaking at Fort Jesus during celebrations to mark the opening of a KTB office at Moi International Airport in early December 2007 (Ndurya 2007).

14. I have known everyone associated with that free mark closely since 2001, and I was fortunate enough to talk to Mama Wachira on the phone briefly in 2014 just weeks before she passed away.

15. Unless otherwise noted, all quotes in this section from the public relations officer came from an interview conducted in his office on October 10, 2005.

16. In the *Mombasa District Monitoring and Evaluation Report* of 2004–2005, the writers pointed to progress made in licensing around tourism areas—a major part of their initiative. They discussed 180 "tour guides," 123 "tour operators," and 115 "curio shops" registered with the Municipal Council and the Ministry of Tourism in order to "install order on the beach and minimize harassment of Tourists" (Kenya 2004–2005:17).

17. The government plan made quite clear that the initial regulation and formalization process was intended to "restrict the trade to genuine operators only while the second phase involving relocating the operators away from the beach is underway" (Kenya 2004–2005:17).

CHAPTER 5. NEW MOBILITIES, NEW RISKS

Much of the information in this chapter also appears in Dillon Mahoney, 2016, "Mobilities and Risks in Coastal Kenya: Jumping Scales versus Staying Local," *PoLAR: Political and Legal Anthropology Review* 39 (2): 176–89.

1. In recent years, a large body of research has emerged that debates the validity of ICT4D (see Burrell 2008, 2012; Donner and Escobari 2010; Heeks 2002; Horst and Miller 2006; Mazzarella 2010; Porter 2012). Research has found that most users of new digital technologies are rarely successful at developing businesses with new media technologies (Burrell 2012; Horst and Miller 2006; Molony 2008). As patron-client networks were redrawn during the time of my research (2001–present), I witnessed some businesses expand and others be outcompeted. Many had been in the business for decades and were transforming the handicrafts trade in dynamic ways. Indeed, the success of the few demonstrated that economic development has less to do with access to new digital technologies and more to do with access to profitable social networks and the willingness to innovate both artistically and economically.

CHAPTER 6. CRAFTING ETHICAL CONNECTION AND TRANSPARENCY IN COASTAL KENYA

1. There has been a fair amount of recent research on the balancing of visibility and invisibility or transparency and ambiguity (Archambault 2013; Burrell 2012; Ginsburg 2012; Goggin and Newell 2003; Molony 2009a). For example, trust has undeniably become even more important within global economic relations as business interactions are increasingly mediated over long distances (Chepaitis 2002; Molony 2007, 2009a; Porter 2012). Indeed, while cell phones can reduce travel costs (Esselaar et al. 2007; Jensen 2007; Kamga 2006; Porter 2012), they also reduce face-to-face communication and personal oversight while empowering intermediaries (Donner and Escobari 2010; Jagun, Heeks, and Whalley 2008; Molony 2007; Overå 2008). My interest is in highlighting the increasing importance of transparency and trusting ethical connectivity within global socioeconomic networks. It is important to demonstrate how digital technologies have a certain politics and play a central role in current ideas of ethical citizenship and digital modernity (Horst and Miller 2012).

2. As mentioned in the previous chapter, I use *microinformality* to refer to informal economic development through the more recently reformulated ideas of the micro and small enterprise sector and microcredit. See Elyachar 2002; Hansen and Vaa 2004; King 1996.

3. See letter from the Co-operative Officer, Coast Province, to the Town Clerk, Mombasa, May 4, 1967, document 17 in the file "Akamba Handicraft Industry Co-operative Society, Ltd. 1963–1978," Ministry of Co-operative Development, Kenya National Archive, Nairobi, serial number TR/8/816, box 236, shelf 6658, room 2.

4. See "Handcraft Co-operatives: A Survey on Potentials for Expansion and Development," January 1978, page 7, Development Planning Division, Ministry of Co-operative Development, Kenya National Archive, Nairobi, serial number TR/20/29, box 509, shelf 6749.

5. See report from Ole Lindberg, Nordic Team Leader to the Handicraft Unit, Dec. 2, 1982, document 91 in the file "Handicrafts Development Plan—Ministry of

Co-operatives 1972–1984," Kenya National Archives, Nairobi, serial number TR/10/24, box 413, shelf 6717.

6. In both shops, all carvings were marked with a number, identifying the cooperative member who would be compensated once a carving had been sold. A single carver could work independently, producing his own masks every day to place in the cooperative's shops. Or a group of carvers working together could produce a large number of masks, which could together be purchased directly by a local business owner through the wholesale shop. The cooperative functioned to negotiate the sale and then redistribute the money to the carvers, who rarely had face-to-face contact with shop owners, and who were officially identified by their membership ID number, scratched or written on the bottom of the items they'd carved.

7. For more on ethical consumerism, see Barnett et al. 2010; Lewis and Potter 2010; and Carrier and Luetchford 2015.

CHAPTER 7. FROM ETHNIC BRANDS TO
FAIR TRADE LABELS

Much of this chapter was previously published in Dillon Mahoney, 2012, "Changing Strategies in Marketing Kenya's Tourist Art: From Ethnic Brands to Fair Trade Labels," *African Studies Review* 55 (1): 161–90.

1. If there is an "art of disconnection," or a set of styles and motifs that display the disconnections and inequalities of life in Kenya and in the world today (such as political art), it would be a great topic for future research.

2. MacCannell's broader claim was that the tourist is one of the best models available for understanding "modern-man-in-general" (1976:1).

3. For more on Kenyan ethnic politics through the early 2000s, see Haugerud 1995 , Bravman 1998 , Ndegwa 1997, 1998b , Nyangira 1987 , Oucho 2002 , and Throup and Hornsby 1998 .

4. I found discussions of national politics to often take on an ethnoregional bias, which was reflected as well through the differences between the various ethnic cooperatives. Many of these groups, irrespective of ethnic difference, were not indigenous to the coast, and many feared being targeted as migrants to Mombasa. Migrants from a variety of backgrounds were targeted in political violence in Mombasa and on the coast, especially in 1997 and 2007, although which particular groups were targeted depended on nuances in national politics. In all cases, lingering frustrations and animosities surfaced, at times in the form of targeting businesses run by people of noncoastal ethnic backgrounds, whether or not they or their families were born in Mombasa.

5. Wood carvings made by Makonde carvers of present-day Mozambique and Tanzania were common before the onset of European influence (Kasfir 1999:109–110; Kingdon 2005). Several decades after the conquest of the Makonde by the Portuguese in 1917, European patronage of the wood-carving industry and the developments of the *shetani,* or spirit figures invented by Samaki Likankoa in

the 1950s, made Makonde carvings famous internationally (Kingdon 2005:53). Zachary Kingdon (2005:52–53) differentiated the various types as *shetani, ujamaa,* and *mawingu* forms, the first representing demons or spirits, the second interconnected people, and the third more abstract forms, said to have been inspired by cloud formations.

6. See letter from F. O. Okwiri of the Handicraft Unit dated November 28, 1980, document 15 in file "Handicrafts Development Plan—Ministry of Co-operatives 1972–1984," Kenya National Archives, Nairobi, serial number TR/10/24, box 413, shelf 6717.

7. Michael Chibnik (2003:242–43) has discussed how Oaxacan wood carvings, generally carved by Spanish speakers of no particular indigenous background, are often marketed as Zapotec or Indian. Kathy M'Closkey (2000) has written of how Zapotec artisans have, by copying Navajo designs, essentially put Navajo weavers out of business. Sidney Kasfir (1996:154–55) similarly described how in much of West Africa, objects based loosely on traditional symbols but embellished and carved for the tourist and export market are called *"nyamanyama"* or "Kenya," whereas in Kenya, many of the same pieces are thought to come from Ghana, although they most likely come from Senegal.

8. See "Monthly Report for April 1964," by W. D. Mwasi, Co-operative Officer, Mombasa, to Ag. Commissioner for Co-operative Development, May 5, 1964, document 136 in the file "Monthly Reports Mombasa—Department of Co-operative Development 1957–1967," Kenya National Archive, Nairobi, serial number TR/19/292, box 489, shelf 6743.

9. Cited on page 12 of "Handcraft Co-operatives: A Survey on Potentials for Expansion and Development," January 1978, Development Planning Division, Ministry of Co-operative Development, Kenya National Archive, Nairobi, serial number TR/20/29, box 509, shelf 6749.

10. Akamba Industry's head of records and books supplied this statistic during author's interview, September 26, 2005, Mombasa.

11. See Simpson (2004:681–82) for an in depth look at gap-year traveling as well as volunteer tourism programs. "Gap-year traveling" is the increasingly common phenomenon in the United States and Western Europe of students to taking a year off after high school or college to travel and "see the world."

12. Kenya Tourism Board, "KTB Marketing Plan 2005/2006" (internal document for KTB partners, first presented January 2005), National Museums of Kenya at Fort Jesus, Mombasa.

CONCLUSION

1. See the Fair Trade Organization of Kenya (http://www.ftok.org/) and Fair Trade Eastern Africa (http://www.fairtrade.or.ke/), although much of the focus on Fair Trade certification in Kenya focuses on commodities like coffee and tea.

2. If one policy lesson should come from this study, it is that there is a need for risk management, particularly among the small businesses that are the lifeblood of a great deal of international exchange, trade, and connections today. Could we reimagine government as a risk manager? While digital technologies are enabling new generations of very smart and savvy entrepreneurs to access online and offline communities through their websites and social networking, these new connections come with all types of new risks. The government could, for example, help cooperatives stabilize and manage themselves efficiently in a way that is innovative, avoids corruption, and provides the risk management so important to the small business class. Akamba Industry had once worked well as an institution of risk management for Kamba migrants to Mombasa looking to get a start in the curio business. While the cooperative has changed since the 1960s along with the broader political and economic environment, the importance of the risk management provided to the cooperative members is as important as ever.

BIBLIOGRAPHY

Adey, Peter, David Bissell, Kevin Hannam, Peter Merriman, and Mimi Sheller. 2014. Introduction. In *The Routledge Handbook of Mobilities,* edited by Peter Adey, David Bissell, Kevin Hannam, Peter Merriman, and Mimi Sheller, 1–20. New York: Routledge.

Akama, John S. 1999. "The Evolution of Tourism in Kenya." *Journal of Sustainable Tourism* 7: 6–25.

———. 2002. "The Role of Government in the Development of Tourism in Kenya." *International Journal of Tourism Research* 4: 1–13.

Alila, Patrick O., and Dorothy McCormick. 1999. "Firm Linkages in Kenya's Tourism Sector." Discussion Paper No. 297. Nairobi: Institute for Development Studies, University of Nairobi.

Allen, James de Ver. 1993. *Swahili Origins: Swahili Culture and the Shungwaya Phenomenon.* London: James Currey.

AMREF (African Medical and Research Foundation). 1999. *Mombasa District Participatory Poverty Assessment.* Nairobi: AMREF.

"The Anti-corruption Collapse." 2006. *Africa Confidential* 47 (21): 1–3.

Appadurai, Arjun, ed. 1986. *The Social Life of Things: Commodities in Cultural Perspective.* Cambridge, UK: Cambridge University Press.

Archambault, Julie. 2013. "Cruising through Uncertainty: Cell Phones and the Politics of Display and Disguise in Inhambane, Mozambique." *American Ethnologist* 40 (1): 88–101.

Arens, William. 1975. "The Waswahili: The Social History of an Ethnic Group." *Africa* 45 (4): 426–38.

———. 1976. "Changing Patterns of Ethnic Identity and Prestige in East Africa." In *A Century of Change in Eastern Africa,* edited by William Arens, 65–76. Paris: Mouton.

Ballestero, Andrea. 2012. "Transparency in Triads." *PoLAR: Political and Legal Anthropology Review* 35 (2): 160–66.

Barasa, Lucas. 2007. "Tourism to Get Boost." *Daily Nation,* March 15.

Barkan, Joel D., ed. 1984. *Politics and Public Policy in Kenya and Tanzania.* Rev. ed. New York: Praeger.

———. 1993. "Kenya: Lessons from a Flawed Election." *Journal of Democracy* 4 (3): 85–99.

———. 1998. "Toward a New Constitutional Framework in Kenya." *Africa Today* 45 (2): 213–26.

———. 2004. "Kenya After Moi." *Foreign Affairs* 83: 87–100.

Barkan, Joel D., and Njuguna Ng'ethe. 1998. "Kenya Tries Again." *Journal of Democracy* 9 (2): 32–48.

Barnett, Clive, Paul Cloke, Nick Clarke, and Alice Malpass. 2010. *Globalizing Responsibility: The Political Rationalities of Ethical Consumption.* Malden, MA: Wiley-Blackwell.

Bascom, William. 1976. "Changing African Art." In *Ethnic and Tourist Arts: Cultural Expressions from the Fourth World,* edited by Nelson Graburn, 303–19. Berkeley: University of California Press.

Beck, Ulrich. 1992. *Risk Society: Towards a New Modernity.* London: Newbury Park.

———. 2000. *The Brave New World of Work.* Cambridge, UK: Polity.

Behrend, Heike. 2000. "Feeling Global: The Likoni Ferry Photographers of Mombasa, Kenya." *African Arts* 33: 70–79.

Belcher, Brian, Anthony Cunningham, and Bruce Campbell. 2005. "Livelihoods, Carving and Conservation." In *Carving Out a Future: Forests, Livelihoods and the International Woodcarving Trade,* edited by Brian Belcher, Anthony Cunningham, and Bruce Campbell, 1–9. London: Earthscan.

Berg, F. J. 1968. "The Swahili Community of Mombasa, 1500–1900." *Journal of African History* 9: 35–56.

Bernard, H. Russell. 2002. *Research Methods in Anthropology: Qualitative and Quantitative Methods.* 3rd ed. New York: Altamira Press.

Bessire, Dominique. 2005. "Transparency: A Two Way Mirror?" *International Journal of Social Economics* 32 (2): 424–38.

Biebuyck, Daniel P, ed. 1969. *Tradition and Creativity in Tribal Art.* Berkeley: University of California Press.

Bond, Patrick. 2014. "Africa Rising? Afro-Optimism and Uncivil Society in an Era of Economic Volatility." In *The Handbook of Civil Society in Africa,* edited by Ebenezer Obadare, 233–51. New York: Springer.

Bowen, M. K. 1999. "Risk as a Constraint to Micro-Enterprise Growth." IDS Working Paper No. 522. Nairobi: Institute for Development Studies, University of Nairobi.

Branch, Daniel. 2011. *Kenya: Between Hope and Despair, 1963–2011.* New Haven, CT: Yale University Press.

Brantley, Cynthia. 1981. *The Giriama and Colonial Resistance in Kenya, 1800–1920.* Berkeley: University of California Press.

Bravman, Bill. 1998. *Making Ethnic Ways: Communities and Their Transformations in Taita, Kenya, 1800–1950.* Portsmouth, NH: Heinemann.

Bright, Jake, and Aubrey Hruby. 2015. *The Next Africa: An Emerging Continent Becomes a Global Powerhouse.* New York: Thomas Dunne.

Bruijn, Mirjam de, and Rijk van Dijk. 2012. "Connectivity and the Postglobal Moment: (Dis)connections and Social Change in Africa." In *The Social Life of Connectivity in Africa,* edited by Mirjam de Bruijn and Rijk van Dijk, 1–20. New York: Palgrave Macmillan.

Bruner, Edward M. 1991. "Transformation of Self in Tourism." *Annals of Tourism Research* 18 (2): 238–50.

———. 2001. "The Maasai and the *Lion King*: Authenticity, Nationalism, and Globalization in African Tourism." *American Ethnologist* 28 (4): 881–908.

Bruner, Edward M., and Barbara Kirshenblatt-Gimblett. 1994. "Maasai on the Lawn: Tourist Realism in East Africa." *Cultural Anthropology* 9 (4): 435–70.

Buluku, Allan. 2005. "Help Artisans Improve Skills, Govt Urged." *Coast Express,* March 18.

Burrell, Jenna. 2008. "Problematic Empowerment: West African Internet Scams as Strategic Misrepresentation." *Information Technologies and International Development* 4 (4): 15–30.

———. 2012 *Invisible Users: Youth in the Internet Cafés of Urban Ghana.* Cambridge, MA: MIT Press.

Burrell, Jenna, and Ken Anderson. 2008. "'I Have Great Desires to Look beyond My World': Trajectories of Information and Communication Technology Use among Ghanaians Living Abroad." *New Media and Society* 10 (2): 203–24.

Caldeira, Teresa. 2000. *City of Walls: Crime, Segregation, and Citizenship in São Paulo.* Berkeley: University of California Press.

Caplan, Patricia. 2004. Introduction. In *Swahili Modernities: Culture, Politics, and Identity on the East Coast of Africa,* edited by Patricia Caplan and Farouk Topan, 1–18. Trenton, NJ: Africa World Press.

Carrier, Neil. 2005. "The Need for Speed: Contrasting Timeframes in the Social Life of Kenyan Miraa." *Africa* 75 (4): 539–58.

Carrier, James, and Peter Luetchford, eds. 2015. *Ethical Consumption: Social Value and Economic Practice.* New York: Berghahn.

"Celtel Raises the Stakes in Tariff War." 2007. *Daily Nation,* May 15.

Chabal, Patrick, and Jean-Pascal Daloz. 1999. *Africa Works: Disorder as Political Instrument.* Oxford: James Currey.

Chepaitis, Elia V. 2002. "Soft Barriers to ICT Application in Development: Trust and Information Quality in Russia." *Journal of International Development* 14: 51–60.

Chibnik, Michael. 2003. *Crafting Tradition: The Making and Unmaking of Oaxacan Wood Carvings.* Austin: University of Texas Press.

Choge, Simon K. 2002. "Study of the Economic Aspects of the Woodcarving Industry in Kenya: Implications for Policy Development to Make the Industry More Sustainable." MSc thesis, University of Natal, Durban, South Africa.

Choge, Simon K., Anthony Cunningham, and William Ellery. 2005. "Chasing the Wooden Rhino: The Case of Woodcarving in Kenya." In *Carving Out a Future:*

Forests, Livelihoods and the International Woodcarving Trade, edited by Anthony Cunningham, Brian Belcher, and Bruce Campbell. London: Earthscan.

Chowdhury, Shyamal K. 2006. "Investments in ICT-Capital and Economic Performance of Small and Medium Scale Enterprises in East Africa." *Journal of International Development* 18: 533–52.

Chowdhury, Shyamal K., and Susanne Wolf. 2003. "Use of ICTs and the Economic Performance of SMEs in East Africa." Discussion Paper No. 2003/06. Helsinki: United Nations University, World Institute for Development Economics Research.

Clark, Gracia. 1988. Introduction. In *Traders Versus the State: Anthropological Approaches to Unofficial Economies,* edited by Gracia Clark. Boulder, CO: Westview Press.

Clifford, James. 1988. *The Predicament of Culture.* Cambridge, MA: Harvard University Press.

Coleman, Gabriella. 2010. "Ethnographic Approaches to Digital Media." *Annual Review of Anthropology* 39: 487–505.

Comaroff, John L., and Jean Comaroff. 2009. *Ethnicity, Inc.* Chicago: University of Chicago Press.

Cooper, Frederick. 1977. *Plantation Slavery on the East Coast of Africa.* New Haven, CT: Yale University Press.

———. 1980. *From Slaves to Squatters: Plantation Labor and Agriculture in Zanzibar and Coastal Kenya, 1890–1925.* New Haven, CT: Yale University Press.

———. 1987. *On the African Waterfront: Urban Disorder and the Transformation of Work in Colonial Mombasa.* New Haven, CT: Yale University Press.

———. 2001. "What is the Concept of Globalization Good For? An African Historian's Perspective." *African Affairs* 100: 189–213.

———. 2002. *Africa Since 1940: The Past of the Present.* Cambridge, UK: Cambridge University Press.

Crick, Malcolm. 1989. "Representations of International Tourism in the Social Sciences: Sun, Sex, Sights, Savings, and Servility." *Annual Review of Anthropology* 18: 307–44.

Crowley, Daniel J. 1970. "The Contemporary-Traditional Art Market in Africa." *African Arts* 4 (1): 43–49, 80.

Cunningham, Anthony. 2005. "Global Overview: Tradition, Technology and Trade." In *Carving Out a Future: Forests, Livelihoods and the International Woodcarving Trade,* edited by Anthony Cunningham, Brian Belcher, and Bruce Campbell, 11–29. London: Earthscan.

Cunningham, Anthony, Bruce Campbell, Brian Belcher, and Ramadhani Achdiaman. 2005. "Ecological Footprints: Carving, Sustainability and Scarcity." In *Carving Out a Future: Forests, Livelihoods and the International Woodcarving Trade,* edited by Anthony Cunningham, Brian Belcher, and Bruce Campbell, 199–228. London: Earthscan.

Dabiri, Emma. 2014. "Why I'm Not an Afropolitan." *Africa Is a Country,* January 21. http://africasacountry.com/why-im-not-an-afropolitan/.

Daniels, Lisa. 1999. "The Role of Small Enterprises in the Household and National Economy in Kenya: A Significant Contribution or a Last Resort?" *World Development* 27: 55–65.

Davis, Elizabeth A. 1999. "Metamorphosis in the Culture Market of Niger." *American Anthropologist* 101 (3): 485–501.

De Blij, Harm J. 1968. *Mombasa: An African City*. Chicago: Northwestern University Press.

Deuze, Mark. 2007. *Media Work*. Cambridge, UK: Polity.

Donner, Jonathan. 2006. "The Use of Mobile Phones by Microentrepreneurs in Kigali, Rwanda: Changes to Social and Business Networks." *Information Technologies and International Development* 3 (2): 3–19.

Donner, Jonathan, and Marcela X. Escobari. 2010. "A Review of Evidence on Mobile Use by Micro and Small Enterprises in Developing Countries." *Journal of International Development* 22: 641–58.

Douglas, Mary, and Aaron Wildavsky. 1982. *Risk and Culture: An Essay on the Selection of Technological and Environmental Dangers*. Berkeley: University of California Press.

Eastman, Carol. 1971. "Who Are the Waswahili?" *Africa* 41 (3): 228–36.

———. 1995. "Tourism in Kenya and the Marginalization of Swahili." *Annals of Tourism Research* 22 (1): 172–85.

Elkan, Walter. 1958. "The East African Trade in Woodcarvings." *Africa* 28 (4): 314–23.

Ellis, Stephen. 2011a. *Season of Rains: Africa in the World*. Chicago: University of Chicago Press.

———. 2011b. "Africa: Progress and Risk." *OpenDemocracy*, May 24. www.opendemocracy.net/stephen-ellis/africa-progress-and-risk.

Elyachar, Julia. 2002. "Empowerment Money: The World Bank, Non-Governmental Organizations, and the Value of Culture in Egypt." *Public Culture* 14 (3): 493–513.

Esselaar, Steve, Christoph Stork, Ali Ndiwalana, and Mariama Deen-Swarray. 2007. "ICT Usage and Its Impact on Profitability of SMEs in 13 African Countries." *Information Technologies and International Development* 4 (1): 87–100.

Eze, Chielozona. 2014. "Rethinking African Culture and Identity: The Afropolitan Model." *Journal of African Cultural Studies* 26 (2): 234–47.

Ferguson, James. 2002. "Global Disconnect: Abjection and the Aftermath of Modernism." In *The Anthropology of Globalization: A Reader,* edited by J. X. Inda and R. Rosaldo, 136–53. Malden, MA: Blackwell.

———. 2004 "Power Topographies." In *A Companion to the Anthropology of Politics,* edited by David Nugent and Joan Vincent, 383–99. Malden, MA: Blackwell.

Ferrand, David. 1996. "A Study of the Missing Middle in Kenya." IDS Working Paper No. 515. Nairobi: Institute for Development Studies, University of Nairobi.

Gaitho, Macharia. 2002. "Tribal Violence Looms at the Coast." *Daily Nation,* February 26.

Gaonkar, Dilip Parameshwar, and Robert J. McCarthy, Jr. 1994. "Panopticism and Publicity: Bentham's Quest for Transparency." *Public Culture* 6 (3): 547–75.

Geschiere, Peter. 1997. *The Modernity of Witchcraft: Politics and the Occult in Postcolonial Africa*. Charlottesville: University Press of Virginia.

———. 2009. *The Perils of Belonging: Autochthony, Citizenship, and Exclusion in Africa and Europe*. Chicago: University of Chicago Press.

Gettleman, Jeffrey. 2007. "Tribal Rivalry Boils Over after Kenyan Election." *New York Times*, December 30.

———. 2008. "Kenya, Known for Its Stability, Topples into Post-election Chaos." *New York Times,* January 3, 2008.

Giddens, Anthony. 1991. *Modernity and Self-Identity: Self and Society in the Late Modern Age*. Stanford, CA: Stanford University Press.

Ginsburg, Faye. 2012. "Disability in the Digital Age." In *Digital Anthropology,* edited by Heather Horst and Dan Miller, 101–26. London: Bloomsbury.

Glick Schiller, Nina, and Noel B. Salazar. 2013. "Regimes of Mobility across the Globe." *Journal of Ethnic and Migration Studies* 39 (2): 183–200.

Goggin, Gerald, and Christopher Newell. 2003. *Digital Disability: The Social Construction of Disability in New Media*. New York: Rowman and Littlefield.

Goldsmith, Paul. 2014. "Constitutional Reform and Minority Exclusion: The Case of the Bajuni and Lamu County." In *Indigenous Peoples in Africa: Contestations, Empowerment and Group Rights,* edited by Ridwan Laher and Korir Sing'Oei, 85–103. Pretoria: Africa Institute of South Africa.

Goldstein, Daniel. 2016. *Owners of the Sidewalk: Security and Survival in the Informal City*. Durham, NC: Duke University Press.

Graburn, Nelson, ed. 1976. *Ethnic and Tourist Arts: Cultural Expressions from the Fourth World*. Berkeley: University of California Press.

"Growth of the Economy Is Laudable, But . . ." 2006. Editorial. *The Standard,* May 26, 12.

Hannam, Kevin, Mimi Sheller, and John Urry. 2006. Editorial: "Mobilities, Immobilities, and Moorings." *Mobilities* 1 (1): 1–22.

Hansen, Karen Tranberg. 2014. Introduction. *City and Society* 26 (2): 150–52.

Hansen, Karen Tranberg, and Mariken Vaa. 2004. Introduction. In *Reconsidering Informality: Perspectives from Urban Africa,* edited by Karen Tranberg Hansen and Mariken Vaa, 7–24. Uppsala: Nordiska Afrikainstitutet.

Harbeson, John W. 1998. "Political Crisis and Renewal in Kenya: Prospects for Democratic Consolidation." *Africa Today* 45 (2): 161–83.

Hart, Keith. 1973. "Informal Income Opportunities and Urban Employment in Ghana." *Journal of Modern African Studies* 11: 61–89.

———. 1992. *Market and State after the Cold War: The Informal Economy Revisited. In Contesting Markets: Analyses of Ideology, Discourse, and Practice*. Edinburgh: Edinburgh University Press.

Harvey, David. 1989. *The Condition of Postmodernity*. Oxford: Blackwell.

———. 2005. *A Brief History of Neoliberalism*. Oxford: Oxford University Press.

Haugerud, Angelique. 1995. *The Culture of Politics in Modern Kenya*. Cambridge, UK: Cambridge University Press.

Haugerud, Angelique, M. Priscilla Stone, and Peter Little, eds. 2000. *Commodities and Globalization: Anthropological Perspectives*. Lanham, MD: Rowman and Littlefield.

"The Hawks Are Circling." 2006. *Africa Confidential* 47 (4): 1–2.

Heeks, Richard. 2002. "i-Development not e-Development." Special Issue on ICTs and Development. *Journal of International Development* 14: 1–11.

Hetherington, Kregg. 2011. *Guerilla Auditors: The Politics of Transparency in Neoliberal Paraguay*. Durham, NC: Duke University Press

———. 2012. "Agency, Scale, and the Ethnography of Transparency." *PoLAR: Political and Legal Anthropology Review* 35 (2): 242–47.

Hodgson, Dorothy. 2001. *Once Intrepid Warriors: Gender, Ethnicity, and the Cultural Politics of Maasai Ethnicity*. Bloomington, IN: Indiana University Press.

Hodgson, Dorothy, and Sheryl McCurdy, eds. 2001. *"Wicked" Women and the Reconfiguration of Gender in Africa*. Portsmouth, NH: Heinemann.

Holmquist, Frank, and Michael Ford. 1998. "Kenyan Politics: Toward a Second Transition?" *Africa Today* 45 (2): 227–58.

Horst, Heather A., and Daniel Miller. 2006. *The Cell Phone: An Anthropology of Communication*. New York: Berg.

———. 2012. "Normativity and Materiality: A View from Digital Anthropology." *Media International Australia* 145: 103–11.

Horton, Mark, and John Middleton. 2000. *The Swahili: The Social Landscape of a Mercantile Society*. Malden, MA: Blackwell.

HRW (Human Rights Watch). 2002. *Playing with Fire: Weapons Proliferation, Political Violence, and Human Rights in Kenya*. New York: Human Rights Watch.

ILO (International Labour Organization). 1972. *Employment, Incomes and Equality: A Strategy for Increasing Productive Employment in Kenya*. Geneva: International Labour Organization.

Jagun, Abi, Richard Heeks, and Jason Whalley. 2008. "The Impact of Mobile Telephony on Developing Country Micro-Enterprise: A Nigerian Case Study." *Information Technologies and International Development* 4 (4): 47–65.

Jensen, Robert. 2007. "The Digital Divide: Information (Technology), Market Performance, and Welfare in the South Indian Fisheries Sector." *Quarterly Journal of Economics* 122 (3): 879–924.

Jules-Rosette, Bennetta. 1984. *The Messages of Tourist Art: An African Semiotic System in Comparative Perspective*. New York: Plenum Press.

Kabecha, Wanjau wa. 1999. "Technological Capability of the Micro-enterprises in Kenya's Informal Economy." *Technovation* 19: 117–26.

Kamga, Osee. 2006. "Mobile Phone in Cote d'Ivoire: Uses and Self-fulfillment." Paper presented at the International Conference on Information and Communication Technologies and Development, Berkeley, CA, May 25–26.

Kanogo, Tabitha, and Robert M. Maxon. 1992. "Co-operatives." In *An Economic History of Kenya*, edited by W. R. Ochieng' and R. M. Maxon. Nairobi: East African Educational Publishers.

Kanyinga, Karuti. 2000. *Re-distribution from Above: The Politics of Land Rights and Squatting in Coastal Kenya*. Uppsala: Nordiska Afrikainstitutet.

Kareithi, Samuel. 2003. "Coping with Declining Tourism, Examples from Communities in Kenya." PPT Working Paper No. 13. Pro-Poor Tourism Partnership. https://www.odi.org/sites/odi.org.uk/files/odi-assets/publications-opinion-files/4030.pdf.

Karp, Ivan. 2002. "Development and Personhood: Tracing the Contours of a Moral Discourse." In *Critically Modern: Alternatives, Alterities, Anthropologies*, edited by Bruce Knauft, 82–104. Bloomington: Indiana University Press.

Kaplan, Caren. 1995. "'A World without Boundaries': The Body Shop's Trans/National Geographics." *Social Text* (43): 45–66.

Kasfir, Sidney L. 1996. "African Art in a Suitcase." *Transition* 69: 146–58.

———. 1999a. *Contemporary African Art*. London: Thames and Hudson.

———. 1999b. "Samburu Souvenirs: Representations of a Land in Amber." In *Unpacking Culture: Art and Commodity in Colonial and Postcolonial Worlds*, edited by Ruth Phillips and Christopher B. Steiner, 67–83. Berkeley: University of California Press.

———. 2004. "Tourist Aesthetics in the Global Flow: Orientalism and 'Warrior Theatre' on the Swahili Coast." *Visual Anthropology* 17 (3/4): 319–43.

———. 2007. *African Art and the Colonial Encounter: Inventing a Global Commodity*. Bloomington: Indiana University Press.

Kazungu, Nyabonyi. 2006. "State and Business Community at Loggerheads over New Requirement for Tax Collection." *Daily Nation*, April 2, 15.

Kenya, Republic of. 1992. Sessional Paper No. 2 of 1992 on "Small Enterprises and Jua Kali Development in Kenya." Nairobi: Government Printer.

———. 2002. *National Development Plan 2002–2008*. Nairobi: Government Printer.

———. 2003. *Economic Survey 2003*. Nairobi: Government Printer.

———. 2004–2005. *Mombasa District Monitoring and Evaluation Report*. Mombasa: Ministry of Planning and National Development.

———. 2005a. *Economic Survey 2005*. Nairobi: Government Printer.

———. 2005b. Sessional Paper No. 2 of 2005 on "Development of Micro and Small Enterprises for Wealth and Employment Creation for Poverty Reduction." Nairobi: Government Printer.

———. 2014. *Economic Survey 2014*. Nairobi: Government Printer.

Kiai, Maina. 1998. Commentary: "A Last Chance for Peaceful Change in Kenya?" *Africa Today* 45 (2): 185–92.

Kibua, Thomas N., and Benjamin K. Nzioki. 2004. "Are Export Processing Zones Relevant in a Liberalized Environment? The Kenyan Case." IPAR Discussion Paper Series, Discussion Paper No. 45. Nairobi: Institute of Policy Analysis and Research.

Kimambo, Isaria N. 1970. "The Economic History of the Kamba, 1850–1950." In *Hadith 2*, edited by Bethel A. Ogot, 79–99. Nairobi: East African Publishing House.

King, Kenneth. 1996. *Jua Kali Kenya: Change and Development in an Informal Economy: 1970–1995*. Athens: Ohio University Press.

Kingdon, Zachary. 2005. "Sculpture and Identity: The Makonde African Blackwood Carving Movement." In *Carving Out a Future: Forests, Livelihoods and the International Woodcarving Trade*, edited by Anthony Cunningham, Brian Belcher, and Bruce Campbell, 53–65. London: Earthscan.

"Kiosk Demolitions Well-Calculated." 2001. Letter to editor. *Daily Nation*, December 31, 10.

Kirkman, James. 1983. "The Muzungulos of Mombasa." *International Journal of African Historical Studies* 16: 73–82.

Kitching, Gavin. 1980. *Class and Economic Change in Kenya: The Making of an African Petite Bourgeoisie 1905–1970*. New Haven, CT: Yale University Press.

Kithi, Ngumbao. 2002. "Millions Lost as Squad Pulls Down More Kiosks." *Daily Nation*, January 15.

———. 2006. "Mombasa Hub for Human Trafficking." *Daily Nation*, November 24.

Klein, Naomi. 2002. *No Logo*. New York: Picador.

Klopp, Jacqueline. 2000. "Pilfering the Public: The Problem of Land Grabbing in Contemporary Kenya." *Africa Today* 47: 7–26.

"Knocking Out the Lion's Teeth." 2006. *Africa Confidential* 47 (25): 1–2.

Krapf, J. L. 1860. *Travels, Researches, and Missionary Labours in Eastern Africa*. London: Trubner.

Larkin, Lance L. 2011. "Carving the Nation: Zimbabwean Sculptors and the Contested Heritage of Aesthetics." In *Contested Cultural Heritage: Religion, Nationalism, Erasure, and Exclusion in a Global World*, edited by Helaine Silverman, 233–59. New York: Springer.

Lemma, Salome. 2013. "Against the Gospel of 'Africa Rising.'" *Africa Is a Country*, November 6. http://africasacountry.com/2013/11/against-the-gospel-of-africa-rising/.

Lewellen, Ted. 2002. *The Anthropology of Globalization: Cultural Anthropology Enters the 21st Century*. London: Bergin and Garvey.

Lewis, Tania, and Emily Potter, eds. 2010. *Ethical Consumption: A Critical Introduction*. London: Routledge.

Leys, Colin. 1975. *Underdevelopment in Kenya: The Political Economy of Neo-Colonialism*. London: Heinemann.

Lindblom, Gerhard. 1920. *The Akamba in British East Africa: An Ethnological Monograph*. Uppsala: Appelbergs Boktryckeri Aktiebolag.

LiPuma, Edward, and Benjamin Lee. 2004. *Financial Derivatives and the Globalization of Risk*. Durham, NC: Duke University Press.

Low, William, and Eileen Davenport. 2005. "Postcards from the Edge: Maintaining the 'Alternative' Character of Fair Trade." *Sustainable Development* 13: 143–53.

Lynch, Gabrielle. 2011. *I Say to You: Ethnic Politics and the Kalenjin in Kenya*. Chicago: University of Chicago Press.

MacCannell, Dean. 1976. *The Tourist: A New Theory of the Leisure Class*. New York: Schocken Books.

MacGaffey, Janet, and Rémy Bazenguissa-Ganga. 2000. *Congo-Paris: Transnational Traders on the Margins of the Law*. Oxford: James Currey.

Macharia, Kinuthia. 1993. *The Informal African City and the Development of Jua Kali Associations: Whither Way?* Nairobi: Institute for Development Studies, University of Nairobi.

———. 1997. *Social and Political Dynamics of the Informal Economy in African Cities: Nairobi and Harare*. New York: University Press of America.

Mahajan, Vijay. 2008. *Africa Rising: How 900 Million African Consumers Offer More Than You Think*. Upper Saddle River, NJ: Pearson Prentice Hall.

Mahoney, Dillon. 2012. "Changing Strategies in marketing Kenya's Tourist Art: From Ethnic Brands to Fair Trade Labels." *African Studies Review* 55 (1): 161–90.

———. 2016. "Mobilities and Risks in Coastal Kenya: Jumping Scales versus Staying Local." *PoLAR: Political and Legal Anthropology Review* 39 (2): 176–89.

Manda, Damiano Kulundu, and Kunal Sen. 2004. "The Labour Market Effects of Globalization in Kenya." *Journal of International Development* 16: 29–43.

Marcus, George, and Michael M. J. Fischer. 1986. *Anthropology as Cultural Critique: An Experimental Moment in the Human Sciences*. Chicago: University of Chicago Press.

Marcus, George, and Fred Myers, eds. 1995. *The Traffic in Culture: Refiguring Art and Anthropology*. Berkeley, CA: University of California Press.

Mas, Ignacio, and Dan Radcliffe (Bill and Melinda Gates Foundation). 2010. "Mobile Payments Go Viral: M-PESA in Kenya." Part 2. *Capco Institute Journal of Financial Transformation* 32 (August), 171–82. http://52.16.200.48/uploads/articlefiles/261/file_0_1420722663.pdf.

Matthews, Paul. 2007. "ICT Assimilation and SME Expansion." *Journal of International Development* 19: 817–27.

Maurer, Bill. 2012. "Mobile Money: Communication, Consumption and Change in the Payments Space." *Journal of Development Studies* 48 (5): 589–604.

Mayoyo, Patrick, and Dominic Wabala. 2006. "Alarm over Port Fraud and Drug Smugglers." *Daily Nation*, January 8, 1–2.

Mazrui, Alamin M., and Ibrahim Noor Shariff. 1994. *The Swahili: Idiom and Identity of an African People*. Trenton, NJ: Africa World Press.

Mazzarella, William. 2010. "Beautiful Balloon: The Digital Divide and the Charisma of New Media in India." *American Ethnologist* 37 (4): 783–804.

Mbembe, Achille. 2007. "Afropolitanism." In *Africa Remix: Contemporary Art of a Continent*, edited by Simon Njami, 26–30. Johannesburg: Johannesburg Art Gallery.

McChesney, Robert. 2000. "So Much for the Magic of Technology and the Free Market: The World Wide Web and the Corporate Media System." In *The World*

Wide Web and Contemporary Cultural Theory, edited by Andrew Herman and Thomas Swiss, 5–35. New York: Routledge.

McCormick, Dorothy. 1987. "Fundis and Formality: Very Small Manufacturers in Nairobi." In *The Political Economy of Kenya,* edited by M. G. Schatzberg. New York: Praeger.

———. 1993. "Risk and Firm Growth: The Dilemma of Nairobi's Small-scale Manufacturers." Discussion Paper No. 291. Nairobi: Institute for Development Studies, University of Nairobi.

McIntosh, Janet. 2005. "Baptismal Essentialisms: Giriama Code Choice and the Reification of Ethnoreligious Boundaries." *Journal of Linguistic Anthropology* 15 (2): 151–70.

———. 2009. *The Edge of Islam: Power, Personhood, and Ethnoreligious Boundaries on the Kenyan Coast.* Durham, NC: Duke University Press.

———. 2010. "Mobile Phones and Mopoho's Prophecy: The Powers and Dangers of Flying Language." *American Ethnologist* 37 (2): 337–53.

M'Closkey, Kathy. 2000. "Part-Time for Pin-Money." In *Artisans and Cooperatives: Developing Alternative Trade for the Global Economy,* edited by Kimberly M. Grimes and B. Lynne Milgram, 143–58. Tucson: University of Arizona Press.

Meiu, George. 2011. "On Difference, Desire and the Aesthetics of the Unexpected: The *White Masai* in Kenyan Tourism." In *Great Expectations: Imagination and Anticipation in Tourism,* Jonathan Skinner and Dimitrios Theodossopoulos, 96–115. New York: Berghahn Books.

Middleton, John. 1992. *The World of the Swahili: An African Mercantile Civilization.* New Haven, CT: Yale University Press.

Migiro, Stephen O. 2006. "Diffusion of ICTs and E-Commerce Adoption in Manufacturing SMEs in Kenya." *South African Journal of Libraries and Information Science* 72 (1): 35–44.

Miller, Charles. 1971. *The Lunatic Express: An Entertainment in Imperialism.* New York: Macmillan.

Miller, Daniel, and Don Slater. 2000. *The Internet: An Ethnographic Approach.* Oxford: Berg.

Miller, Judith von Daler. 1975. *Art in East Africa: A Guide to Contemporary Art.* New York: Africana (Holmes and Meier).

Miller, Norman, and Rodger Yeager. 1994. *Kenya: The Quest for Prosperity.* 2nd ed. Boulder, CO: Westview Press.

Mintz, Sidney W. 1985. *Sweetness and Power: The Place of Sugar in Modern History.* New York: Viking Penguin.

Molony, Thomas. 2007. "'I Don't Trust the Phone; It Always Lies': Trust and Information and Communication Technologies in Tanzanian Micro and Small Enterprises." *Information Technologies and International Development* 3 (4): 67–83.

———. 2008. "Nondevelopmental Uses of Mobile Communication in Tanzania." In *Handbook of Mobile Communication Studies,* edited by James E. Katz, 339–51. Cambridge, MA: MIT Press.

————. 2009a. "Carving and Niche: ICT, Social Capital, and Trust in the Shift from Personal to Impersonal Trading in Tanzania." *Information Technology for Development* 15 (4): 283–301.

————. 2009b. "Trading Places in Tanzania: Mobility and Marginalisation at a Time of Travel-saving Technologies." In *Mobile Phones: The New Talking Drums of Everyday Africa,* edited by M. de Bruijn, F. Nyamnjoh, and I. Brinkman, 92–109. Leiden, NL: African Studies Centre.

Morton, Fred. 1990. *Children of Ham: Freed Slaves and Fugitive Slaves on the Kenya Coast, 1873–1907.* Boulder, CO: Westview Press.

Morton, R. F. 1972. "The Shungwaya Myth of Miji Kenda Origins: A Problem of Late Nineteenth-Century Kenya Coastal History." *International Journal of African Historical Studies* 5 (3): 397–423.

————. 1977. "New Evidence Regarding the Shungwaya Myth of Miji Kenda Origins." *International Journal of African Historical Studies* 10 (4): 628–43.

Mount, Marshall. 1973. *African Art: The Years Since 1920.* Bloomington: Indiana University Press.

Moyi, Eliud Dismas. 2003. "Networks, Information and Small Enterprises: New Technologies and the Ambiguity of Empowerment." *Information Technology for Development* 10: 221–32.

Mueller, Susanne D. 2008. "The Political Economy of Kenya's Crisis." *Journal of Eastern African Studies* 2 (2): 185–210.

Mugambi, Kaburu. 2007. "Tourism Again Tops in Foreign Earnings." *Daily Nation,* February 1.

Muiruri, Mary. 2007. "Kenya: Diffusion, Democracy, and Development." In *Negotiating the Net in Africa: the Politics of Internet Diffusion,* edited by E. J. Wilson and K. R. Wong, 65–84. Boulder, CO: Lynn Reinner.

Munene, Mugumo. 2006. "The 10 Per Cent Who Control Kenya's Riches." *Daily Nation,* May 23, 1.

Munro, J. Forbes. 1975. *Colonial Rule and the Kamba: Social Change in the Kenya Highlands 1889–1939.* Oxford, UK: Clarendon Press.

Muthuma, Elizabeth. 2012. "Do Co-operative Development Policies Really Lead to the Development of Co-operatives? Lessons from Kenya." *Africa Insight* 41 (4): 176–91.

Mutongi, Kenda. 2006. "Thugs or Entrepreneurs? Perceptions of Matatu Operators in Nairobi, 1970 to the Present." *Africa* 76 (4): 549–68.

Mutonya, Njuguna. 2002. "Nassir Era Ends in Humiliation." *Daily Nation,* December 29, 12.

"Mwai's Muddle." 2005. *Africa Confidential* 46 (25): 7.

Mwajefa, Mwakera. 2001a. "Minister Supervises Demolition of Kiosks." *Daily Nation,* December 23.

————. 2001b. "Youths Beat Kiosk Owners in Scuffle at Town Hall." *Daily Nation,* December 25, 3.

Mwajefa, Mwakera and Edmund Kwena. 2001. "Tension Rises over Demolition." *Daily Nation,* December 24, 6.

Mwesige, Peter. 2004. "Cyber Elites: A Survey of Internet Cafe Users in Uganda." *Telematics and Informatics* 21 (1): 83–101.

Nabende, Julius Simiyu, and Martha Wangari Musalia. 1999. "Muslims of Kenya: A Struggle for Identity and Participation." In *The Political Economy of Transition: A Study of Issues and Social Movements in Kenya since 1945*, edited by Eric M. Aseka, Julius S. Nabende, and Martha W. Musalia, 143–52. Nairobi: Eight Publishers.

Nash, June, ed. 1993. *Crafts in the World Markets: The Impact of Global Exchange on Middle American Artisans.* Albany, NY: SUNY Press.

Ndege, George Oduor. 1992. "Tourism in Kenya: Genesis, Growth and Impact." In *An Economic History of Kenya*, edited by W. R. Ochieng' and R. M. Maxon. Nairobi: East African Educational Publishers.

Nation Correspondent. 2007. "KRA Nets Traders over Cash Register." *Daily Nation*, April 6, 2007.

Nation Correspondents. 2002. "Nassir 'Clean-up' Now Targets Slum Dwellers." *Daily Nation*, February 25.

Nation Reporter. 2006. "Deadline on Tax Registers Still Jan. 31." *Daily Nation*, January 10, 21.

Nation Team. 2001a. "Chaos and Death as Kiosk Riots Shut Down Mombasa." *Daily Nation*, December 27.

———. 2001b. "Protests as Kiosks Clear-out Continues." *Daily Nation*, December 26.

———. 2002. "Action Group Plan for new Mombasa City." *Daily Nation*, January 2.

Ndegwa, Stephen N. 1997. "Citizenship and Ethnicity: An Examination of Two Transition Moments in Kenyan Politics." *American Political Science Review* 91 (3): 599–616.

———. 1998a. "The Incomplete Transition: The Constitutional and Electoral Context in Kenya." *Africa Today* 45 (2): 193–211.

———. 1998b. "Citizenship amid Economic and Political Change in Kenya." *Africa Today* 45 (3/4): 351–68.

Ndurya, Mazera. 2007. "Give Coast New Status, Urges KTB." *Daily Nation*, December 10, 2007.

Nelson, Edwin G., and Erik J. de Bruijn. 2005. "The Voluntary Formalization of Enterprises in a Developing Economy—The Case of Tanzania." *Journal of International Development* 17: 575–93.

NMK (National Museums of Kenya). 1990. *A Conservation Plan for the Old Town of Mombasa, Kenya.* Mombasa: Municipal Council of Mombasa, UNESCO, UNDP, and NMK.

Ntarangwi, Mwenda. 2003. *Gender, Identity, and Performance: Understanding Swahili Cultural Realities through Song.* Trenton, NJ: African World Press.

Nurse, Derek, and Thomas Hinnebusch. 1993. *Swahili and Sabaki: A Linguistic History.* Berkeley: University of California Press.

Nurse, Derek, and Thomas Spear. 1985. *The Swahili: Reconstructing the History and Language of an African Society, 800–1500.* Philadelphia: University of Pennsylvania Press.

Nyangira, Nicholas. 1987. "Ethnicity, Class, and Politics in Kenya." In *The Political Economy of Kenya,* edited by M. G. Schatzberg, 15–31. New York: Praeger.

Obara, Alex O., Martina G. Höft, and Robert Höft. 2005. "Neem (*Azadirachta indica,* A. Juss., Meliaceae) and Its Potentials for Sustainable Woodcarving: A Case Study from Malindi." In *Carving Out a Future: Forests, Livelihoods and the International Woodcarving Trade,* edited by Anthony Cunningham, Brian Belcher, and Bruce Campbell, 221. London: Earthscan.

Obunga, Raymond. 1995. *Sustainable Development of the Woodcarving Industry in Kenya.* Technical Project Report for the WWF/UNESCO/Kew People and Plants Initiative. Nairobi: National Museums of Kenya.

Oded, Arye. 2000. *Islam and Politics in Kenya.* Boulder, CO: Lynne Rienner.

Ogot, Bethel A., and John A. Kieran, eds. 1968. *Zamani: A Survey of East African History.* New York: Humanities Press.

Ombongi, Kenneth. 2005. "Radical Change in Mvita." In *The Moi Succession: The 2002 Elections in Kenya,* edited by Hervae Maupeu, Musambayi Katumanga, and Winnie Mitullah, 299–347. Nairobi: Transafrica Press.

Ondicho, Tom G. 1999. "International Tourism in Kenya: Development, Problems and Challenges." *Eastern Africa Social Science Research Review* 16: 49–69.

Orta, Andrew. 2013. "Managing the Margins: MBA Training, International Business, and 'the Value Chain of Culture.'" *American Ethnologist* 40 (4): 689–703.

Osborne, Myles. 2014. *Ethnicity and Empire in Kenya: Loyalty and Martial Race among the Kamba, c. 1800 to the Present.* New York: Cambridge University Press.

Oucho, John O. 2002. *Undercurrents of Ethnic Conflict in Kenya.* Boston: Brill.

Overå, Ragnhild. 2008. "Mobile Traders and Mobile Phones in Ghana." In *Handbook of Mobile Communication Studies,* edited by James E. Katz, 43–54. Cambridge, MA: MIT Press.

Parkin, David. 1972. *Palms, Wine, and Witnesses: Public Spirit and Private Gain in an African Farming Community.* Prospect Heights, IL: Waveland Press.

———. 1989. "Swahili Mijikenda: Facing Both Ways in Kenya." *Africa* 59 (2): 161–75.

Perry, Alex. 2011. "Silicon Savanna: Mobile Phones Transform Africa." *Time,* June 30. http://www.alex-perry.com/silicon-savanna-mobile-phones-transform-africa/.

Phillips, Ruth, and Christopher B. Steiner, eds. 1999a. *Unpacking Culture: Art and Commodity in Colonial and Postcolonial Worlds.* Berkeley: University of California Press.

———. 1999b. "Art, Authenticity, and the Baggage of Cultural Encounter." In *Unpacking Culture: Art and Commodity in Colonial and Postcolonial Worlds,* edited by Ruth Phillips and Christopher B. Steiner, 3–19. Berkeley: University of California Press.

"Phone Sects." 1999. *Africa Confidential* 40 (19): 3.

Poggiali, Lisa. 2016. "Seeing (From) Digital Peripheries: Technology and Transparency in Kenya's Silicon Savannah." *Cultural Anthropology* 31 (3): 387–411.

"Policy Makers Must Close Poor-Rich Gap." 2006. *The Standard,* May 24, 12.

Porter, Gina. 2012. "Mobile Phones, Livelihoods and the Poor in Sub-Saharan Africa: Review and Prospect." *Geography Compass* 6 (5): 241–59.

Porter, Gina, Kate Hampshire, Albert Abane, Elsbeth Robson, Alister Munthali, Mac Mashiri, and Augustine Tanle. 2010. "Moving Young Lives: Mobility, Immobility and Inter-generational Tensions in Urban Africa." *Geoforum* 41 (5): 796–804.

Pouwels, Randall Lee. 2001. "A Response to Spear on Early Swahili History." *International Journal of African Historical Studies* 34 (3): 639–46.

Prestholdt, Jeremy. 2004. "On the Global Repercussions of East African Consumerism." *American Historical Review* 109: 755–81.

———. 2008. *Domesticating the World: African Consumerism and the Genealogies of Globalization.* Berkeley: University of California Press.

Price, Sally. 1991. *Primitive Art in Civilized Places.* Chicago: University of Chicago Press.

———. 2007. "Into the Mainstream: Shifting Authenticities in Art." *American Ethnologist* 34 (4): 603–20.

Pruitt, Sharon, and Thomas Causey. 1993. "Art in Kenya." In *Kenya: The Land, the People, and the Nation,* edited by M. Azevedo. Durham, NC: Carolina Academic Press.

Rakodi, Carole, Rose Gatabaki-Kamau, and Nick Devas. 2000. "Poverty and Political Conflict in Mombasa." *Environment and Urbanization* 12: 153–70.

Rapley, John. (1996) 2002. *Understanding Development: Theory and Practice in the Third World.* Boulder, CO/London: Lynne Rienner.

Raynolds, Laura T., and Michael A. Long. 2007. "Fair/Alternative Trade: Historical and Empirical Dimensions." In *Fair Trade: The Challenges of Transforming Globalization,* edited by Laura T. Raynolds, Douglas L. Murray, and John Wilkinson, 15–32. London and New York: Routledge.

"The Real Digital Divide." 2005. *Economist,* March 10. http://www.economist.com/node/3742817.

Redfern, Paul. 1993. "Holidays in Kenya at Their Cheapest." *Daily Nation,* May 15, 11.

Redfern, Andy, and Paul Snedker. 2002. "Creating Market Opportunities for Small Enterprises: Experiences of the Fair Trade Movement." SEED Working Paper No. 30. Geneva: International Labour Office.

Reichman, Daniel. 2008. "Justice at a Price: Regulation and Alienation in the Global Economy." *PoLAR: Political and Legal Anthropology Review* 31 (1): 102–17.

Richards, Paul. 1998. *Fighting for the Rain Forest: War, Youth, Resources in Sierra Leone.* Oxford, UK: James Currey.

Roy, Anyana. 2005. "Urban Informality: Toward and Epistemology of Planning." *Journal of the American Planning Association* 71 (2): 147–58.

Rudra, Nita. 2008. *Globalization and the Race to the Bottom in Developing Countries: Who Really Gets Hurt?* Cambridge, UK: Cambridge University Press.

Salazar, Noel B. 2011. "The Power of Imagination in Transnational Mobilities." *Identities: Global Studies in Culture and Power* 18 (6): 576–98.

Salim, Ahmed Idha. 1970. "The Movement for 'Mwambao' or Coast Autonomy in Kenya, 1956–63." In *Hadith 2*, edited by Bethel A. Ogot, 212–28. Nairobi: East African Publishing House.

———. 1973. "The Swahili-Speaking Peoples of Kenya's Coast, 1895–1945." Nairobi: East African Publishing House.

Sassen, Saskia. 1998. *Globalization and Its Discontents.* New York: New Press.

Schatzberg, Michael G., ed. 1987. *The Political Economy of Kenya.* New York: Praeger.

Schmitt, Susanne F., and Anthony B. Cunningham. 2002. "Reducing the Ecological Footprint of the 'Wooden Rhino': The Case for Certification of Kenyan Woodcarvings." In *Tapping the Green Market: Certification and Management of Non-Timber Forest Products,* edited by Patricia Shanley, Alan R. Pierce, Sarah A. Laird, and S. Abraham Guillen, 259–64. London: Earthscan.

Schmitt, Susanne F., and David R. Maingi. 2005. "Certification of Woodcarving." In *Carving Out a Future: Forests, Livelihoods and the International Woodcarving Trade,* edited by Anthony Cunningham, Brian Belcher, and Bruce Campbell, 229–48. London: Earthscan.

Sheller, Mimi and John Urry, eds. 2006. *Mobile Technologies of the City.* London: Routledge.

Sheriff, Abdul. 1987. *Slaves, Spices and Ivory in Zanzibar: Integration of an East African Commercial Empire into the World Economy, 1700–1873.* London: James Currey.

Simone, Abdou Maliq. 2001. "On the Worlding of African Cities." *African Studies Review* 44 (2): 15–41.

Simpson, Kate. 2004. "'Doing Development': The Gap Year, Volunteer-Tourists and a Popular Practice of Development." *Journal of International Development* 16 (5): 681–92.

Sindiga, Isaac. 1996. "Domestic Tourism in Kenya." *Annals of Tourism Research* 23 (1): 19–31.

———. 1999. "Tourism." In *Kenya Coast Handbook: Culture, Resources, and Development in the East African Littoral,* edited by J. Hoorweg, D. Foeken, and R. A. Obudho. 223–36 New Brunswick, NJ: Transaction.

Smith, Daniel Jordan. 2006. "Cell Phones, Social Inequality, and Contemporary Culture in Nigeria." *Canadian Journal of African Studies* 40 (3): 496–523.

———. 2007. *A Culture of Corruption: Everyday Deception and Popular Discontent in Nigeria.* Princeton, NJ: Princeton University Press.

Smith, James H. 2008. *Bewitching Development: Witchcraft and the Reinvention of Development in Neoliberal Kenya.* Chicago: University of Chicago Press.

Smith, Neil. 1993. "Homeless/Global: Scaling Places." In *Mapping the Futures: Local Cultures, Global Change,* edited by John Bird, Barry Curtis, Tim Putnam, George Robertson, and Lisa Tickner, 87–119. London: Routledge.

Spear, Thomas. 1978. *The Kaya Complex: A History of the Mijikenda Peoples of the Kenya Coast to 1900.* Nairobi: Kenya Literature Bureau.

———. 1981. "Traditions of Origin and Their Interpretation: The Mijikenda of Kenya." Papers in International Studies, Africa Series No. 42. Athens: Ohio University, Center for International Studies.

————. 2000. "Early Swahili History Reconsidered." *International Journal of African Historical Studies* 33 (2): 257–90.

Spear, Thomas, and Richard Waller, eds. 1993. *Being Maasai: Ethnicity and Identity in East Africa*. London: James Currey.

Steiner, Christopher B. 1994. *African Art in Transit*. Cambridge, UK: Cambridge University Press.

————. 1995. "The Art of the Trade: On the Creation of Value and Authenticity in the African Art Market." In *The Traffic in Culture: Refiguring Art and Anthropology*, edited by George Marcus and Fred Myers, 151–65. Berkeley: University of California Press.

————. 1996. "Discovering African Art ... Again?" *African Arts* 29 (4): 1–5, 93.

Steinhart, Edward I. 2000. "Elephant Hunting in 19th-Century Kenya: Kamba Society and Ecology in Transformation." *International Journal of African Historical Studies* 33 (2): 335–49.

Stiglitz, Joseph E. 2002. *Globalization and Its Discontents*. New York: Norton.

Stoller, Paul. 2003. "Circuits of African Art/ Paths of Wood: Exploring an Anthropological Trail." *Anthropological Quarterly* 76 (2): 207–44.

Stone, M. Priscilla, Angelique Haugerud, and Peter Little. 2000. "Commodities and Globalization: Anthropological Perspectives." In *Commodities and Globalization: Anthropological Perspectives,* edited by Angelique Haugerud, M. Priscilla Stone, and Peter Little, 1–29. Lanham, MD: Rowman and Littlefield.

Swartz, Marc J. 1991. *The Way the World Is: Cultural Processes and Social Relations among the Mombasa Swahili*. Berkeley: University of California Press.

Taylor, Ian. 2014. *Africa Rising?* Oxford, UK: James Currey.

Throup, David W. 1987. "The Construction and Deconstruction of the Kenyatta State." In *The Political Economy of Kenya,* edited by Michael G. Schatzberg, 33–74. New York: Praeger.

Throup, David W., and Charles Hornsby. 1998. *Multi-party Politics in Kenya: The Kenyatta and Moi States and the Triumph of the System in the 1992 Election*. London: James Currey.

Tonelson, Alan. 2002. *The Race to the Bottom: Why a Worldwide Worker Surplus and Uncontrolled Free Trade Are Sinking American Living Standards*. Boulder, CO: Westview Press.

Trillo, Richard. 2002. *The Rough Guide to Kenya*. 7th ed. London and New York: Rough Guides.

Tsing, Anna. 2005. *Friction: An Ethnography of Global Connection*. Princeton, NJ: Princeton University Press.

UNDP (United Nations Development Program). 2002. *Kenya Human Development Report 2001: Addressing Social and Economic Disparities*. Nairobi: UNDP Kenya.

Urry, John. 2007. *Mobilities*. Cambridge, UK: Polity.

Waaijenberg, Henk. 1993. *Land and Labor in Mijikenda Agriculture: Kenya, 1850–1985*. Leiden, NL: African Studies Center.

Wahome, Muna. 2005. "KTB Backs Fully Paid Tours." *Daily Nation,* November 18, 26.

Wahome, Muna, and Samuel Siringi. 2006. "Kenya's Economy Booms as Growth Sets 10-Year Record." *Daily Nation,* May 26, 1, 4.

Wahome, Mwaniki. 2006. "Taxman Faces Showdown with Traders over VAT." *Daily Nation,* December 17.

Wainaina, Binyavanga. 2006. "How to Write about Africa." *Granta 92: The View from Africa,* January 19. http://granta.com/how-to-write-about-africa/.

———. 2007. "Generation Kenya." *Vanity Fair,* July, 84–94.

Wandera, Noel. 2006. "Operators Miss Tourism Gravy Train." *Financial Standard,* January 10, 3.

Wandiba, Simiyu. 1992. "Craft and Manufacturing Industries." In *An Economic History of Kenya,* edited by W. R. Ochieng' and R. M. Maxon, 17–34. Nairobi: East African Educational Publishers.

Warigi, Gitau. 2001. "Baffling Behavior from a Cabinet Minister." *Daily Nation,* December 30, 8.

Wawrzinek, Jennifer, and J. K. S. Makokha, eds. 2010. *Negotiating Afropolitanism: Essays on Borders and Spaces in Contemporary African Literature and Folklore.* Amsterdam: Rodopi.

Webb, Martin. 2012. "Activating Citizens, Remaking Brokerage: Transparency Activism, Ethical Scenes, and the Urban Poor in Delhi." *PoLAR: Political and Legal Anthropology Review* 35 (2): 206–22.

Weis, Toni. 2008. "The Results of the 2008 Kenyan General Election." *Journal of Eastern African Studies* 2 (2): 1–41.

Weiss, Brad. 2002. "Thug Realism: Inhabiting Fantasy in Urban Tanzania." *Cultural Anthropology* 17 (1): 93–124.

Willis, Justin. 1993. *Mombasa, the Swahili, and the Making of the Mijikenda.* Oxford, UK: Clarendon Press.

Wilson, Ernest J., and Kelvin R. Wong, eds. 2007. *Negotiating the Net in Africa: The Politics of Internet Diffusion.* Boulder, CO: Lynne Reinner.

Wolf, Eric R. 1982. *Europe and the People without History.* Berkeley: University of California Press.

Wolf, Thomas. 2000. "Contemporary Politics." In *Kenya Coast Handbook: Culture, Resources, and Development in the East African Littoral,* edited by Jan Hoorweg, Dick Foeken, and Robert A. Obudho, 129–54. New Brunswick, NJ: Transaction.

Wright, Kristina Dziedzic. 2008. "Cleverest of the Clever: Coconut Craftsmen in Lamu, Kenya." *Journal of Modern Craft* 1 (3): 323–43.

Wrong, Michela. 2009. *It's Our Turn to Eat: The Story of a Kenyan Whistle Blower.* London: Fourth Estate.

Zilberg, Jonathan. 1995. "Shona Sculpture's Struggle for Authenticity and Value." *Museum Anthropology* 19 (1): 3–24.

INDEX

advertising: as ethical, 197–198; as more
important now than location, 94–95; of
M-PESA, 149F11; of dating sites to
young Kenyans, 124–125; of digital
technologies, 1, 8–9
Africa: changing global understandings of,
164, 175, 179, 198, 202; gender relations
in, 22, 35, 49–50; ideological construction of, 3–4, 13–14; representations of,
2–5, 13–14, 40, 107; and as a frontier of
investment, 4; and as a place for discovery, 13–14; and as cosmopolitan and
globally connected, 21, 184; and as
marginalized and impoverished, 170–
175, 196–198, 201; and as needy, 175,
196–198, 201; and as primitive, "tribal,"
or closer to nature, 2, 4–5, 13–14, 70,
174–178, 182–183, 188–189, 197–198, 201;
and as produced by Kenya's tourism and
crafts industries, 2, 11, 13–14, 25, 41, 70,
175–176, 198, 201; and as transparent
and honest, 40; and as violent, 3–5
African art: as categorized as "curios," 11,
178; as global commodity, 10–14, 177–
181, 184; as tribal, 31, 174; discovery of,
13; and historical erasure, 13; ethnic
networks for producing and selling, 42,
144; traders of, 10–14; value of, 10–14,
180–181; and in Europe and North
America, 10–14
African blackwood (*Dalbergia melanoxylon*), 23, 192–195, 194*fig.*, 195*fig.*
Africans: as global businesspeople, 4–5, 10,

54, 74; as tourists in Africa, 184, 198–
201; being given a voice by Afropolitanism, 5, 178; representations of, 4–5; and
as marginalized, 170–173, 175; and as
modern, global, and connected, 4–5,
175, 178; and as primitive, "tribal," or
closer to nature, 2, 4–5, 13–14, 174, 178,
182–183, 188–189, 201; and as produced
by Kenya's tourism and crafts industries,
13–14, 175; and as violent, 5; and holding
cell phones, 2–4, 11, 162, 175
African woodcarving industries, 10–11, 68,
73, 221–222n5
Africa rising narrative, 3, 107, 209n4; as a
magazine cover story, 3–5, 162; and
Afro-optimism and pessimism, 3–4, 6,
40; and digital technologies, 3–4, 8, 153,
155–156, 162; and global connection, 165;
and historical erasure, 13–14; critiques
of, 4, 153, 155, 170–173, 175, 201, 204,
209n8; and Kenya's crafts industry, 165,
170–173, 175, 201
Afropolitanism, 3–5, 210n9: and Kenyan
crafts, 15, 91, 165, 178, 183–184, 198–201;
and domestic tourism, 180, 198–202; as
giving Africans a voice, 5; as handmaiden of the Africa Rising narrative, 5,
201; as modern and global, 5, 165, 183–
184, 201; as representing hybridity, 4,
178; balancing Afro-optimism and
pessimism, 4–5, 40; critiques of, 4–5,
200
Airtel, 130, 132

art of connection, 14–17, 165; as artistic motif, 15, 174–175, 185–187; and roots of, 187–191; and representation of connection, 15; and transparency, 188, 203; and simplification, 203; and interethnic cooperation, 191; as strategy, 14, 52, 165; and ethics, 165, 201; and Fair Trade, 16, 165, 203; predigital, 28, 31, 64; as shaped by risk and insecurity, 30, 52, 53; and sex, 119

Arusha, Tanzania, 34*map*, 143

Authenticity: and domestic tourism, 198–202; and labeling, 165; appearance of crafts as authentically African, 70, 179, 183; claims to by upcountry curio vendors, 60–62; of being modern, 183, 185–186; of wood, 193–194; questioning, 174; "shifting authenticities" in art, 176, 179–180, 183

autochthony, 63–64

Balala, Najib, 86–87

banking: bank accounts, 149–150; banking industry, 4, 153, 205; and value placed on investing in risky environments, 9; and M-PESA, 131, 149–153, 205; and microfinance, 152; Kenya's banking sector, 150–151; telecom companies functioning as banks, 150–153, 205

"beach boys", 59–61, 115–116

beach curio vendors, 115; licensing of, 115–117

branding: ethical, 16–17, 154, 170, 201, 204; Fair Trade, 16–17, 203; ethnic brands, 165, 184, 200–201, 204

bribery, 90, 97, 102–107, 117, 122, 140–141; as eating, 104, 152

Burrell, Jenna, 133

business cards, 6, 28, 129, 136; and exporting, 155, 160, 165

cell phones, 1–8, 11; and trust, 139, 144; as collateral, 122–123; as risk-saving technologies, 132; as travel-saving technologies, 131; expansion in access to phones in Kenya, 132–133

Chaani, 30, 36*map*, 84, 159, 167, 169

Changamwe, 21, 30, 33*map*, 36*map*, 40

Christianity, 28–29, 90–91; and revivalist churches, 141–142

citizenship, 14–15, 31, 38, 59, 101; citizen-consumers, 131; ethical citizenship, 157

"city cleaning," 21, 64, 65–66, 82–83; and beautification, 93; and spatial reconfiguration, 142

Class: African middle class, 4–5, 150; and Afropolitanism, 178, 184; and ethnic politics, 56, 90–92; leisure class, 13; small-business class, 6, 52–54, 164; working class migrants, 46

Clifford, James, 180

colonial history: and gender, 22, 49; of cooperatives, 71–74; of crafts industry, 10, 68–74, 210n19; of Mombasa, 27, 31–39, 213n16; of tourism industry, 12; of urban demolitions, 8, 86, 93; of construction of African communities, 23, 32, 37–38, 48, 59; of imagination and understandings of Africa, 2, 13–14, 70, 191

competition: ethics of, 166; individual, 58, 113, 163, 165; in Old Town, 89; interethnic, 59–64; within cooperatives, 160–162, 168–169. *See also* market burnings; witchcraft accusations

connection: and digital technologies, 4, 129; and risk, 4, 117, 126, 204; and trust and transparency, 17, 160, 165; as dangerous, 117–120; as precarious, 129; as symbolically global, 1, 25, 63, 156, 165, 188, 191; to the global economy, 1, 4, 15, 63, 164, 190–191, 201

consumption: and meaning, 11, 13; as participatory, 175; by tourists in Old Town, 47; of African art in the West, 13; of experience, 176, 180, 187; of leisure, 62, 122; patterns of tourists, 41–42

cooperative development: history of, 2, 7, 71, 78–79, 89, 157–158; cutting of support for cooperatives, 156

corruption: local, Mombasa, 29; and Kibaki, 15, 24, 96–97, 108; versus transparency, 17

cosmopolitanism, 18, 27, 32, 41. *See also* Afropolitanism

crafts industries, 2, 5, 7, 10–11, 22, 66–67, 209n1. *See also* Kenyan crafts industry

race, 67, 118–119; and the tourism industry, 200

religion, 28–29, 47; and selling curios, 52, 90–91; complexity of, 141

risk, 31; and digital technologies, 9; as emerging from new global connections, 4, 117–120, 147, 204–205; globalization of, 9; of economic (in)formality, 9, 66, 81, 103, 109, 124, 140; of investment, 9; of exporting, 144–145; of mobility, 9, 46, 126, 147; of money transfers, 150; of not adapting to new economic contexts, 166; lived experiences of, 1; strategies for mitigating, 53, 57, 60, 132, 147; types of risk, 132

risk management, 102; need for, 205; placement upon citizen-consumers, 131, 152; and M-PESA, 153, 205

roadside economy, 50, 54–57, 66, 104, 176

rosewood, 188*fig.*, 192–194

Safaricom, 132, 134; debt to, 152–153; marketing by, 130, 150; resembling a bank, 149–150

Salazar, Noel, 9, 12, 46, 210n13

Second World War, 12, 69–75, 193

security, 27, 50, 53, 56–65, 80–81; and mobility, 88–89, 140; and modernity, 182; and M-PESA, 148, 153; and the informal economy, 103; as permanence, 143

semiformality: of roadside traders, 7, 9, 66, 97, 99; of global economy, 9; and risk, 102, 140

sex tourism, 117–118, 120–125; and online dating, 124–125

sex work, 116–119, 120–125; accusations of, 117, 122–123; and online dating, 124–125

soapstone, uniqueness of, 78; as medium for experimentation, 147

social media, 4, 8, 117, 136–137; Facebook, 8, 88, 137; WhatsApp, 8; YouTube, 199

South Coast, Mombasa, 29, 80; Diani Beach, 81; Ukunda, 33*map,* 81

souvenirs, 6, 129, 175–176, 197; art, 70, 75, 215n4; stalls and shops, 32, 47

Steiner, Christopher, 10–13

structural violence, 65, 93

study abroad, 20, 40, 180

Swahili: as lazy, 32, 37, 48, 52, 58–60, 63; as marginalized, 32, 63; ethnonationalism, 59; Coast, 22–23; etymology, 31, 37; history, 31–33, 37; identity, 23, 37; independence politics, 38–39; language, 38, 61, 64; and acquisition of, 20; woodcarving, 52, 181

Symbolic capital, 40; and modernity, 182; of artisans, 128; of marginality, 59

Tabaka, 34*map,* 42, 53, 55, 78, 143–144

taxation, 37–38, 60, 62, 97; and semiformality, 99; electronic tax registers, 106; tax holidays for foreign investors, 109; traders' views of, 106–107; VAT, 105

telecommunications: development in Kenya, 132–135; policy and deregulation, 130; politics of, 130, 133

terrorism, 217n26, 27–28, 81

Theneshara Taifa, 32–33, 35, 37

Time, 3, 162, 175

tour guides, 41, 59–61; regulation of Fort Jesus guides, 113–115

tourism: and game hunting, 12; as global experience, 187–188; as public good, 12; in Kenya, 2; mass tourism, 12, 67; and all-inclusive packages, 94, 109; sexualization of, 185. *See also* Kenyan tourism industry

tourist imagination, 12–13, 26, 70

trafficking, 27, 118–119

transparency, 14–18, 171; and digital technologies, 15–16, 165; and ethics, 15–17, 40, 203, 166; and Fair Trade, 160, 165, 195–198; and neoliberalism, 15; and the art of connection, 14–17, 31, 165, 171, 188, 203; as ethical scene, 15, 170; as fleeting experience, 15; as invisibility, 157; as political technology, 157; as simplification or erasure, 16–18, 31, 40; definition of, 17, 157; performance of, 17, 160

travel advisories, 27–28, 93–94

"tribalism," 21, 91, 62, 146, 182

trust: and connection, 17; and cooperatives, 165; and digital technologies, 139; and Fair Trade, 165; and formalization, regulation, and licensing, 116; and transparency, 151, 165; as essential, 126; crisis of, 144

Tsing, Anna, 3, 5, 130

Tudor Estate, Mombasa, 46, 49, 75–77

Uganda, 34*map*, 70, 177

Uhuru Gardens, Mombasa, 56, 78–79, 169

Uhuru Park, Nairobi, 109

Ukambani, 45, 68–71, 158

United Nations, 12, 192

United States, 30, 129, 136, 147, 196

value: of African art as authentic, 10–14, 180–184; of appearing modern, 184; of ethnic or tribal symbolism, 166, 174–177, 184; of Fair Trade, 14, 195–197; of mystification, discovery, and revelation, 14; of trusting and transparent connection, 15, 197; of uniqueness, 146–147; of wood, 193–194

visibility (and invisibility), 17, 155–156, 220n1. *See also* transparency

Vodafone, 132, 150, 153

Wainaina, Binyavanga, 4–5, 109–110

Wamunyu, 45, 69, 72–74, 181, 215n2

witchcraft, 85; accusations, 154–155, 162, 172; and ethics, 164; and neoliberalism, 155

work ethic, 48, 57–58, 63

World Bank, 132, 206

Zaramo, 69

Zimbabwe, 143, 177, 190; Shona carvers of, 189